FORSYTH LIBRARY

D0904856

MYTH IN INDO-EUROPEAN ANTIQUITY

PUBLICATIONS OF THE UCSB INSTITUTE OF RELIGIOUS STUDIES

Gerald James Larson (ed.), *Myth in Indo-European Antiquity*. 1974.

Myth in Indo-European Antiquity

edited by GERALD JAMES LARSON
coedited by C. SCOTT LITTLETON and JAAN PUHVEL

UNIVERSITY OF CALIFORNIA PRESS
Berkeley Los Angeles London 1974

University of California Press
Berkeley and Los Angeles, California

University of California Press, Ltd.
London, England

ISBN: 0-520-02378-1
Library of Congress Catalog Card Number: 72-93522
Printed in the United States of America

Preface

The University of California, Santa Barbara, supports work in the academic study of religion through both the Department of Religious Studies, which offers undergraduate and graduate degree programs, and the Institute of Religious Studies, an organized research unit, which encourages interdisciplinary research related to the general theme, "Religion and the Transmission of Culture." In March 1971 the institute sponsored a symposium focusing on issues growing out of the so-called new comparative mythology. Scholars representing various disciplines in Europe and the United States were invited to participate. Most important, Professor Georges Dumézil, at that time a visiting professor at the University of California, Los Angeles, took part in the symposium, which had for its subject: "Comparative Indo-European Mythology: A Symposium with Georges Dumézil." In addition to the Institute of Religious Studies, the symposium was sponsored by the Center for the Study of Comparative Folklore and Mythology (UCLA), the Forschungskreis für Symbolik (Heidelberg University), and the Wenner-Gren Foundation of New York.

The essays in the present collection grow out of that symposium. As even a casual reading shows, however, the essays are not concerned solely with Dumézil's own work, although most of them, to be sure, are inspired by one or another of Dumézil's articles or books. They represent rather an effort to break some new ground in various aspects of Indo-European mythology, taking as a clue the comparative studies of Dumézil. As a result, the contributions to this volume are at times quite technical and move into areas not often discussed. Moreover, they represent a variety of disciplines: linguistics, anthropology, religious studies, sociology, and others. Interestingly enough, the very diversity in subject matter and discipline testifies eloquently to the profound contribution of Professor Dumézil to Indo-European studies as well as to the exciting new areas of research which have been opened in response to the new comparative mythology.

I am grateful to all the sponsoring organizations for making the symposium possible. Special thanks are due Professor Walter Capps, director of the Institute of Religious Studies, who first conceived the idea for the symposium and who planned and organized the entire affair. I am also indebted to Professors C. Scott Littleton and Jaan Puhvel who collaborated with me not only in selecting the essays included in this volume but also in rendering invaluable assistance throughout the process of preparing the manuscript for publication.

G. J. L.

Contents

Introduction: The Study of Mythology and Comparative Mythology

GERALD JAMES LARSON,
University of California, Santa Barbara

THE DEFINITION OF MYTH

The word "myth" in the history of religions is a crucial technical term requiring careful and precise treatment, but unfortunately, in the scholarly literature on the subject, an intellectually bewildering variety of interpretations and definitions of the term have been suggested. Anthropologists, psychoanalysts, sociologists, classicists, and theologians have often used the term carelessly or casually. As a result, when including the word "myth" in the title of a book, the connotations are almost limitless.

It is important, therefore, to indicate briefly how the term is being used in this collection of essays. In this context a myth or a mythology means a narrative or a collection of narratives about the gods or supernatural beings used by a people—clan, tribe, or ethnic community—for purposes of interpreting the meaning of their experience and their world, both individually and corporately. Such narratives may describe the creation of the world or of man, the destruction of demonic forces, the origin of death, the beginning of sacrifice, the exploits of heroic figures, and so on. What is fundamental in the definition of "myth," however, and what distinguishes mythical narrative from other kinds of stories, is that myth articulates the basic self-understanding of a people and thereby operates as a kind of charter for the total cultural life. As a result, various components of a people's mythology are often used in the context of cultic life; that is, a myth or a group of myths may function as a means of giving symbolic expression to a set of continuing religious actions. Moreover, a myth or a mythology often reflects the structure of the social life of a people and shows how this structure relates to the world of the gods or supernatural forces. The function of myth, says Dumézil,

> . . . is to express dramatically the ideology under which a society lives; not only to hold out to its conscience the values it recognizes and the ideals it pursues from generation to generation, but above all to express its very being and structure, the elements, the connections, the balances, the tensions that constitute it; to justify the rules and traditional practices without which everything within a society would disintegrate.[1]

In time, of course, the mythology of a people undergoes considerable transformation for a variety of reasons, including cultural borrowing, group migrations, and individual genius. Sometimes, as in much of Greek mythology, only late literary traditions of myth remain, and the task of reconstructing the original context of a myth is nearly impossible. At any rate, in this volume the term "myth" is to be clearly distinguished from such terms as "tale," "fable," or any good story. What Malinowski says about the meaning and function of myth among "primitives" is to a large extent true of myth in general:

> [A myth is] a narrative resurrection of a primeval reality, told in satisfaction of deep religious wants, moral cravings, social submissions, assertions, even practical requirements. Myth fulfills in primitive culture an indispensable function: it expresses, enhances, and codifies belief; it safeguards and enforces morality; it vouches for the efficiency of ritual and contains practical rules for the guidance of man. Myth is thus a vital ingredient of human civilization; it is not an idle tale, but a hard-worked active force.[2]

PERSPECTIVES IN THE STUDY OF MYTHOLOGY

Related to the problem of definition, of course, are the issues of method and perspective, and again it is useful to locate the essays in this collection in the larger context of the many approaches to the study of mythology. This is not to suggest that the essays here presented follow only one method but, rather, to indicate that the papers have a methodological and perspectival identity which differentiates them from certain other kinds of studies. On one level, to be sure, this identity can be easily characterized. The essays in this volume address themselves to problems in Indo-European mythology and, more specifically, to problems growing out of the work of Georges

[1] Georges Dumézil, *The Destiny of the Warrior*, trans. Alf Hiltebeitel (Chicago, 1970), p. 3.

[2] B. Malinowski, *Magic, Science and Religion and Other Essays* (New York, repr. of 1948 Free Press edition), p. 101.

Dumézil. On a deeper level, however, the essays reflect a certain orientation to the study of mythology which goes far beyond Indo-European studies. They reflect an effort to treat the meaning of myth in an interdisciplinary manner which takes seriously not only structural and sociological analysis but also linguistic, anthropological, historical, and theological analysis. Such an effort is, indeed, ambitious; it presupposes a critical appropriation of a wide variety of previous work in the field.

One way of characterizing earlier work would be to present a historical account of the development of the field of comparative mythology, but such an approach is hardly workable in the context of a short introduction. Moreover, a number of books and articles are readily available which provide such historical treatment.[3] What is more appropriate in this context is simply a brief survey of some of the more important perspectives in the study of comparative mythology which have emerged as the field has developed. As will become evident, many of these perspectives have been surpassed in subsequent research, but all of them have been important either as methodological breakthroughs—or sometimes, indeed, as significant methodological failures— or as important initial intuitions that led in later times to more solid results. Such a brief survey will provide a convenient introductory framework within which the methods and the analyses of Dumézil and his colleagues can be located.

These varying perspectives may be described as follows:

1) *Myth as a symbolic portrayal in sensual and primarily visual language of the phenomena of nature—of celestial and atmospheric forces (sun, storm, thunder, etc.) but also to some extent of terrestrial forces—in Indo-European sources (i.e., in Indic, Germanic, Celtic, and Greek texts, etc.).* This now discredited perspective, prevalent in the middle and later nineteenth century, included the solar theories of F. Max Müller, the storm-gods of A. Kuhn, and so on. Methodologically, it proceeded by comparing and analyzing names of gods in various Indo-European languages (most of which etymologies were subsequently proved wrong); philosophically, it was little more than the popular romantic naturism characteristic of the time. Jaan Puh-

[3] See, e.g., Jan de Vries, *The Study of Religion: A Historical Approach,* trans. Kees W. Bolle (New York, 1967); Richard A. Dorson, "The Eclipse of Solar Mythology," in *Myth: A Symposium,* ed. T. A. Sebeok (Bloomington and London, 1958), pp. 25–63; Mircea Eliade, "The History of Religions in Retrospect: 1912 and After," in *The Quest* (Chicago, 1969), pp. 12–36; R. A. Georges, ed., *Studies on Mythology* (Homewood, Ill., 1968); S. H. Hooke, ed., *Myth, Ritual and Kingship* (Oxford, 1958), especially pp. 1–21, 149–158, 261–291; S. E. Hyman, "The Ritual View of Myth and the Mythic," in *Myth: A Symposium,* pp. 136–153, etc. For an older but still valuable survey of the field see Wilhelm Schmidt, *The Origin and Growth of Religion: Facts and Theories,* trans. H. J. Rose (London, 1931), *passim.*

vel, in describing this early phase in comparative mythology, offers the following assessment.

> The earlier scholarly history of such study is a sad, not to say an embarrassing chapter. In the middle of the nineteenth century the first intoxication of the discovery of Vedic Sanskrit, the then current naturist doctrine of myth interpretation, and personal idiosyncrasy coalesced in the fertile brain of F. Max Müller to produce a first flowering of comparative Indo-European mythology; it was essentially a loose derivation of Greek mythic names from Sanskrit prototypes, propped up by the tenet of the omnipresence of sungods and solar allegory, and the doctrine of the disease of language and the decay of metaphors. By the time when Max Müller was gathered to his sungods soon after the year 1900, this Victorian gingerbread of mythology had come crashing down in the Darwinian landslide, and fate dealt no more kindly with the rival Indo-European stormgods of Adalbert Kuhn, the moon myths of Georg Hüsing, the animal allegories of Angelo de Gubernatis, or the "Arische Feuerlehre" of Johannes Hertel.[4]

It should be said in defense of this perspective, however, that it at least opened up the field of comparative studies, albeit most subsequent work has had to proceed by *not* following the methods of this first exuberant phase in the scholarly study of comparative mythology.

2) *Myth as a symbolic representation of ancient Near Eastern astral speculations in Akkadian and Hebrew sources (i.e., Pan-Babylonianism).* This perspective in the study of mythology, also now discredited, emerged in the late nineteenth and early twentieth centuries. According to it, myth grows out of ancient Babylonian man's attempt to articulate his knowledge of the stars and planets (i.e., Babylonian astrology and astronomy) and to see how this knowledge affected both his self-understanding and his understanding of the world. These astral myths spread by diffusion throughout the ancient Near East and influenced many religious communities, including the religion of the Hebrews in the Old Testament. The primary exponent of this perspective was Hugo Winckler, and one of his disciples, E. Stucken, extended the theory to include astral myths throughout the world. In other words, it was asserted that these Babylonian astral myths spread by diffusion not only in the ancient Near East but to all nations and to archaic or "primitive" contexts as well:

> For Stucken the constellation of the Pleiades is the key to the diffusion. Stucken even believed in a precise date when the influence diffused from Babylon. The date was an equinox when the sun was in the sign of Taurus, to which the Pleiades belong, in about the year 3000 B.C.; the calendar reform connected with the equinox was established by Stucken at 2800 B.C. on the basis of cuneiform documents. So we may thank the Pleiades and

[4] Jaan Puhvel, "Indo-European Prehistory and Myth," in *Yearbook of the Estonian Learned Society in America* (New York, 1968), IV, 51–62.

> the accuracy of Babylonian astronomers, which inform us of the starting point of a worldwide mythological development![5]

Although obviously naïve and uncritical with respect to ethnology, even the ethnology characteristic of the late nineteenth and early twentieth centuries, this perspective at least called attention to the rich materials for the study of comparative mythology in the ancient Near East and thus provided important data for subsequent research. Moreover, it cannot be doubted that astral phenomena played an important role in the social, religious, and cultic life of the ancient Near East, and that some of these astral motifs did indeed diffuse widely in the ancient Near East. The serious error in the perspective clearly centered in claiming too much for such motifs and in extending them to absurd limits.

3) *Myth as a symbolic articulation of institutional structures and communal thought in archaic or preliterate sources (i.e., the sociological perspective).* Beginning with the work of W. Wundt (*Völkerpsychologie*) and J. J. Bachofen (*Das Mutterrecht*), this perspective in the study of religion and mythology was given a more systematic treatment in Durkheim's *The Elementary Forms of the Religious Life* and in the French sociological school. The latter included such scholars as Lévy-Bruhl, H. Hubert, M. Mauss, and M. Griaule.[6] It should also be noted that this perspective was influential in shaping the sociological dimension of Georges Dumézil's work in comparative mythology, especially the notion of *le fait social total.* The focus in this perspective is on myth as an expression of a people's social experience. An objective analysis of the social structure of a people provides important insights and clues with respect to interpreting their religious experience and the articulation of that experience in such phenomena as cult, totem, and myth.

Myth legitimates the social system and provides a symbolic articulation of the corporate religious experience. In other words, there is a close correlation between the religious experience and mythology of a people and the social reality. Indeed, Durkheim and other early theorists went so far as to suggest that religious experience and mythology are merely symbolic representations of the social experience of a tribe or group; that is, they explained away religious experience and myth as derivatives of social experience. Most contemporary scholars of comparative mythology and anthropology who make use

[5] De Vries, *op. cit.*, p. 97.

[6] Emile Durkheim, *The Elementary Forms of the Religious Life*, trans. J. W. Swain (New York, 1961). For good discussions of the French sociological school, see de Vries, *op. cit.*, pp. 15–17; and Emile Durkheim and Marcel Mauss, *Primitive Classification*, trans. Rodney Needham (Chicago, 1963), esp. Needham's introduction, pp. vii–xlviii.

of sociological analysis have, however, rejected such reductionism. That is to say, it is now generally recognized that the social dimension of a mythology, though one important focus in the task of interpretation, is not at all the only focus:

> Durkheim and his colleagues and pupils were not content to say that religion, being part of the social life, is strongly influenced by the social structure. They claimed that the religious conceptions of primitive peoples are nothing more than symbolic representations of the social order. . . . This postulate of sociologistic metaphysic seems to me an assertion for which evidence is totally lacking.[7]

Similarly, the early theories of the French sociological school regarding the importance of totemism have also been modified and toned down by subsequent interpreters, mainly as a result of the work of historical ethnologists who have demonstrated that totemism is neither universal nor the oldest form of religious organization. Apart from these later corrections of the excesses of Durkheim and his early followers, however, it cannot be doubted that this perspective in the study of mythology represented an important breakthrough methodologically and continues to be an important perspective and a productive method in studying comparative mythology.

4) *Myth as a symbolic expression of profound psychic needs and longings in archaic and ancient sources and in contemporary psychoneurotics.* About the time that Durkheim and his colleagues were setting forth the sociological dimensions of religion and mythology, both Freud and Jung were beginning to relate their psychoanalytic researches to the study of mythology. Freud, by synthesizing in an ingenious manner (*a*) his findings derived from clinical work with psychoneurotics, (*b*) his interpretations of the meaning of symbols, fantasies, and dreams, and (*c*) his reading of certain current works in anthropology (Frazer, W. R. Smith, etc.), produced a theory of the origin of religion and mythology which emphasized motifs like primal murder, cannibalism, sexual promiscuity, and the psychological correlates of guilt, fear, and repression. In Freud's work, as a result, myth has little value in and of itself, although, if interpreted properly, myth does provide important clues for discovering the content of certain repressions and instinctual drives in individuals and ethnic groups. Jung, on the other hand, assessed the meaning of myth in quite a different manner. Fascinated by certain images that appear universally in ancient mythology as well as in contemporary psychoneurotics, he developed an interpretation of mythology which emphasized certain "archetypes" and "patterns of behavior" common to all men. Myth is a way of giving symbolic expression to certain basic

[7] E. E. Evans-Pritchard, *Nuer Religion* (London, 1956), p. 313.

psychological needs, such as integration, conflict, and freedom. In contrast with Freud, Jung asserted that myth is an important medium in itself for providing man in his individual and collective experience with an integrative vision of the meaning of existence. Like the early sociological perspectives, however, the psychoanalytic interpretation was initially carried too far; it was justly criticized for its excesses, especially by ethnologists and anthropologists. In more recent work, however, the errors and excesses of the early period have been modified and corrected, and many helpful insights into the study of comparative mythology have emerged in the work of such figures as H. Zimmer, Joseph Campbell, Karl Kerényi, and Erich Neumann.[8] Few serious scholars of comparative mythology ignore the rich insights and productive directions for further investigation which this perspective has provided, although most scholars would also stress that the psychoanalytic perspective is only one among many productive disciplines to be employed in the study of comparative mythology.

5) *Myth as a symbolic rationalization (legomena) of the dramatic actions (dromena) of ritual in ancient Near Eastern and classical sources (i.e., "patternism" or the "myth and ritual school")*. Although the so-called myth and ritual school is technically linked with studies of ancient Near Eastern religion and mythology by British and Scandinavian scholars (beginning with the publication of S. H. Hooke's *Myth and Ritual* in 1933), the antecedents of the school can be traced back to the work of anthropologists and classicists like J. G. Frazer, Jane Harrison, F. M. Cornford, and Gilbert Murray, whose work established an intimate relationship between myth and ritual. It was suggested that myth emerges out of the cultic life of a people. Myth is "the spoken correlative of the acted rite, the thing done; it is *to legomenon* as contrasted with or rather as related to *to dromenon*."[9] A myth is never basically an etiological explanation of something in nature. It appears, rather, as an effort to render intelligible the complex action and drama of ritual. A myth functions as an important expression of a total cultural reality which has its foundation in cultic action. The myth in time may become separated from its ritual context, but it is never originally far removed from cult. With respect to the more specific "myth and ritual school" in ancient Near Eastern studies, an effort was made to reconstruct the basic myth and ritual

[8] For good examples of the application of psychoanalytic principles to areas like myth, dream, fantasy, etc., see Sigmund Freud, *Delusion and Dream and Other Essays*, ed. Philip Rieff (Boston, 1956), and C. G. Jung, *Two Essays on Analytical Psychology*, trans. R. F. C. Hull (New York, 1961). See also de Vries, *op. cit.*, pp. 142–146, and Eliade, *op. cit.*, pp. 19–22.

[9] Jane Harrison, *Themis* (New York, 1962), p. 328.

pattern that diffused widely throughout Egypt, Israel, and Mesopotamia in ancient times. As culture was transmitted in the Near East, according to Hooke, the three processes of "adaptation," "disintegration," and "degradation" occurred.[10] Nevertheless, certain common elements remained, including the great New Year festivals, enthronement rituals, and such motifs as the overwhelming importance of the king as a sacred figure, the death and resurrection of a god, an elaborate ritual combat, a sacred marriage, and a triumphal procession. This basic pattern of myth and ritual existed in Crete, Egypt, and Mesopotamia, and traces of the pattern can be found among the Hittites, the Elamites, and the Israelites, and as far away as Mohenjo-daro in the Indus Valley. In addition to Hooke, other names of importance linked with this perspective in the study of mythology are Mowinckel, Engnell, Geo Widengren, E. O. James, and to a lesser extent S. G. F. Brandon. Like the other perspectives that have been surveyed, there were numerous exaggerations of the theory in the early years, especially among the Scandinavians, but, again, it cannot be seriously questioned that significant progress was made in understanding ancient Near Eastern mythology as a result of the work of the patternists.

6) *Myth as important evidence for piecing together the history of preliterate cultures (i.e., Kulturkreislehre, the Vienna school, etc.).* This is not so much a perspective regarding the meaning of myth qua myth as it is an important tradition of scholarship using the study of myth in an attempt to do a "history" of preliterate peoples. Building on the work of Leo Frobenius and Fritz Graebner, it was primarily Wilhelm Schmidt in his *Der Ursprung der Gottesidee* who first developed a systematic presentation of this perspective.[11] Subsequently, further work in the same tradition was produced by W. Koppers, P. Schebesta, Josef Haekel, and others. Basic to the perspective is the claim that it is possible to isolate historical stratifications among archaic cultures. A culture has its own identity made up of customs, myths, images, weapons, social institutions, food-raising techniques, and geographical extent. Careful investigation of such configurations reveals that interaction and diffusion have taken place over long periods of time and over great distances. Moreover, it is possible to relate the interaction and diffusion in such a way that a history of these archaic or preliterate cultures can be determined, although ethnologists disagree as to its precise articulation. Schmidt's own scheme isolates (*a*) oldest "primitive-cultures" or "food-gatherers"

---

[10] S. H. Hooke, ed., *Myth and Ritual* (London, 1933), pp. 3 ff.

[11] Wilhelm Schmidt, *Der Ursprung der Gottesidee*, 2d ed. (Münster, 1926–1955), esp. sections of Volume I.

(e.g., Southeast Australians); (*b*) the younger "primary-cultures" or "food-producers" (e.g., "city" and "village" cultures of Melanesia and Indonesia as well as patrilineal pastoral nomad cultures of the Hamito-Semites and Indo-Europeans); (*c*) "secondary cultures" (e.g., the free patrilineal cultures in western Asia and southern Europe); and (*d*) "tertiary cultures" (e.g., oldest civilizations of Asia, Europe, and America).[12] Although much controversy still surrounds this perspective, especially the efforts to provide an overall history of preliterate cultures, students of comparative mythology have learned a great deal from this tradition of historical ethnology as well as from other excellent work in ethnography and general anthropology.

7) *Myth as a symbolic account of the structured ideological system of tripartition characteristic of Proto-Indo-European culture, a system reconstructed by means of comparative (historical, sociological, philological, and theological) analysis (i.e., the comparative Indo-European mythology of Georges Dumézil*). In order to characterize the methods and content of Dumézil's work it is useful initially to call attention to some of the influences and presuppositions that shaped his early work. First, although the original Indo-European comparative mythology of Max Müller and his followers had failed because of a naive philological/etymological method as well as the other reasons outlined above, Dumézil was nevertheless convinced that there was a common Indo-European cultural heritage and that it could be investigated, if correct methods could be devised. Second, as mentioned earlier, Dumézil was influenced by the French sociological school and, more specifically, by the work of M. Mauss. As a result of this influence, Dumézil was convinced that the mythology of the Indo-Europeans was closely allied with and reflected the social structures and institutions of their common cultural heritage. Third, Dumézil disagreed with evolutionary theories regarding the origins of religion and with the tendency among some scholars to discuss Indo-European culture and myth in terms of "primitive" religion. He believed, rather, that far from being primitive, the Proto-Indo-European people possessed a structured social and political organization and had accepted agriculture or at least at an early period had ruled over an agricultural population.[13] The discovery of the Boghazköy documents, which included a list of Indic deities (Mitra-Varuṇa,

[12] See introduction to Schmidt, *The Origin and Growth of Religion.*

[13] For a general survey of Dumézil's theories, see Georges Dumézil, *L'idéologie tripartie des Indo-Européens*, Collection Latomus, vol. 31 (Brussels, 1958). See also Puhvel, *op. cit.*, pp. 58–60; C. Scott Littleton, *The New Comparative Mythology: An Anthropological Assessment of the Theories of Georges Dumézil* (Berkeley and Los Angeles, 1966; 2d ed., 1973), *passim*; de Vries, *op. cit.*, pp. 181–186; and Eliade, *op. cit.*, pp. 32–34.

Indra, and the two Nāsatyas) and thus established the existence of an Indic rather than an Indo-Iranian community prior to the Aryans in India, tended to support the idea that the Indo-Europeans had an organized society in ancient times and had been in contact with the high Mediterranean civilizations in the early part of the second millennium B.C. Dumézil sought, then, to bring together a set of methods that would allow the investigator to go beyond the study of names—à la Max Müller and company—in order to analyze concepts, functions, and institutions making up the total historical-cultural experience of the Indo-Europeans. What emerged as Dumézil developed his work was an essentially historical method supplemented by insights from sociology, anthropology, and philology, focusing on concepts and functions within the various Indo-European mythological traditions and attempting to reconstruct the common ideological system characteristic of Proto-Indo-European culture before its separation into nations and tribes. As his research continued—research that ranged into the history and philology of almost all of the Indo-European peoples—Dumézil became convinced that in the Indo-Iranian (especially the Vedic), the Roman, and the Germanic traditions, enough evidence was available for reconstructing a structured, tripartite ideology which integrated the total cultural (i.e., social, political, economic, and mythological) experience of the Proto-Indo-Europeans. This structured ideology included three primary socioreligious functions: (1) dual sovereignty including both magical and contractual or juridical dimensions; (2) warrior force; and (3) economic productivity. Each function manifested itself both on the level of sociopolitical organization and on the level of theological or mythological system. A summary scheme of this structured ideology would be the following:

	INDIC	IRANIAN	ROMAN	SCANDINAVIAN
(1) DUAL SOVEREIGNTY	Varuṇa-Mitra (*brāhmaṇa* priesthood)	Vohu Manah Aša	Jupiter-Dius Fidius	Odin Týr
(2) WARRIOR FORCE	Indra and the Maruts (*kṣatriya* or warriors)	Xšathra	Mars	Thor
(3) ECONOMIC PRODUCTIVITY	Aśvins and the goddess Sarasvatī (*vaiśya* or producers)	Amərətāt-Haurvatāt and the goddess Armaiti	Quirinus	Njördr-Freyr and the goddess Freyja

It should be emphasized that Dumézil's structured ideology is a reconstruction. That is to say, extensive source criticism and detailed comparative analyses of specific mythological motifs in various traditions had to be completed before the tripartite scheme could be asserted with plausibility.[14] Many changes in social and political life as well as in the content and manner of presentation of the mythology occurred after the separation of the Proto-Indo-Europeans. In Roman traditions, for example, the use of myth almost completely disappeared, but Dumézil was able to reconstruct the mythological system from Roman legendary history. Similarly, according to Dumézil, in ancient Iran, because of the Zoroastrian reform, the tripartite structured ideology was transmuted, reappearing in the scheme of the Aməša Spəntəs, the archangels who assist Ahura Mazdāh. Moreover, the various mythological traditions of the Indo-European groups evidence tension on several levels, suggesting that the tripartite scheme was often characterized by instability. For example, the first and second functions frequently were in conflict with the third. As a result of such reconstructions and the obvious criticisms that could be and have been leveled at this kind of research, Dumézil himself has emphasized that such comparative Indo-European mythology is an unfinished task. The scholar who follows this perspective must continually double back over his own work, changing, modifying, and correcting his results as new materials become available and as new insights emerge from the ongoing comparative analysis. In spite of these difficulties, however, much clarification has been gained regarding Indo-European mythology and culture. One has only to think of Jan de Vries's work in Germanic mythology, or Duchesne-Guillemin's in Iranian studies, or Stig Wikander's work with the *Mahābhārata*, to realize the productive results of this perspective in the study of mythology.[15] Subsequent research may indeed reveal that the basic Dumézilian perspective needs further elaboration and conceptual clarification, but, in any event, Dumézil and his co-workers have made a massive and important contribution to the study of comparative mythology.

In addition to this brief survey of perspectives in the study of comparative mythology, mention should also be made of the work of a few important scholars in related fields who have worked on problems

---

[14] For good examples of the specific application of the methods, see Dumézil, *Destiny of the Warrior*; see also Dumézil's essay in this volume.

[15] See, e.g., J. Duchesne-Guillemin, *The Western Response to Zoroaster* (Oxford, 1958), pp. 20–51; Jan de Vries, *Keltische Religion*, Die Religionen der Menschheit, vol. 18 (Stuttgart, 1961); and Stig Wikander, "Pāṇḍava-sagan och Mahābhāratas mytiska förutsättningar," *Religion och Bibel* 6 (1947), 27–39.

that touch upon the theoretical interpretation of mythical thinking but whose work cannot easily be confined to any one of the above perspectives. In the field of philosophy of culture, for example, Ernst Cassirer's work, which compares and contrasts mythical discourse with scientific and philosophical discourse, has proved useful as a philosophical clarification of the structure and intelligibility of myth. Dissatisfied with interpretations of myth which dismiss mythical thinking as subjective or as illusionist, Cassirer sets out in volume 2 of *The Philosophy of Symbolic Forms* to relate and assess the significance of mythical thinking to other "basic forms of cultural life."[16] Art, ethics, law, language, science, and technology are related in their genesis "to a stage in which they all resided in the immediate and undifferentiated unity of the mythical consciousness."[17] To develop an adequate philosophical account of the symbolic forms of culture by means of which man constitutes himself, therefore, it is essential to have an adequate account of the significance of mythical thinking. According to Cassirer, mythical thinking has coherence as does philosophical or scientific thinking, but its coherence is of a different symbolic structure and intention:

> . . . mythical thinking shows itself to be concrete in the literal sense: whatever things it may seize upon undergo a characteristic concretion; they grow together. Whereas scientific cognition seeks a synthesis of distinctly differentiated elements, mythical intuition ultimately brings about a *coincidence* of whatever elements it combines. In place of a synthetic unity, a unity of different entities, we have a material indifference. And this becomes understandable when we consider that for the mythical view there is fundamentally but one dimension of relation, one single "plane of being."[18]

Cassirer's work draws upon the findings of many of the approaches to myth surveyed above, but his important contribution is in the direction of overall theoretical clarification or what he calls "the systematic problem of the *unity* of this manifold and heterogeneous material."[19]

Second, in the field of the general history of religions, Mircea Eliade has written extensively on the problem of the meaning and significance of myth and especially on the problem of how the interpretation of myth contributes to an adequate description of that which is uniquely religious. As a phenomenologist of religion Eliade is interested in the structures of religious consciousness, and thus he interprets myth and the function of myth from the perspective of its religious intention or from the perspective of *homo religiosus*. Myth,

---

[16] Ernst Cassirer, *The Philosophy of Symbolic Forms*, trans. Ralph Mannheim, II (New Haven, 1955), xiv.
[17] *Ibid.*, p. xv. [18] *Ibid.*, p. 63. [19] *Ibid.*, p. xiv.

according to Eliade, is a sacred narrative that gives shape and articulation to religious man's self-understanding, and hence there is a religious dimension in the apprehension of myth which cannot be reduced to other than a religious intuition. The interpretation of myth, in other words, requires a sensitive description and assessment of the religious apprehension involved in the phenomenon. Typical of Eliade's perspective in the interpretation of myth is the following passage:

> The myth relates a sacred history, that is, a primordial event that took place at the beginning of time, *ab initio*. . . .
>
> . . . it is always the recital of a creation; it tells how something was accomplished, began to *be*. It is for this reason that myth is bound up with ontology; it speaks only of realities, of what *really* happened, of what was fully manifested.
>
> Obviously these realities are sacred realities, for it is the *sacred* that is pre-eminently the *real*. Whatever belongs to the sphere of the profane does not participate in being, for the profane was not ontologically established by myth, has no perfect model.[20]

Eliade draws freely upon many of the approaches to the study of comparative mythology mentioned earlier (e.g., patternism, Dumézilian comparative research, psychoanalytic approaches, etc.), but throughout his work is the recurring assertion that the historian of religions brings a unique perspective and an important contribution to the study of myth, that is, an interpretation of myth which takes seriously the uniquely religious dimension of experience.

Finally, in the field of anthropology the work of Claude Lévi-Strauss has provided not only a new methodological perspective but also a number of provocative insights into the meaning and significance of myth. Like Cassirer and Eliade, Lévi-Strauss also is dissatisfied with any interpretation of myth which "amounts to reducing mythology either to idle play or to a crude kind of philosophic speculation."[21] Myth, according to Lévi-Strauss, is a mode of symbolic communication which is as logical and intelligible as modern scientific discourse. The difference between the two lies

> . . . not in the quality of the intellectual process, but in the nature of the things to which it is applied. This is well in agreement with the situation known to prevail in the field of technology: What makes a steel ax superior to a stone ax is not that the first one is better made than the second. They are equally well made, but steel is quite different from stone. In the same way we may be able to show that the same logical processes operate in myth as in science, and that man has always been thinking equally well;

---

[20] Mircea Eliade, *The Sacred and the Profane*, trans. Willard R. Trask (New York, 1961), pp. 95–96.

[21] Claude Lévi-Strauss, *Structural Anthropology*, trans. C. Jacobson and B. G. Schoepf (New York, 1967), p. 203.

> the improvement lies, not in an alleged progress of man's mind, but in the discovery of new areas to which it may apply its unchanged and unchanging powers.[22]

To study myth with the intention of probing to the deeper levels of the logical or intellectual processes involved, Lévi-Strauss employs a structural method. It is necessary to collect all the variants of a particular myth—which Lévi-Strauss calls "gross constituent units"—and then to analyze the "relations" and "bundles of such relations" in order to determine the fundamental essence or the logical structure of the myth which abides in spite of the diversities of historical form.[23] Edmund Leach has aptly summarized Lévi-Strauss's methods and findings as follows:

> If we accept Lévi-Strauss's view, the heart of the matter is that myth furnishes a "logical" model by means of which the human mind can evade unwelcome contradictions, such as that human beings cannot enjoy life without suffering death or that rules of incest (which specify that legitimate sex relations can only be between members of opposed kin groups) conflict with a doctrine of unilineal descent. The function of myth is to "mediate" such contradictions, to make them appear less final than they really are and thus more acceptable. This end is not served by isolated myths but by clusters of myths that are similar in some ways but different in others so that, in accumulation, they tend to blur the edges of real (but unwelcome) category distinctions.[24]

Despite the controversy that continues to surround Lévi-Strauss's ideas, his work has clearly come to represent not only a potent critique of functionalism in anthropology but also an interesting complement to the comparative Indo-European mythology of Dumézil.[25]

Much more could be said about approaches to the study of comparative mythology, but enough has been said with respect to the limited intention of this introduction to place the essays in this volume in the larger framework of research in the field. But perhaps enough has also been said to indicate that the study of comparative mythology is still very much a living issue in humanistic and social scientific studies. Especially in the work of Dumézil, Cassirer, Eliade, and Lévi-Strauss, it becomes obvious that the interpretation of myth is intimately allied with modern man's continuing search for self-understanding. What Robert Zimmerman asserts specifically about Lévi-Strauss and the field of anthropology is surely applicable to re-

[22] *Ibid.*, p. 227.

[23] *Ibid.*, p. 207.

[24] Edmund Leach, "Lévi-Strauss in the Garden of Eden," in E. N. Hayes and T. Hayes, eds., *The Anthropologist as Hero* (Cambridge, Mass., 1970), pp. 50–51.

[25] For a recent and valuable discussion of the relationship between Dumézil and Lévi-Strauss see P. Smith and D. Sperber, "Mythologiques de Georges Dumézil," *Annales économies sociétiés, civilisations,* 26 (May–August, 1971), 559–586.

searchers in the humanities and the social sciences who are interested in the larger enterprise of the study of mythology and comparative mythology:

> Is primitive man then a savage different *in kind* from us, or is he essentially identical with us? The work of Lévi-Strauss does not provide us with the answer—but then, neither does the work of any anthropologist. This, however, should produce a cynicism about anthropology within us only if we misconceive the nature of the question, that is, if we believe it to be a rather straightforward empirical question amenable to the methods of scientific inquiry. It should be clear by now that the matter is not at all as simple as that. Rather, the nature of the question is perhaps best defined by its resemblance to such perennial philosophical questions as, "What is man?" "What is nature?" and "What is the relation between man and nature?" And with respect to these questions it is as important that we confront them and *attempt* to answer them as it is that we answer them conclusively. For only in that continuing confrontation do we define and redefine ourselves; and only by grappling with these questions of identity do we create an identity worth bothering about.[26]

ARRANGEMENT OF THE ESSAYS

The essays in the present collection fall into three rather distinct groups. The first includes methodological or theoretical discussions that address themselves to issues of approach or method in the study of mythology. Dumézil's own contribution is the first in this group, and he takes up the problem of one-eyed and one-handed figures in Indo-European mythology, a problem to which he has returned on several occasions throughout his career. The essay is especially interesting as an example of Dumézil's comparative method, which is bold in its sweep but cautious in its attention to detail and to precise comparison. Also noteworthy is Dumézil's continuing critical appreciation of views that differ from his own theoretical position and his continuing willingness to rework his formulations as new evidence and new comparative insights appear. The contributions of Strutynski and Polomé follow up Dumézil's in this first group and assess the significance of Dumézilian comparative method in contrast with other approaches and in response to some of the criticisms of Dumézil's work in the field of Germanic mythology. The second group includes historical and comparative discussions of selected traditions in Indo-European mythology. These essays (the contributions of Ford, Puhvel, Gimbutas, Greenebaum, Evans, Gerstein, and Talley) explore specific problems and issues in various mythological traditions and offer a variety of new findings and insights with respect to our

---

[26] Robert L. Zimmerman, "Lévi-Strauss and the Primitive," in Hayes and Hayes, eds., *The Anthropologist as Hero*, pp. 233–234.

knowledge of various Indo-European mythological traditions. Some of the essays follow Dumézil's methods closely (e.g., those of Ford and Puhvel) while others employ a variety of perspectives. Finally, the interdisciplinary discussions by Littleton and Vereno relate Dumézilian comparative mythology to the fields of anthropology and the general history of religions.

"Le Borgne" and "Le Manchot": The State of the Problem*

GEORGES DUMÉZIL,* *Professor Emeritus, Collège de France*

The comparative study of the several Indo-European mythologies continually brings to light new and exciting matters for discussion. But it also drags with it some old impedimenta, some of them dating from the very beginning of the discipline. Thus, while always on the lookout for new themes and patterns, I still cherish a number of problems that have, from time to time, occupied my attention over many years. One of these involves the figures I have labeled "le Borgne" and "le Manchot," the one-eyed and one-handed figures that occur in several Indo-European traditions. I began my inquiry here some thirty-two years ago, and I have returned to the matter at least four times since,[1] repeating, adding, rectifying, cutting, without reaching an entirely satisfactory formulation. My initial solution to the problem in question, proposed with great confidence, has been subject to doubt, my own and that of others. In any event, with this background in mind, I should like to discuss what I take to be the present state of this old and restive problem.

The facts that led me to assume that at least part of the Germanic and Italic societies had inherited one-eyed and one-handed figures from their common Indo-European past are as follows: The two sovereign gods of ancient Scandinavia, Odin and Týr (who derive from

---

*The materials included in this paper correspond in part to those treated in *Mythe et épopée*, III (Paris, 1973), 267–281; see Introduction, *ibid.*, p. 16. Thanks are due C. Scott Littleton for help with editing the final English text.

[1] From the first edition of *Mitra-Varuṇa* (Paris, 1940), pp. 163–188, to *Mythe et épopée* I (Paris, 1968), 423–428.

the common Indo-European sovereign gods), were both maimed, and each disability was paradoxically connected with the particular god's character and role in the pantheon. Odin is the great sorcerer—to speak broadly—and Týr is the god of the political and juridical contentions in the *thing* and of the nonviolent contentions in war; these two notions are very closely related in the ancient Germanic world. Odin is one-eyed because he deprived himself of an eye, which became a source of knowledge; compensatorily, he acquired the gift of clairvoyance, science, and so on. Týr is one-handed because he deliberately imperiled and lost his right hand in a kind of heroic perjury, in an attempt to make a lie be taken for a truth. It was a lie of vital importance, one required for the salvation of the whole divine society. When the wolf Fenrir was born, the gods, who knew that he was to devour them, decided to tie him up. Odin had a magic cord made, a cord so thin that it was invisible, but one strong enough to resist all tests. Then the gods proposed to the young Fenrir that, as a sport, he let himself be bound with this apparently harmless fetter so that he might have the pleasure of breaking it. More distrustful than is usual among the young, the wolf accepted only on the condition that one of the gods put a hand in his mouth while the operation took place, *at veði*, "as a pledge," so that all should transpire without deceit. None of the gods showed sufficient devotion to the commonweal until Týr stretched forth his right hand and put it into the wolf's mouth. Naturally the wolf could not free himself: the harder he tried, the tighter the magic fetter became. And so he stays until the end of time, those gloomy days when all the forces of evil will be liberated and will destroy the world and the gods with it. Then the wolf will have his revenge and devour Odin, if not Týr, who is destined for a mutual killing in a fight against another wolf or monstrous dog, Garmr. But for the present the gods were saved, and all of them laughed, Snorri asserts, all but Týr, who lost his hand and resented it. As a result of this loss, Snorri concludes, Týr can no longer be called "peacemaker."

In 1940 I discovered a Roman parallel to this theme, not in divine mythology, which hardly exists, but, as usual, in Roman epic, itself transformed into history. During the first war waged by the republic, Rome, in the mortal peril into which it was thrown by Porsenna and his Etruscans who supported the expelled last king, is successively saved by two heroes, one of whom is one-eyed and the other one-handed: Horatius the Cyclops (Cocles) and Mucius the Left-Handed (Scaevola). While the Roman army retreated in disorder across the Tiber bridge, Cocles disconcerted the enemy by casting terrifying looks at it: *circumferens truces minaciter oculos*, as Livy puts it. The other hero, Mucius, who had entered the enemy camp to stab Porsenna and had been captured after being tricked, deliberately burnt his right hand in the king's brazier in order to persuade him, by this proof of heroism, that 300 young warriors, equally resolved, stood ready to repeat the act (which seems not to have been true, but rather a sudden contrivance on Mucius's part). In so doing Mucius convinced the Etruscan king to consent to an honorable peace with Rome.

These, then, are the facts. The next step is to review the balance sheet of the comparative process.

It seems to me that I have three strong points in my argument:

1) In both Scandinavia and Rome the two sets of figures just discussed are the only mythological (or, in Rome, pseudohistorical) ones who are maimed. And their mutilations are the same (even if, according to most of the variants, Cocles' thigh is wounded at the end of the heroic deed, which would render him lame as well as one-eyed; nevertheless, this secondary bodily fault, which is not a mutilation in the strict sense of the term, has no effect whatsoever upon his performance).

2) Both sets of figures are on the same hierarchical level and can be opposed to figures occupying other levels:

a) In Scandinavian mythology Odin and Týr (as I understand them and for quite different reasons)[2] are heirs to a pair of complementary sovereign gods, the only chief gods on their level.

b) At Rome, in spite of Marie Delcourt's denial,[3] it can hardly be fortuitous that the two deeds involving these two mutilations are located in the same war, give birth to parallel *cognomina* with similar honors (both heroes were rewarded by the same sort of privilege), and are accomplished by two men of the same level, that is, outside the normal *militaris disciplina*. Neither is an officer, and both volunteer to perform their respective acts. They are, as it were, *allowed* to perform them rather than *ordered* to do so. And they act alone, willingly.

3) The idea underlying at least one of the panels of the diptych is the same. Professor Littleton objects: ". . . indeed, the only common denominators seem to be the absence of an eye and a hand and a concern for the maintenance of sovereignty."[4] No. Týr and Scaevola have

[2] *Les dieux des Germains* (Paris, 1959), chap. 2 ("La magie, la guerre et le droit"), augmented in the Danish edition, *De nordiske Guder* (1969).

[3] *Hommages à Waldemar Deonna*, Collection Latomus, vol. 28 (Brussels, 1957), pp. 169–180.

[4] C. Scott Littleton, *The New Comparative Mythology: An Anthropological Assessment of the Theories of Georges Dumézil* (Berkeley and Los Angeles: University of California Press, 1966) , p. 86. Sovereignty as such does not appear in the case of Cocles and Scaevola in this legend of the first war fought by the republic, a war against royal power wherein even the heroes who correspond to the sovereign gods act only as "citizens"; they save the state but do not dominate it.

more in common than the absence of a hand. Each sacrifices his right hand in order to make the enemy believe a false statement and thus induce him to engage in behavior absolutely necessary to Rome's or to the gods' salvation—behavior that he would never engage in were he not led by this dramatic warrant to take the lie for truth. This is indeed substantial, more substantial than the "absence of a hand," and not so common in world literature.

There are the strong points. Now to the weak ones.

1) The disparity, in meaning and location, of the other mutilation, the eye mutilation, and how it is put to use by the maimed figure cannot be overlooked. What I have just said of Týr's and Scaevola's right hand cannot be said of Odin's and Cocles' eye. We no longer have symmetry. What Odin gains by the sacrifice of an eye, we are told, is science, clairvoyance, and so on. Cocles sacrifices nothing; he is already one-eyed when he performs his deed, either as a result of a former wound or because his eyes or eyebrows were shaped by nature in such a way that he seemed and was accounted one-eyed although not in fact so afflicted. And when he casts *truces minaciter oculos* over the Etruscans he does not make use of a new or permanent gift; he only disconcerts and paralyzes them. This is, of course, quite different from the situation in which Odin finds himself.

I tried to lessen the difference by recalling that Odin also paralyzes the enemy; indeed, it is his chief technique when he interferes in battles. But for Odin the voluntary loss of one eye and his power to paralyze are separate matters. His quality of one-eyedness is, as far as I know, nowhere related to this *herfjöturr*, or "army fetter." To be sure, in the *Hávamál*, Odin himself tells us that his magic runes can stop an arrow flying against an army merely by looking at it. This claim resembles in a more marvelous form the description of Cocles' performance in Livy 2.10 (according to Livy, Cocles escapes without suffering a wound):

> He withdrew to a place of safety on a small portion of the bridge still left. Then casting his stern looks round the officers of the Etruscans in a threatening manner, he sometimes challenged them singly, sometimes reproached them all, "the slaves of haughty tyrants, who regardless of their own freedom, came to oppress the liberty of others." They hesitated for a considerable time, looking round one at the other, to commence the fight. Shame then put the army in motion, and a shout being raised, they hurled their weapons from all sides on their single adversary. And when they all stuck in the shield held before him, and he with no less obstinacy kept possession of the bridge with firm step, when at once the crash of the falling bridge, at the same time a shout of the Romans raised for joy at having completed their purpose, checked their ardour with sudden panic.

> Then Cocles [after a short prayer addressed to Father Tiber], armed as he was, leapt into the Tiber, and, amid showers of darts hurled on him, swam across safe to his party.

Here Cocles seems to be endowed with an Odinic power to make arrows and darts ineffective. But this partial concordance does not alter the main difference between the two figures: even in the *Hávamál* the power of stopping airborne arrows with a single look is not explicitly connected with Odin's divine affliction but rather, it seems, with his general capacity as a divine sorcerer. Moreover, normal two-eyed figures are often credited with similar powers. For example, Odin's troop, the Berserkir, are (according to the *Ynglingasaga*) able to blunt the sword of their adversary before or during battles or single combats; the same is told of many Vikings by Saxo and in various sagas.[5]

In short, I must repeat that as far as I know the sacrifice of Odin's eye is not the cause of this paralyzing privilege and results only in intellectual (or better, perhaps, superintellectual) benefits.

2) The second weak point in my proposal has been well defined in Littleton's book. The comparison is limited to Rome and Scandinavia. Only in Rome and in Scandinavia do we find, at the same level, a one-eyed and a one-handed hero or god. Even in Ireland, where Nuada, the one-handed king of the Túatha dé Danann, is an obvious counterpart of Týr, I am still unable to point to a one-eyed hero on the same level. My earlier proposals—first Balor, then Lug—do not stand. When Lug shuts an eye, it is only a magical grin, not a mutilation; and Balor is evil-eyed rather than one-eyed. One of his eyes is malevolent, and he is obliged to keep it shut when he does not want to harm the people in front of him. Furthermore, Balor is not one of the Túatha dé Danann and is therefore not homologous to Nuada; indeed, he fights in the other camp.

As for India, I have long since retracted my first proposal, namely, that the one-eyed and one-handed gods were represented, respectively, by Bhaga and Savitar. Bhaga, the god of destiny, is entirely blind, and Savitar, whose job is to put any process in motion, loses both hands. These afflictions have nothing to do with the one eyed sorcerer ~ one-handed guarantor theme, save for the general idea of a mutilation paradoxically qualifying a being for the very kind of activity it would appear to preclude in the bodily sense.

This difficulty has not been resolved until now. I am still in quest of a one-eyed member of the Túatha dé Danann counterpoising

[5] S. Seligman, *Die Zauberkraft des Auges und das Berufen* (Hamburg, 1922), pp. 377–378.

Nuada and, more generally, of one-eyed figures balancing one-handed figures in other Indo-European mythologies, as Cocles balances Scaevola and Odin balances Týr. But is it really an objection? Mythical, legendary, and ritual correlations are numerous. Most are found between India (or, more broadly, the Indo-Iranian zone as a whole) and Scandinavia, or between India and Ireland—to say nothing of the many Indic-Roman correspondences, the chief pillar of our constructions. Thus, while the one-eyed and one-handed structure can perhaps be rejected on internal grounds (e.g., if the parallel is not thought strict enough), it cannot be rejected simply because it is exemplified only in Rome and in Scandinavia. Nevertheless, it would be better if I had a third example, but I do not. More ambitious than Diogenes, I look for a pair—my maimed pair.

As it happens, I may have discovered a new variant, not of the whole structure, but of Scaevola's and Týr's performance therein. The text may be found in Arthur Christensen's book, *Les types du premier homme et du premier roi dans l'histoire légendaire des Iraniens* (Pt. I [1917], 184–189). This legend displays, in a distorted form, some striking similarities to the myth of Týr. The full account is preserved in a very late Parsi *rivayāt*, but, as often happens, the episode may be much older.

Already in the Avesta we read that the second of the oldest mythical kings, not of Iran, but of the world, Taxma Urupi ("Urupi the Valiant"), succeeded not only in conquering demons and sorcerers but also in "riding Angra Mainyu as a horse for thirty years, from one end of the earth to the other" (*Yašt* XV, 12–13, and *Yašt* XIX, 29, where this privilege is granted respectively by the god Vayu and the *Xᵛarənah*; cf. Christensen, *op. cit.*, pp. 133–134). Neither the Avesta nor any Pahlavi text nor any Persian text of Islamic times tells us what occurred at the end of the thirty years, not even why and how these *haute-école* exercises had an end, or why and how Angra Mainyu rid himself of this slavery. But in the Parsi *rivayât* published by Friedrich von Spiegel and translated by Christensen, we read much more. The text, though long and verbose, can easily be summarized:

Taxmoruw (Taxma Urupi) succeeded in binding Ahriman (Angra Mainyu)—we are not told how he accomplished this feat—and kept him in this condition for thirty years. Three times a day the king would saddle, bridle, and girth him as if he were a horse and would ride throughout the world. After returning home he would unsaddle, unbridle, and ungirth his mount, put a kind of lasso on him, and again bind him strongly. After thirty years had elapsed, Ahriman, winning Taxmoruw's wife with a gift of splendid costume jewelry—as only the devil is able to manage—learned that his rider always had a short fit of dread at a certain point, an especially dizzying place on the daily ride. The next day, when they reached this point, Ahriman reared, unseated Taxmoruw, devoured him, and freed himself. Taxmoruw's devoted brother Jamshid searched for him throughout the world and finally was told what had happened by Srôsh, a very close collaborator of God. Jamshid asked Srôsh for a magic trick in order to take his brother's corpse out of Ahriman's abominable belly. "The devil is fond of two things," Srôsh said, "music and pederasty. Sing as soon as he comes and propose to have a bit of intimacy with him." Following Srôsh's advice, Jamshid sang, and Ahriman rushed to him and started to play with what in French is termed "les bagatelles de la porte." But, as he had been advised to do, Jamshid imposed a condition on Ahriman: "Grant me a gift, and thereafter I'll do it." We have to understand that the request was to take Taxmoruw out of Ahriman's anus before operating in the opposite direction. Ahriman was already too aroused to object to anything or to bargain; he immediately took the required position and bent forward, waiting for the extraction, then for the pleasure. Jamshid thrust one hand (we are not told whether it was the right or the left) through Ahriman's anus and into his belly as far as the stomach, drew out Taxmoruw's corpse, put it on the ground, and fled. Ahriman pursued him, but Jamshid ran on, taking care not to turn his head toward his pursuer or to look him in the face, in accordance with the advice Srôsh had given him beforehand. Ahriman realized that he had failed and dived into hell. Then Jamshid built a high tower—the prototype of Mazdean towers of silence—and put the corpse on it. But looking at his hand, the hand that had been in Ahriman's body, he saw it had dried up and stank, having been destroyed by a kind of leprosy. He became sad and fled from people, dwelling on mountains and in deserts, and his disease grew more and more painful. Fortunately, one night while he was asleep an ox urinated on him and he was healed (this was the discovery of the famous *gōmēz,* or "ox urine," the remedy par excellence according to Mazdaism).

We have here not the Scandinavian plot, but, in reverse order, the points around which the Scandinavian plot develops: a devilish, dangerous being will devour the universal king as soon as it is free; this being is temporarily neutralized by the universal king, who stoutly binds it; but it finally unbinds itself and devours its opponent; then another man, the victim's relative, wanting at least to recover the corpse and pay last honors to the dead, induces the devilish being by a deceitful promise to allow him to thrust his hand into its—let us say —lower mouth in order to draw out the corpse; then, breaking the contract, he flees. But after doing so, his hand has dried, and he would remain a cripple if the specific Mazdean remedy had not appeared fortuitously and healed him.

Thus the first part of the Scandinavian plot—binding the monster, loss of the arm in a bold, heroic act, violation of an agreement—is divided in two, and the second part of the Scandinavian plot—the monster unbinding itself and devouring the sovereign god—is inserted between the two halves, that is, between the binding and the loss of the arm. As a consequence, the link between the binding and the loss of the arm, which latter occurs in the context of another kind of heroic and pious treachery, one necessitated by the effort to save a Mazdean corpse from its devilish container, is broken. The considerable differences here between the Iranian and Scandinavian plots may reflect the profound and important differences between Iranian and Scandinavian eschatological conceptions. For Mazdaism shaped a new and quite specific pattern for the end of the world and for the permanent struggle between Good and Evil, between God and Ahriman. As a result, Ahriman could not be thought of as bound from the beginning to the end of time, and the episode of his binding by the second universal king was doomed to lose any eschatological or cosmic implications. Thus I am tempted to suggest that this Iranian story has been inherited from very ancient times, but that it lost its ancient import as a consequence of the Mazdean reform.

But I am once again unable to find the one-eyed hero on the same level as the hero with the dried hand; and thus here, as in every other example of the comparative process, it is necessary to balance the concordances and the discrepancies and to evaluate their respective weights.

In any event, in spite of this possible new datum, there remain only two binary structures, the Scandinavian and the Roman. In these two structures one of the terms (one-handedness) shows a good correspondence, both in form and in meaning; the other (one-eyedness) shows the same physical element but with divergent meanings: one-eyed Odin enjoys supernatural knowledge, one-eyed Horatius paralyzes enemies (a power also characteristic of Odin, but not as a consequence of his mutilation). Commenting on the same point, Littleton notes: "If Jupiter and Dius Fidius, or even Romulus and Numa, exhibited these characteristics, or if there were some evidence that Varuṇa and Mitra or their Iranian counterparts were so afflicted, the theory would be more convincing."[6]

Yes and no. As for India, I agree. Neither Varuṇa and Mitra nor the heroes in the *Mahābhārata* whom I consider as the epic transposi-

[6] *Op. cit.*, p. 86.

tions of the sovereign Vedic pair are one-eyed and one-handed.[7] Moreover, nothing in the Indic tradition prevented them from being so afflicted; indeed, India does not lack for monstrous or mutilated gods. But, as for Rome, Littleton's objection is more questionable. When we first know them, Jupiter and Dius Fidius have no more mythical features than the other Roman deities, for Rome had lost the whole of the divine mythology. But in Roman pseudohistory not only Romulus and Numa, but other heroes and narratives of much later times (at least until the Gaulish catastrophe and a little later; let us say until the middle of the fourth century), are entirely or partly epic transformations of lost mythical figures or theological structures.[8] The fact that Cocles and Scaevola, during the totally fictitious first war of the republic, and the not totally fictitious Romulus and Numa, at the very beginning of so-called Roman history, are concerned makes little difference. To reinforce this assumption, it is necessary to demonstrate that the two figures and deeds in question were grounded in religious ideology and ritual.

It is, as I have just said, sometimes possible to suggest that some action by a Roman consul or dictator is the epic projection of an old lost myth. This assertion may seem to be contradictory; a lost myth is lost and is consequently unavailable to us. Still, what allows us to speak of "old lost myth" is the fact that Roman lost mythology is not completely lost. It left traces, imprints, if you will, which are still perceivable in well-preserved rites. When the Romans came into contact with Greek civilization, especially its religion and literature, they readily abandoned or altered their own myths. But they were too cautious and pious to incur the risk of making any god angry by changing his traditional rites or festival.[9] In the legends of Cocles and Scaevola, it is probable that we can detect such ritual imprints.

As far as Mucius Scaevola is concerned, this idea is an old and still likely hypothesis. Ettore Pais, W. F. Otto, Salomon Reinach, M. F. Münzer in the *Realencyclopaedie*, and many others have suggested, most often with unlikely extensions, that the loss of Scaevola's right hand as a means of corroborating a heroic and necessary lie must have something in common with the well-known yearly rite in the cult of the goddess Fides (probably *Fides publica*), herself closely connected with Dius Fidius (whom Professor Littleton wanted to see involved in the problem). In the two editions of my *Mitra-Varuṇa* (1940, 1948)

---

7 *Mythe et épopée* I, 145–175.

8 *Archaic Roman Religion* I (Chicago, 1970), 47–78.

9 Cf. the rites of the festival of Mater Matuta (*Archaic Roman Religion* I, 50–55, 337–339).

I quoted at length Münzer's statement about the matter and emphasized Pais's illuminating remark that Dius Fidius had a temple on a hill called Collis Mucialis, this name being obviously related to the gens Mucia. As for the cult of Fides, once a year the three *flamines maiores* went to offer a joint sacrifice at her chapel under very special and surely archaic conditions.[10] According to Livy (1.21), "Numa established an annual worship of Fides, to whose chapel he ordered that the *flamines maiores* should proceed in a two-horse hooded carriage, and that they should offer the sacrifice with their right hands wrapped up as far as the fingers." This suggests that the Scaevola half of the diptych, at least, had a ritual (and consequently, in older times, mythical) background.

For Cocles we have no rite, but this lack of ritual correspondence may be plausibly accounted for by the fact that his action involves a kind of magic strength of body. If the effect of his one-eyedness was, as in Scandinavia, a deep view, the sight of things invisible, we could expect some rite, for instance, in the *ius augurale*. But, as I have said, Cocles' privilege is different. He does not exactly possess the "evil eye," but he is endowed with a very effective and very terrible look, and the Romans did not like men (or gods) who fell outside the normal pattern. To be sure, the Roman gods performed many miracles. But these were accomplished by means of their will and through invisible actions and not with an exceedingly developed or altered organ. Only at a lower level, in unofficial, individual practices, where magic was more acceptable, may we hope to meet what we miss as far as the gods and public rites are concerned.

In 1969, in the first of the three volumes of the *Hommages à Marcel Renard* (Collection Latomus, vol. 101, pp. 443–448), my colleague Jacques Heurgon, with whom I so often cordially disagree in matters of early Roman history, published a very interesting and elegant paper, "Les sortilèges d'un avocat sous Trajan" ("The Magic Practices of a Barrister-at-Law in Trajan's Time"). The barrister in question, M. Aquilius Regulus, who died in A.D. 105, was a *dilator* under Nero and Domitian and a very despicable man. According to Pliny the Younger, who dealt with him in one of his letters (VI.2), Regulus was not devoid of gifts as an orator, but he was lacking in *inventio* and *memoria* and for this reason was easy to disconcert when he was pleading in court. Moreover he was extremely superstitious, a good customer for the soothsayers, and before pleading he used to take a strange precaution: "He had a practice, Pliny says (2), of paint-

[10] As opposed to the very personal treatment to which Kurt Latte has subjected this text, as well as many others in his *Römische Religionsgeschichte* (1960); see also *Archaic Roman Religion* I, 144–146.

ing round his right or left eye, according to whether he was to plead for the plaintiff or the defendant, and of wearing a mobile white patch over one eyebrow or the other."

Professor Heurgon connects this practice with the *malocchio*, the evil eye, although he confesses he found no convincing parallel in the books concerning the evil eye. He does not mention the fact—abundantly exemplified—that to be one-eyed often involves qualities related to the evil eye.[11] But I do not think we can here speak of the evil eye. To be sure, outside the court of justice, before the trial, defendant and plaintiff, or their respective counsels, were like all Romans, entirely free to attempt to cast a spell or a charm on their adversary or his counsel. Heurgon gives a good example of this, and I know of some other Roman cases of this sort of thing. But it is inconceivable that, during the trial, *praetore aut judicibus praesentibus*, anyone would dare—let alone be allowed—to publicly practice malefices, evil spells, or the evil eye with the declared intent of hurting the other side. Heurgon is on firmer ground when he refers to Cocles:

> In Pliny's account only one eye is concerned. To understand that, we do not need to go back as far as the Cyclopes, but only remember one-eyed Horatius Cocles. We read in Livy's history that, when he was the sole defender of the bridge between the Janiculum and Rome, he continued assailing the Etruscans with the strength of his threatening and terrifying look, *circumferens truces minaciter oculos.*

Then Heurgon quotes my interpretation of Cocles and concludes:

> Is this not exactly what Regulus does, conforming to a tradition related, since time immemorial, to the fascinating power of the "single eye," a tradition which magic had probably well preserved? Regulus makes up only one of his eyes so as to touch up its brightness (*nitorem addere*) and, at the same time, he suppresses one of his eyebrows, evidently the other one. For it is in this sense that we have to understand the words *splenium candidum,* which are generally translated "white patch." To be sure, Marivaux's and Watteau's "love patch" ("les mouches galantes de M. et de W.") are already mentioned by Martial (VII.33.22), but *splenium,* as well as Greek *σπλήνιον,* is properly a compress or a bandage, one broad enough, according to Martial again (II.29.5–10), to hide dishonorable scars. The piece of adhesive plaster Regulus used to paste now on his right, now on his left eyebrow was not intended to enhance the whiteness of his complexion, but rather to make the eyebrow vanish from his face.

For the rest, I must repeat that I do not fully agree with Heurgon's opinion that Regulus pretended to be a *jettatore*. More probably, knowing his own weaknesses (little *inventio,* poor *memoria*), he merely wanted to make himself impressive and terrifying, to protect him-

[11] Seligman, *op. cit.,* pp. 231–233; see also his earlier work *Der Böse Blick und Verwandtes* (Berlin, 1910), 1 (see "Einäugigkeit" in the index).

self against the opposite party and keep them—morally—at a distance and on the defensive.

Thus, in default of a rite, Rome provides us with a magical practice very similar to Cocles's figure and behavior. We may imagine that, before being thus degraded and at a time when the religion of early Rome, or even that of the pre-Romans, admitted more witchcraft than it did in later times, both public and private rites existed with this meaning and intent. But this extension is unprovable, whereas Regulus's makeup and compress are attested facts. And that is enough, as far as I am concerned.

In any event, the existence of the ritual of veiled right hands in the cult of Fides, together with the magical initiation of a one-eyed face by Regulus in the oratory battles at the bar of justice, reinforces the assumption that the structure "Scaevola ~ Cocles" had a religious origin and consequently brings it closer to the Scandinavian mythical structure "Týr ~ Odin."

Having presented the latest facts relative to "le dieu borgne" and "le dieu manchot," I must conclude without reaching a decision; the problem remains open. To sum up: on the one hand, the difficulties that arise from (1) the difference in meaning between Odin's and Cocles' mutilations and (2) the absence of any comparable pair of figures in a third Indo-European mythology or folklore persist. But on the other hand, (1) the dossier of Týr and Scaevola seems to have been enriched with an Iranian narrative (one that reminds us more of the Týr episode than of that of Scaevola, but with the same import as both), and (2) the religious origin of Cocles' and Scaevola's figures and mutilations seems to be strengthened by the existence of what is surely a very old rite, a magical observance probably much older than the instance preserved through Pliny the Younger's taste for tittle-tattle.

History and Structure in Germanic Mythology: Some Thoughts on Einar Haugen's Critique of Dumézil

UDO STRUTYNSKI, *University of California, Los Angeles*

It is well known that Georges Dumézil has been active in the subfield of Germanic mythology for a great many years. His first book-length investigation of this segment of the Indo-European continuum appeared in 1939.[1] Since then numerous publications dealing with this area have come from his pen.[2] Scholarly activity of this range and depth does not exist without attracting critical comment from colleagues in the field. In Europe, Dumézil's work has won the respect of a number of eminent scholars of Germanic antiquities, including E. O. G. Turville-Petre, Jan de Vries, Stig Wikander, and Werner Betz. In the United States, however, there has been a minimum of scholarly response.[3]

The first comprehensive critical reaction to Dumézil's work, covering not only its entire range but also the principles underlying it, from this side of the Atlantic came in 1962 with the publication of E. A. Philippson's "Phänomenologie, vergleichende Mythologie und

1 *Mythes et dieux des Germains: Essai d'interprétation comparative*, Mythes et Religions, 1 (Paris, 1939).

2 See Jaan Puhvel, ed., *Myth and Law among the Indo-Europeans: Studies in Indo-European Comparative Mythology* (Berkeley, Los Angeles, and London, 1970), pp. 250–259.

3 Dumézil publishes only in French, but a number of his works have been translated into other languages, including German (see *ibid.*). In 1970 the University of Chicago Press came out with two of Dumézil's works in English translation: *The Destiny of the Warrior* and *Archaic Roman Religion*.

germanische Religionsgeschichte."[4] The intensity with which Philippson takes up the argument against Dumézil can perhaps be explained by the fact that Dumézil's 1959 *Les dieux des Germains* contains serious criticism of views that Philippson expounded in an earlier work.[5] In 1964 C. Scott Littleton presented Dumézil's side of the story in an article reviewing the work of the new comparativists up to that date.[6] Since then a number of publications, both favorable and critical, have appeared, attesting the growing influence of Georges Dumézil in American scholarly circles.[7]

One of these is a paper published in 1967 by Einar Haugen under the title, "The Mythical Structure of the Ancient Scandinavians: Some Thoughts on Reading Dumézil."[8] Of the works critical of Dumézil, Haugen's is the most interesting because its argument combines the historicism of pre-Dumézil days with the present structuralist vogue which has spread from linguistics to folklore, anthropology, mythology, and, in fact, to any field that allows (and bears) structural analysis.[9] As a result of this mésalliance of approach the reader receives a warped image of Dumézil, the protostructuralist who somewhere went astray, an image that is as unfair as it is untrue. Unfortunately this image has survived in some circles.[10] A corrective to Haugen is therefore needed, one that will again put Dumézil's thought into perspective.[11]

Einar Haugen's article can logically be divided into two distinct parts. The first part gives an analysis and critique of Dumézil's work;

---

4 *PMLA* 77 (1962), 187–193.

5 See E. A. Philippson, *Die Genealogie der Götter in Germanischer Religion, Mythologie und Theologie*, Illinois Studies in Language and Literature, XXXVII, 3 (Urbana, 1953).

6 "The Comparative Indo-European Mythology of Georges Dumézil," *Journal of the Folklore Institute* 1 (1964), 147–166. In 1966 Littleton published a book-length introduction to Dumézil: *The New Comparative Mythology: An Anthropological Assessment of the Theories of Georges Dumézil* (Berkeley and Los Angeles). It does not seem likely that Haugen had an opportunity to see this book, since in fact it did not appear until 1967.

7 See bibliography in Puhvel, *op. cit.*

8 Einar Haugen, "The Mythical Structure of the Ancient Scandinavians," in *To Honor Roman Jakobson: Essays on the Occasion of His Seventieth Birthday, 11 October 1966*, II (The Hague, 1967), 855–868.

9 See Jacques Ehrmann, ed., *Structuralism* (New York, 1970).

10 See Michael Lane, ed., *Introduction to Structuralism* (New York, 1970), esp. p. 19, where the editor hopes that "the taste of . . . [Dumézil] is conveyed by Einar Haugen," whom he includes in his collection.

11 Haugen and his students have translated Dumézil's *Les dieux des Germains: Essai sur la formation de la religion scandinave*, Mythes et Religions, 38 (Paris, 1959), as *Gods of the Ancient Northmen* (Berkeley, Los Angeles, London, 1973). It seems not unreasonable, therefore, to suppose that Haugen's views regarding Dumézil have undergone certain modifications.

the second presents a structural system of Haugen's own making which offers an alternative to Dumézilian tripartition.

Haugen begins by admitting that he is no expert in mythology and that his only connection with this field is "that he has from time to time taught a course in Scandinavian mythology" (p. 855). His lack of expertise, however, has not prevented Haugen from speaking out on those points of Dumézil's theory which he finds disquieting. His principal objections may be summarized as follows:

1) He is concerned with Dumézil's claim to have made a structural analysis of mythology and is inclined to question whether Dumézil has in fact found the correct structures of the Indo-European daughter mythologies, specifically Germanic mythology (p. 856).

2) He is uncomfortable with Dumézil's "insistent argumentation against what he calls the evolutionary approach which his own is supposed to supersede." "Dumézil," claims Haugen, "argues repeatedly against 'historicism,' as if this were incompatible with structuralism" (p. 856).

3) Haugen finds it a weakness in Dumézil's method that "his comparisons refer to the functions alone: it is as if the mythology consisted wholly of slots ('functions') which could be filled by a variety of gods. However similar Indra and Thor may be in function, their identity as gods is dependent on their having the same name" (p. 858).

4) The one apparent exception to the etymological discontinuity of divine names from Indo-European times to Germanic attested evidence seems to be the case of Týr. Haugen, however, is not convinced that Týr can successfully be traced back to the Indic sky-god Dyauḥ. He further strengthens this point by quoting Jan de Vries's statement: "die Rechnung stimmt nicht genau" (p. 858).

5) Finally, Haugen questions Dumézil's choice in placing Týr alongside Odin as the Germanic god of justice, paralleling the Latin Dius Fidius and the Indic Mitra. "Týr's participation in the binding of Fenrir," he writes, "is not an act of justice; it is part of a trick played on Fenrir by the gods, an episode in their war against the giants, and therefore part of Thor's sphere of activity" (p. 861).

It seems that the common denominator of these objections is a lack of sympathy on Haugen's part (or a lack of understanding) for the curious admixture of abstract and concrete which characterizes Dumézil's system of thought. It should be remembered that Dumézil himself is a linguist of no mean repute[12] and that the influence of Durk-

---

[12] Haugen acknowledges Dumézil's linguistic ability (*op. cit.*, p. 856), but this does not deter his misunderstanding of Dumézil's diachronism, both in linguistics and in mythology.

heim, Mauss, Granet, and Meillet has formed his mind along marked sociological and functional lines.[13] Dumézil, therefore, is no strict algebraist.

Although Haugen is, on the whole, quite fair in his outline sketch of Dumézil's thought, his interpretation of it shows that he has failed to heed his own warning, namely that "the full import of [Dumézil's] terms does not become clear without *extensive reading of the text*" (p. 856; italics mine). The "terms" of Dumézilian mythology to which Haugen refers are the catchwords for the "three functions": sovereignty, force, and fecundity. In Dumézil's sociologically oriented system of mythical interpretation ancient Indo-European society was characterized by a triad of classes: priest, warrior, and herdsman-cultivator. In his analysis of Indic myths, Dumézil found that the social structure paralleled the structure of the Vedic and pre-Vedic pantheon. Following Durkheim, Dumézil postulated that since religion is a communal affair, the society of men and the society of gods should, in effect, logically reflect each other. While traces of Proto-Indo-European social tripartition remain in the Indic *varṇa* system, they have been absent or vestigial in the societies of other Indo-European peoples following the centum/satəm differentiation and the great migrations. On the other hand, mythological tripartition seems to have been much better preserved. The Indic triad of Mitra and Varuṇa, representing the juridical and magico-religious aspects of the sovereign function, respectively; Indra, representing the warrior function; and the two Nāsatyas representing the third function of fecundity, health, and riches, find parallel reflections in Rome in the gods Dius Fidius and Jupiter for the first function, Mars for the second, and Quirinus for the third. In the Scandinavian area the first-function gods are Týr and Odin, the second-function god is Thor, and the third function is represented by the divinities Njördr, Freyr, and Freyja.

Haugen does not directly argue with these points. Sometimes, however, he subtly shifts their meaning, and at other times he ignores them entirely. In commenting on the *Rígsþula*, for example, he states that the caste system of India is reflected in Scandinavia in the division of society into kings, earls, and farmers (p. 857). He seems not at all disquieted by the fact that the class of kings is not really comparable to the Indic *brāhmaṇa* or priestly class.[14]

13 See Littleton, "Comparative Indo-European Mythology," p. 148 n. 6.

14 Edgar Polomé, "The Indo-European Component in Germanic Religion," in Puhvel, *op. cit.*, p. 60, following R. Derolez (*De Godsdienst der Germanen* [Roermond and Maaseik, 1959], pp. 28–29), gives evidence that can be used to support Haugen's division of Germanic society: "At the head of every tribe was a king or

In 1958 Dumézil examined this Eddic poem and concluded that the social structure had experienced a gradual shift.[15] The three children of the god Heimdallr are characterized as (1) Thraell (slave), (2) Karl (peasant), and (3) Jarl (nobleman). It is the son of Jarl who might possibly represent the lost priestly class[16] since his name is Konr-ungr (cf. ON *konungr* = king, conceivably magician-king).[17]

What is of course interesting is that this change in the form of Germanic social organization had little or no effect on the nature of the functions as conceived supernaturally, that is, in the differentiation among Odin, Thor, and Freyr.[18] The fact that social change is reflected here cannot, however, be doubted. The "thrall" (Thraell) or slave is best paralleled in Indic tradition by the śūdra, those who are outside and "beyond the pale" of the Indo-European tripartite social organization. The karl, who represents the farmer class, is paralleled in the Indo-European system by the "third-function" herdsman-cultivator. The earl is clearly a warrior. The colors associated with the three sons of Heimdallr are black, red, and fair. Dumézil has shown that colors such as black, blue, and green are associated with the third function; the color red is a warrior color; and the color

---

a group of heads of smaller tribal units, but in the latter case, a suitable commander was chosen among them in time of war. Various religious elements appeared in the direction of the state: the king was 'sacred,' the priests kept order and peace in the 'thing' assemblies and punished all crimes. . . . Political power belonged in principle to the 'thing'; all important decisions were taken in those assemblies, in which all free men appeared in arms, but among these free men a smaller group of influential families controlled in fact the direction of public affairs, tending to make this situation permanent by isolating themselves from the lower classes and claiming they were born noblemen. Below the free men were the half-free taxpayers, and on the lowest level, the slaves." Note, however, that Indic kings were chosen from the warrior class, indeed from a special segment of that class, the influential *rājanya*, after which they assumed total sovereignty for all functions.

[15] See Dumézil, "La *Rigsþula* et la structure sociale indo-européenne," *Revue de l'histoire des religions*, 154 (1958), 1–19. The shift might be viewed as an upward one; conversely, the canonic colors (black, red, white) have been debased, and there is "downward mobility" in the pantheon: Odin becomes a war god and Thor a fertility deity.

[16] The *goðar* of Iceland were as much warrior-farmer chieftains (*hersir*) as they were priests; in the sagas practically nothing is made of their sacral duties or "functions," nor is there any hard evidence that they were considered a class apart (see Peter Hallberg, *The Icelandic Saga* [Lincoln, 1962], *passim*).

[17] See L. Gerschel, "Une episode trifonctionnelle dans la saga de Hrolfr Kraki," in *Hommages à Georges Dumézil*, Collection Latomus, vol. 45 (Brussels, 1960), pp. 104–116. See also Lee M. Hollander, trans., *The Poetic Edda* (Austin, 1962), p. 127 n. 36.

[18] Jan de Vries, "Sur certains glissements fonctionnels de divinités dans la religion germanique," in *Hommages à Georges Dumézil*, pp. 83–95, indicates that conservatism is not an absolute but a relative factor in myth.

white is reserved for the priestly class.[19] Thus, in the *Rígsþula,* the slave is given a third-function color, the farmer a second-function color, and the warrior assumes a color (fair hair) which most closely resembles the white reserved for the priests.

Another instance of supernatural tripartition which Haugen points out is the configuration from eleventh-century Uppsala where Thor is seen as the central one of three figures, with Odin and Freyr on either side (p. 860). While Haugen argues that this configuration asserts the supremacy of Thor, it is clear that it is also tripartite and represents another instance of mythological conservatism, as well as adding another parallel to the already extensive list of Indo-European triads Dumézil has collected.[20]

The new emphasis Dumézil places on the structural correspondences between the society and the myth of a linguistically homogeneous group such as the Indo-Europeans unites structural thinking with historical thinking. Dumézil's investigation proceeds in two phases. The aim of the first phase is to reconstruct from the comparative evidence of a people diffused across the temporal and spatial boundaries of the Indo-European spectrum the *idéologie* that informed both the sacred and the profane aspects of their lives in earliest times.[21] The second phase moves centrifugally from the reconstructed *idéologie* outward and restores, in Haugen's words, "to Scandinavian and other Indo-European mythologies their backward perspective" (p. 856). In light of this it seems that both of Haugen's major objections to Dumézil, which touch upon the areas of structure and historicism and their relationship or lack of it, are unfounded.

On the issue of historicism Haugen actually echoes Philippson,[22] although he refrains from mentioning his name. Therefore, Dumézil's response to Philippson's objections can adequately serve as response to Haugen's as well.

In the first place, it seems absurd to call Dumézil antihistorical. When Dumézil says that he and Höfler, de Vries, and Betz "résistent à cette vue historicisante,"[23] he refers to the approach of the evolutionary school.[24] Further, it cannot be overstressed that Dumézil's

[19] *L'idéologie tripartie des Indo-Européens,* Collection Latomus, vol. 31 (Brussels, 1958), pp. 25–27.

[20] Cf. Jan de Vries's sobering comments on this (*Altgermanische Religionsgeschichte,* 2d ed. [Berlin, 1956–1957], I, 385–387; II, 86–87, 287–288). See also Dumézil, *Les dieux des Germains,* pp. 116, 117, esp. p. 117.

[21] See Haugen, "Mythical Structure of the Ancient Scandinavians," pp. 855–856, on Dumézil's dependence on the nineteenth-century school of linguistic reconstruction.

[22] See Philippson, "Phänomenologie," and *Die Genealogie der Götter.*

[23] Dumézil, *Les dieux des Germains,* p. 16.

[24] See Jan de Vries, *The Study of Religion: A Historical Approach,* trans. Kees Bolle (New York, 1967), pp. 92–93. The historical school believed that what seemed

objections to this approach are related to specific issues. In this instance the issue is Philippson's discussion of the war between the Aesir and the Vanir.[25] Philippson's argument is that the difference between the religion of the Vanir and the Aesir is a fundamental one. The Vanir represent an older stratum; they are autochthonous, and they produced an agricultural civilization. By contrast, the Aesir are more recent and serve as the expression of a virile, warlike epoch which at the same time manifested strong spiritual traits. Dumézil's response is that this view represents euhemerism in reverse.[26] Philippson would have the reader believe that the war between the Aesir and the Vanir actually took place within a historical context. Dumézil finds this assumption unjustified. He bases his reasons on a careful examination of the texts that recount the battle. These texts, he proceeds to show, treat the event as having taken place either in mythical time and space or in time and space so indefinite that it is clear the author (in this instance Snorri), who otherwise is very careful about historical detail, could not have been writing history.[27]

It is unreasonable to assume that Dumézil has rejected all forms of evolution. He has never said so, and those texts that might bear this implication have not been cited by Haugen as supportive evidence. In fact, an example of evolution which Dumézil quite clearly recognizes is the "évolution du 'dieu juriste,' " Týr. The lie that the god of justice perpetrates on Fenrir in order to bind the monster is not really punished by Týr's self-sacrificing loss of his hand. What in effect occurs is that Týr loses his primary position among the gods. Apparently the moral consciousness of the Germans was developed to so

---

to be ubiquitous was a primitive and barbaric religiosity, that the various I-E tribes began their existence cut off from their common heritage, and that the real gods had only recently evolved. Dumézil does not reconstruct only I-E elements; however, his keen eye for historical nuances is more apparent in his studies on Indo-Iranian and Roman mythology (see his *Archaic Roman Religion*).

25 Philippson, *Die Genealogie der Götter*, p. 19; see also Philippson, "Phänomenologie," p. 189.

26 Dumézil and Wikander (see Stig Wikander, "Pāṇḍava-sagan och Mahābhāratas mytiska förutsättningar," *Religion och Bibel* 6 [1947], 27–39) have shown that the survival of myth in epic garb is a form of euhemerism. What once were divine figures of the Vedic pantheon appear transformed as epic heroes in the *Mahābhārata*. In Roman tradition, no Latin myth parallels the exploits of Romulus, Numa, the three Horatii, and the three Curiatii, or of the Sabines as they are recounted by Livy, yet enough functional and structural parallels exist in the myth of other I-E traditions (notably Indic and Germanic) that it is safe to consider early Roman "history" as euhemerized myth (see Littleton, *New Comparative Mythology*, for further references). Philippson stands closer to the position of Euhemerus: that the gods were originally great men who achieved apotheosis as a reward for the great tasks performed in service of mankind. A similar view is also expressed by Snorri Sturluson in the prologue to his *Prose Edda* (see Kees W. Bolle, "In Defense of Euhemerus," in Puhvel, *op. cit.*, pp. 19–38).

27 Dumézil, *Les dieux des Germains*, pp. 17–21.

high a point that they would not tolerate a god of justice who violated the precepts of his own function.[28]

The second issue raised by Haugen's objection is that Dumézil's structural approach is a likely cause of his antihistoricism and that Dumézil fails to realize how wrong he is in assuming the two are incompatible. A number of scholars have commented on this issue:[29] Turville-Petre, Philippson, Kees Bolle, and Werner Betz.

Turville-Petre's reaction is generally supportive of Dumézil, in commenting on the work of the evolutionist Eugen Mogk who contended that since Snorri Sturluson knew as much or perhaps less about Nordic mythology than we do today, his works, rather than being first-class sources, are mere inventions. While Turville-Petre admits that it is hard to refute such arguments since "tangible evidence in support of Snorri's stories was scarcely to be found,"[30] he himself welcomes the alternative Dumézil presents. This alternative consists of not looking at the literature of ancient Iceland as a Germanic specialist but as an Indo-European comparativist. The parallels that Dumézil was able to draw among the Aesir-Vanir conflict, the Roman-Sabine war, and the Aśvinic conflict with the "two forces" in ancient India,[31] as well as the dual mutilation of Odin and Týr which finds parallels in both Roman and Celtic mythologies, to mention just two examples, are indicative of a methodological approach that cuts across time and space in the Indo-European continuum but, perhaps more important, is supportive of Snorri's reputation as a reliable mythographer. In short, in spite of Snorri's euhemerizing tendencies, as well as his obvious Christian education, a third influence other than his imagination would have to be posited as the source for his mythological writings. Turville-Petre is happy to suggest that this source is Germanic oral tradition.[32]

In E. A. Philippson one finds an apologist for the evolutionist school engaged in a polemic attack[33] on what he chooses to call the "phenomenological approach" of Dumézil. It is ironic that Philippson winds up doing for Dumézil what Mogk did for Snorri: he accuses Dumézil of having invented *Gelehrtenmärchen*. While this accusation

---

[28] *Ibid.*, pp. 74–76, esp. p. 74: " 'Mars,' Týr sont pratiquement descendus au rang de 'Hercules,' de Thórr." See also Dumézil, " 'Le Borgne' and 'Le Manchot,' " elsewhere in this volume.

[29] E. O. G. Turville-Petre, "Professor Dumézil and the Literature of Iceland," in *Hommages à Georges Dumézil*, pp. 209–214. Although Haugen seems to depend on Turville-Petre for his exposition of the evolutionist viewpoint (compare *ibid.*, p. 210, with Haugen, "The Mythical Structure of the Ancient Scandinavians," p. 857), he ignores Turville-Petre's conclusions favoring Dumézil's approach.

[30] *Op. cit.*, p. 210.

[31] See Dumézil, *L'idéologie tripartie*, p. 56.

[32] *Op. cit.*, pp. 213–214.

[33] See "Phänomenologie," pp. 187–193.

puts Dumézil in good company, it does not solve the apparent conflict between Dumézil's structuralism and his alleged antihistoricism.

Kees Bolle, in his somewhat original approach to this problem, takes as his starting point the defense of Euhemerus.[34] His argument —that euhemerism, properly considered, is neither blasphemous nor rationalizing but rather a mythical *aggiornamento* (the updating of a myth whose meaning is nearly lost so that it may survive *as myth*)— concludes with the following comment on Dumézil: "The 'genetic approach'[35] is valid, of course, in the study of euhemerizing documents, but its limit becomes visible when it disregards the form and structure of the document under discussion by focusing only on what may have been left of the 'original' myth" (p. 37). In other words, Dumézil's approach is prone to suffer from the same weakness that characterized earlier evolutionism: neither approach can illuminate the total religious phenomenon. Bolle suggests that an even more radical solution to the problem of how to transcend evolutionism might be the structural way of Claude Lévi-Strauss, who proposed to study all the versions of a given myth, so that Sophocles and Freud, with respect to Oedipus, would form variants of each other. The profits gleaned from such an endeavor are limited, however, by the nature of the intellectual game that makes them possible.[36]

Edgar Polomé sees the problem as representing an irreconcilable dichotomy. On the one hand he finds that Karl Helm views Germanic religion as an evolved organism whose Indo-European genetic component is largely vestigial; on the other hand he finds that Dumézil "has recognized a definite structure as basic to and specific of Indo-European society and by comparison of the various attested systems tries to back up his deductions on the survival of the original tripartition in the most disparate traditions of the Indo-European peoples."[37]

A possible resolution to this dichotomy, suggested by Werner Betz, is cited by Polomé:[38] "Beide Wege sind notwendig. Der Germanist wird versuchen, die Gefahren beider zu vermeiden: geschichtsloses Strukturieren oder historisierendes Auflösen in auseinanderfallende

[34] *Op. cit.* Bolle supports Snorri's validity in an exciting new way which might be supported by recalling that Snorri's integrated compendium of myth reflects the earlier gospel harmonies such as Tatian's *Diatessaron*, translated into East Frisian circa 830, and Otfried von Weissenburg's *Evangelienharmonie*, written in South Rhenish Franconian between 863 and 871. It seems inconceivable that Snorri, easily one of the most learned men of his age, would be unfamiliar with these earlier models or that they exercised no influence on him.

[35] See C. Scott Littleton, "Georges Dumézil and the Rebirth of the Genetic Model," elsewhere in this volume.

[36] Bolle, *op. cit.*, p. 38.

[37] Polomé, *op. cit.*, p. 61.

[38] *Ibid.*, p. 61. See also Werner Betz, "Die altgermanische Religion," in W. Stammler, ed., *Deutsche Philologie im Aufriss*, 2d ed. (Berlin, 1962), III, col. 1558.

Details—und dafür sich bemühen, die Vorteile beider fruchtbar zu machen: Herausarbeiten der grossen Zusammenhänge und Überprüfung des Beschlossenen am geschichtlich Bezeugten."

While the flexibility of Dumézil's approach vis-à-vis historicism has not escaped Haugen's notice, Haugen has unfortunately not been able to rise above puzzlement. After admitting (p. 858) that "even in Dumézil's thinking there is room for a historical change in the functions," he makes a gigantic leap from the displacement of functions to the replacement of gods and presents evolutionist hypothesis for fact: "But what is equally striking is that the gods themselves have not only been 'un peu déplacées' [*sic*], they have quite simply been replaced by others. This is what the evolutionists have been saying all along" (p. 858). Yet this is not what Dumézil has been saying, nor is it what Dumézil has wittingly or unwittingly implied.

Dumézil's structural analysis excludes the possibility of evolution in this sense: no matter how much or how little evolution was at work, if the structure of a daughter mythology reflects a parental structure in whole or in part, then it is more reasonable to assume that the daughter structure represents a genetic phenotype than it is to assume an evolutionary or polygenetic development. And should evolution ever be proved in this or in that instance, the persistence of the "old" structure into which the divine "replacements" arrange themselves will reveal only that ontogeny is just as prone to recapitulate phylogeny in myth as it is in living organisms. And this is the point that Dumézil has been making all along.[39]

As a direct consequence of his failure to recognize the complementary roles that historicism and structuralism play in the thought of Dumézil, and also as a consequence of his failure to understand the *analogous* relationship Dumézil sees as existing between linguistic reconstruction and mythological reconstruction, Haugen chooses to make an issue of Dumézil's reluctance to employ the onomastic etymological approach to the names of the divinities in the Germanic pantheon.

Haugen objects to the fact that Dumézil's mythic identifications of deities do not depend on onomastic as well as on functional correspondences.[40] If Dumézil is really a comparativist along the lines of the nineteenth-century philologists who established the genetic relation-

[39] Cf. Dumézil's studies on the post-Zoroastrian pantheon in Iran. Tripartition shines through in the structure of the Aməša Spəntsa. See *L'idéologie tripartie*, pp. 40–46.

[40] Haugen's criticism is inconsistent with his statement in "Mythical Structure of the Ancient Scandinavians," p. 858: "It is perhaps his [Dumézil's] greatest contribution that he has separated the gods from their functions and shown that the latter can be analyzed independently of the former."

ship among Indo-European daughter languages, then he should religiously stick to their method of historical reconstruction, whether the objects of that reconstruction are words, structures, or myths (p. 857). The common denominator of words such as Latin *pater*, Sanskrit *pitā́*, and English *father* is that they all mean the same thing. Their differences can be explained by historical sound laws. Thus the common denominator of gods should be "that their names correspond linguistically and their functions with a degree of approximation comparable to that of word meanings" (p. 857).

With respect to the gods, Haugen's demand may be a little steep. Words are after all names; the names of gods, however, are simply words. Gods themselves are much more than their names. Haugen himself has pointed out (p. 858) that the etymon of Týr might be **dejew-* 'shining,' **djēw-* 'day,' or **deiw-* meaning simply 'god'; the name reveals little. And even were it possible to trace Týr back directly to Dyauḥ (who is linguistically related to the Greek Zeus and the Latin Jupiter), what would be accomplished? Not even the last three gods, in whose case the onomastic links are indisputable, correspond in function. Their having the same name does *not* make them identical as gods.[41] This same error of depending overly and exclusively on onomastic evidence was made earlier by the solarist school of comparative mythologists.

The functional view eliminates any need for onomastic correspondence; on the other hand, it does not reject it. Examples of this point are correspondences that Dumézil has found, both functionally and etymologically, for Indic kṣatriya and Iranian Xšathra; Indo-Iranian Aryaman and Irish Eremon; Indo-Iranian Apā́ṃ Nápāt, Irish Nechtan, and Latin Neptunus.[42]

The names of the gods are far from being of no interest or importance to Dumézil. In fact, Antoine Meillet's 1907 study of Mitra,[43] which determined that the name meant 'contract,' helped provide the base for Dumézil's later distinguishing him from Varuṇa 'oath' and led him to the insight that the first function was divided into magico-religious and juridical aspects.

In Germanic myth, it is unfortunate that no onomastic-etymologi-

[41] Haugen is very vague on this point. *Ibid.*, p. 857, he establishes both onomastic and functional criteria for determining the identity of two or more gods, yet on the next page he drops the functional criterion: "Two successive village priests do not become identical even though they may perform the same function."

[42] Cf. Georges Dumézil, *Le troisième souverain* (Paris, 1949), p. 167; Jan de Vries, "La valeur religieuse du mot germanique *irmin*," *Cahiers du Sud* 36 (1952), 18–27; Jan de Vries, "Über das Wort 'Jarl' und seine Verwandten," *La Nouvelle Clio* 4 (1954), 461–469; Dumézil, "Le puits de Nechtan," *Celtica* 6 (1963), 50–61; *Mythe et épopée*, III (Paris, 1973), 19–89.

[43] "Le Dieu indo-iranien Mitra," *Journal asiatique*, ser. 10, 10 (1907), 143–159.

cal correspondences can be adduced. Their lack, however, does not negate the functional correspondences that are present, and it would be remiss of Dumézil if he did not point them out. In fact, it is clear to Dumézil that if one had to choose between the two, there is no question but that functional correspondences are far more reliable than onomastic ones.[44] Thus Dumézil's method of mythological reconstruction is analogous to the method of the nineteenth-century philologists; it is not identical with it.

It seems, then, that when Haugen says that Dumézil's "thèse structuraliste" excludes the possibility of historical development, he is actually equating comparative mythology with comparative linguistics: "So long as the names of the trinities in each of the daughter languages are demonstrably different," he says, "there is room for a study of the changes that led to the gradual displacement of one god by another" (p. 858). The logical consequence of this kind of displacement is that the structure Dumézil has unearthed for Germanic myth is not necessarily the correct one. And the reason for this is paradoxically that Dumézil's structure is *too* historical, being general and Indo-European rather than specifically Germanic. And this, too, is what Haugen means when he again resorts to the linguistic touchstone and calls Dumézil's attention to the fact that the rift between structural-descriptive linguistics and historical-comparative linguistics has been healed (p. 858). But when Haugen quotes Betz[45]—"Der Gegensatz von Helm und Dumézil ist z.T. der Gegensatz von Historikern auf der einen und Strukturisten und Komparatisten auf der anderen Seite"—he fails to note the shift in terms which at least implies that the opposite of Dumézil is not an historical comparativist but a descriptive historicist.

It would seem that this latter term (bizarre as it is) serves as an adequate definition of Haugen's own position vis-à-vis Germanic mythology. In the first place, Haugen stipulates historical change from Indo-European times, the lack of onomastic correspondences being sufficient proof. Thus the role that history plays in Haugen's thought is merely to smooth the way for his conclusion that the Indo-European structure cannot validly be applied to the Germanic pantheon. This leads to the second point. Historicism, having already negated

[44] See Dumézil, *Les dieux des Germains*, pp. 57–58, for an answer to Haugen's objections on this point. It is surprising that Haugen, whose bibliography indicates an awareness of this book, makes no reference to what Dumézil has to say in defense of his "functional" position. Note also that name-taboos universally associated with divinities make names the least stable element in mythico-religious studies.

[45] See Betz, *op. cit.*, 2d ed. (1962), III, cols. 1557–1558; Haugen, "Mythical Structure," p. 858 n. 7.

comparativism, continues in its negative role by its inability to offer an alternative structure. Thus the new structure that is to be determined for the Germanic pantheon must proceed along synchronic, descriptive lines. The unity of a *Weltanschauung* is necessarily assumed—although again there is no historical justification for the assumption—and Germanic mythology is perforce compared only with itself. In the end, the result is that a very valuable point of reference has been lost; ironically, it is the very point on which Haugen had earlier praised Dumézil, that he had restored to Germanic mythology its backward perspective (p. 858).

Turning now to Haugen's original contribution to the question of what is the proper structural analysis of the Germanic pantheon, it is interesting to observe that he attempts to base his own proposals on a principle (binary opposition) which can also be found in Dumézil. Citing Dumézil's comments on the Aesir-Vanir conflict, he finds that binary opposition can be traced back to Indo-European times: the first two functions allied against the third (p. 860). Haugen stops short, however, of quoting further in Dumézil's sentence: "séparation initiale, guerre; puis indissoluble union dans la *structure tripartie hierarchisée.*"[46] In effect, Dumézil still winds up with tripartition; the full text contains no hint of the possibility of reducing the structure to a bipartite 2:1 tree diagram. This diagram, however, is exactly what Haugen has in mind, and, in order to establish it as a viable alternative, he asks if the conflict cannot be viewed *historically*. It is difficult to determine what Haugen means by this. In Dumézil's comparative sense the Aesir-Vanir myth is historical, with earlier parallels adduced for India and Rome.[47] But Haugen ignores these parallels. Could it be that the clash between two groups of gods represents the clash between migrating and sedentary peoples which later was recounted on the level of myth? Haugen does not say so explicitly. His interests lie in another direction. The truce effected between the Aesir and the Vanir becomes for him the "mythical way of describing that higher unity into which they have entered, in which the opposition is neutralized" (p. 860). And as he further develops the argument for his new structure, he calls on the support of Lévi-Strauss and cites him: "Mythical thought always works from the awareness of oppositions towards their progressive mediation."[48] So it is clear that once again history has served as the missile to be hurled indiscriminately at Dumézil. Its cogency as an issue here must be seriously doubted,

46 *L'idéologie tripartie*, p. 56 (italics mine).

47 *Ibid.*, pp. 56–57.

48 Claude Lévi-Strauss, "The Structural Study of Myth," in Thomas A. Sebeok, ed., *Myth: A Symposium* (Bloomington and London, 1968), p. 99.

just as the cogency of Haugen's prior objections deserves to be doubted. From an ethnographic point of view, for example, it is impossible to conceive of a highly specialized warrior class that is not provided with sustenance by a correspondingly developed group of herdsmen or cultivators.

It might be useful at this stage in the discussion to point out that the role of history in the study of myth has often been confused with the role history plays in mythical thinking itself. The role of history in the study of myth is the concern of scholars and mythographers. Here myth is seen as a human activity which like any other human activity takes place in time and thus is subject to historical investigation. While methodological premises might make it necessary to ignore (or in Husserl's sense to "bracket out") history, the neglect of history does not diminish its role. In the second case, however, mythical thinking goes beyond history. Viewed in this light, what is remarkable about Dumézil's insight is not that the Indo-European pantheon reflects the social structure but that both social structure and pantheon reflect each other. For, despite the sociological base on which Dumézil's structure rests, the action of a real myth has a way of occurring *per omnia saecula saeculorum*: in places that are at once nowhere and now here.

The implication for structure is clear. A structure may have a historical base, but when structure is considered as an indissoluble part of myth *qua* myth then it is ahistorical: myths are enunciated in the aorist.[49] Thus, following Dumézil's approach, a historically inherited structure will mythify a possible historical event like the Aesir-Vanir conflict and dehistoricize it. It does not really matter whether the conflict ever took place. What matters is whether the structure was inherited or represents a new development, and the comparative evidence is in Dumézil's favor.

Haugen's idea of structure is based on the phonological principles of the Prague school of linguistics, which also proved to be formative for the work of Claude Lévi-Strauss.[50] It is an approach that leaves little room for history. The Prague school is ahistorical inasmuch as its principles, unlike Grimm's Law or Verner's Law which account only for unique and unrepeatable historical occurrences, exist on a more abstract level and describe not only past but possible future linguistic developments. Lévi-Strauss, working with these principles and applying them to mythical thinking, has scrapped the historical

[49] I am indebted to Professor Jaan Puhvel of the University of California, Los Angeles, for this insight.

[50] See Haugen, "Mythical Structure," p. 856, esp. nn. 5 and 6.

in favor of the cyclical view.[51] And Einar Haugen, who depends on both these predecessors for his structural insights, is compelled by this adopted methodology to forgo the justification of a historical model for his analysis of the Germanic pantheon. His structure resides on a more abstract level than Dumézil's. It is not historically grounded but logically grounded. Thus at the same time its applicability is not limited to the Germanic area or, as for Dumézil, to the Indo-Europeans, but extends to any product of human thinking no matter where or when it occurred. Further, its logic is not the logic of myth or even the logic found within myth, but something imported from the outside. Its relevance to any form of ratiocination makes Haugen's structure predictable and a priori (as opposed to Dumézil's which is empirical and a posteriori), but that hardly makes it more "correct" than Dumézil's structure.

Had Haugen but realized the insignificance of history as a base for his structural proposals, he might not have devoted so much space to a criticism of Dumézil which not only misses the mark but also is not germane to his purpose. Still, in the exposition of his pantheon, he persists in dredging up historico-structural complaints on two more occasions and deserves to be answered on both points.

The first point concerns Týr. Haugen places this god at the side of Thor rather than at the side of Odin because he feels that the act of binding Fenrir is not concerned with justice but rather with the gods' war against the giants, which is Thor's realm. Further, Týr's martial function is attested by his *interpretatio romana* "Mars Thincsus" and is strengthened by the paralleling of Tuesday (= Týr's day) with *dies Martis* (p. 861).

In view of the closeness of the Indo-European parallels which Dumézil has adduced for this incident,[52] it is at least reasonable to suspect that Haugen has bisected a mythologem which in addition to the "Fenrisginning" also includes the story of how Odin lost his eye and which has been characterized as the dual first-function mutilation.

In looking more closely at Týr's Roman counterpart Scaevola, one might be able to argue that in sacrificing his hand so that the enemy king Porsenna will believe the lie that his life is endangered by 300

[51] Claude Lévi-Strauss, *The Savage Mind* (Chicago, 1969), esp. pp. 245–269. Lévi-Strauss states that in Sartre's dialectical system history plays the part of myth. His own position is that objective history is total chaos. The savage mind totalizes: the entire process of human knowledge assumes the character of a closed system of cyclically self-regenerating structures.

[52] See pp. 35–36, above, and also Dumézil, *Les dieux des Germains*, pp. 66–77; for his latest word see " 'Le Borgne' and 'Le Manchot,' " elsewhere in this volume.

fanatic assassins, Scaevola is acting in the martial context of the war between the Romans and the Etruscans. But does the context alone characterize both lie and sacrifice as an act of force? And in Týr's case, is Fenrir bound because he was constrained by force to submit to the fetters? Did either Týr or Scaevola lose his hand while physically fighting? It seems that in both instances force had already been tried and had failed to gain the desired objective. Thus it became necessary to find precisely someone who was *outside* Thor's or Mars's sphere of activity, rather than someone who was part of it. The means whereby Týr and Scaevola succeeded were false oaths, and these fall into the realm of judicial trickery, that is, into Mitra's sphere of activity. Haugen, by interpreting Týr's loss of his hand as contextually related to the class of "acts of force," has invented thereby the very kind of *Gelehrtenmärchen* which Philippson has accused Dumézil of inventing.

Nor is Haugen's point valid that Týr's "role as a god of war is confirmed by the use of his name to replace that of Mars in the weekday names" (p. 861). Týr appears under the aspect of Mars Thincsus as the protector of law and order. This protector in Indic tradition was Mitra, and Mitra's helper was Aryaman. In Germanic tradition the god cognate to Aryaman was Irmin. And Irmin has been interpreted as being none other than Týr himself. The last piece of evidence concerning Týr's juridical function is that the "thing" or court would meet on the third day of the week, the day that was called "Týr's day."[53]

The final issue with Haugen concerns Heimdallr. Haugen (p. 862) regards him as belonging to an earlier, undifferentiated stratum (before "force" separated Thor from the unmarked Odin). Looking at the argument from a more historical and more Dumézilian point of view, it seems to make little sense. If differentiation into functions took place prior to the individuation and migration of the various Indo-European peoples, then how is one to explain Heimdallr's regression to the undifferentiated state unless one posits that he is more ancient (while still being Indo-European) than any other attested god? Yet this is difficult to imagine (much less establish), since the name appears in a language that is clearly later than the premigration period. Thus if Heimdallr remains undifferentiated it is not because he is a relic of a time when differentiation had not been thought of, but because tradition has placed him at the side of differentiated gods. The differentiation Haugen is looking for cannot be used as a touch-

[53] Betz, *op. cit.*, III, cols. 1579–1580; de Vries, "Sur certains glissements"; de Vries, *Altgermanische Religionsgeschichte*, II, 13–16; Jakob Grimm, *Deutsche Rechtsalterhümer* (Göttingen, 1854), pp. 818–819.

stone for differentiation per se. Heimdallr has his own characteristics which should serve to differentiate him from the other gods, just as his Roman counterpart Janus is individuated in his pantheon. Certainly there is no need for the hypothesis that Heimdallr existed prior to differentiation.

In summation, then, the following points may be recapitulated:

1) Haugen's belief that Dumézil's argumentation against the evolutionary approach amounts to a rejection of historicism in favor of structuralism is not quite the same argument linguists use when they speak of diachronic versus synchronic approaches. At its best, Dumézil's approach is a combination of both, while at its worst it is most strongly biased toward the realm of diachronism. After all, the entire concept of *idéologie* which serves as the base for Dumézil's comparative reconstructions seems at times to be no more than a logical and methodological tool to "explain" how a tripartite pantheon or how tripartite formulas can exist among a people whose social structure no longer exhibits the tripartite division that presumably once characterized Proto-Indo-European society. Indeed, it is difficult to maintain that some of these Indo-European peoples ever actually exhibited a tripartite social structure. Thus the *idéologie* of which Dumézil speaks, unless it is a religiomythical "renewal," refers more to the detritus of a common Indo-European inheritance (which is historical) than to the functional reflection of social and mythological conditions (which is synchronic).

2) Haugen's central premise seems to be that if Dumézil can follow the path that comparative philology has made smooth in order to construct a comparative mythology along similar lines, then Haugen can make use of the concepts of more modern linguistics in order to set up a mythological structure as a counterpart to Dumézil's. The basic fallacy of this approach lies in the fact that his dependence on Roman Jakobson is not comparable to Dumézil's dependence on the early comparative philologists. Both Dumézil and his predecessors were engaged in what might be called Indo-European studies; the specific objects of these studies (civilization, language, mythology) were but the means toward an illumination of the whole of this group of people. Linguistic studies dominated the field because more thorough preliminary work had been done in this area and because the data, by their very nature, were more plentiful and more reliable. Yet it seems safe to say that these philologists were more concerned with studying the nature of the Indo-Europeans than they were with studying the nature of language as such. The latter is a more modern preoccupation, arising, in part, together with the neopositivist and analytic movements in philosophy.

This sort of diachronic approach contrasts heavily with that of Roman Jakobson (p. 856), whose concern with "minimal oppositions," "distinctive features," and "neutralization of contrasts" reflects a synchronic, analytical, and abstract interest in the nature of language itself. Thus Jakobson's structural principles are not ideally limited to the Indo-European language family; they are much less applicable to the relationship of the languages to Indo-European civilization as a whole. If Jakobson's approach can be fruitfully applied to myth, then the results of that application must be recognized as existing on a supraliteral level and as depending not on the comparative evidence of history but purely and simply on the rules of logic and on the correctness of the starting premises.

It is unfortunate that Einar Haugen does not defend the correctness or *unerbittliche Notwendigkeit* of the premise that binary opposition (which convention has made a workable Hegelian tool in linguistics) is validly applicable to the data of myth. Such a defense seems unnecessary to him for perhaps two reasons. First, and more mundanely, a paper in a Festschrift should say something laudatory about the man who is being honored. Second, if binary opposition can be applied to Germanic myth with as much success as tripartition (and Haugen argues that this system is even more successful than Dumézil's), then all the proof necessary for validity has been established. It would be helpful to recall that the historical name for this kind of reasoning is "begging the question." Thus, while Haugen may conclude his article with the statement, "at no point is a tripartite division necessary" (p. 866), saying it does not make it true. It might just as easily be said of Haugen: at no point is a bipartite division necessary.[54]

3) It is in distinguishing Dumézil from Haugen that the notion of levels becomes important. The very abstractness of Haugen's approach makes its concrete value negligible. Literary critics have shown that analyses that depend on self-evident oppositions such as light/dark, love/hate, and life/death are at best uninspired and at worst banal. If the binary approach is worth anything at all, it is worth something only inasmuch as it delineates a mode of behavior which is either not all that self-evident and/or which is common to all humans. That is to say, it must be universally applicable, though not universally recognized. What one ends up with here is a structure à la Lévi-Strauss (to whom Haugen [p. 856] makes his proper bow of

[54] Cf. Rudolf Carnap, "Empiricism, Semantics, and Ontology," *Revue internationale de philosophie* 4 (1950), 20–40. If one assumes the existence of a framework, he cannot make value judgments about it without recourse to a different framework.

obeisance)[55] which represents even at its best the error that the more literal-minded Dumézil would call a "departure from the text." Thus Haugen, seemingly unconsciously, universalizes (= identifies the already universal elements of) Germanic myth, while Dumézil particularizes already concrete elements found in other Indo-European areas by showing their parallels in Germanic in a straightforward, literal manner. In the end it is Dumézil who looks the historian rather than Haugen, who would pose as history's defender.

Bearing these objections in mind, the question arises whether one can still make some valid use of Haugen's binary scheme. Its real (albeit vague) value on the abstract level has already been alluded to, provided the descent to the concrete in conclusions is cautious and minimal. On the concrete and literal level, however, an abstract system is of dubious value unless the abstractions themselves are already present in the text as abstractions, not as potential abstractions awaiting an interpreter.

Such a text seems to exist in Germanic tradition. It is the prose preface to the Middle High German *Heldenbuch*.[56] It recounts how God came to create dwarfs, giants, and heroes. Dwarfs appeared first; they were given control of land and mountains and charged with the maintenance of the earth's treasure. When dragons threatened the existence of the dwarfs, however, God created giants to kill the dragons. Then the giants' evil nature got the better of them and they in turn began to threaten the dwarfs, taking their riches and making them slaves. God again had to send a mediating force into the field, and so he created heroes who are described as *ein mittel volck vnder der treier hant volck*. The dwarfs were rescued and the giants became their servants. The text then drops all mention of giants and dwarfs and turns to the courtly and heroic exploits of knights: the tournaments, battles, the rescue of maidens. The text concludes with a series of cryptic statements: (1) the nobility from the emperor on down is de-

[55] For a criticism of the Lévi-Straussian approach, see Bertel Nathhorst, *Formal or Structural Studies of Traditional Tales: The Usefulness of Some Methodological Proposals Advanced by Vladimir Propp, Alan Dundes, Claude Lévi-Strauss and Edmund Leach*, Acta Universitatis Stockholmiensis, Stockholm Studies in Comparative Religion, 9 (Stockholm, 1969), pp. 37–59 and esp. p. 71, where Nathhorst concludes that the problem of Lévi-Strauss lies in "the impossibility . . . of definitely connecting the analysis with any human condition except that of his own mind."

[56] Adelbert von Keller, ed., *Das deutsche Heldenbuch nach dem Muthmasslich ältesten Drucke*, Bibliothek des Literarischen Vereins in Stuttgart, 87 (Stuttgart, 1867), pp. 1–2 (see appendix to this paper for the full German text). I am grateful to Stephen P. Schwartz for calling this text to my attention, and to Professor Georges Dumézil for his comments and suggestions on how it might be interpreted. See also Haugen, "Mythical Structure," pp. 863–864.

scended from giants; (2) *Vnd was kein held nie kein paur,* which could either mean that the nobility were neither heroes nor peasants, or that no hero was ever a peasant; and (3) from these (the antecedent is ambiguous, but presumably it is either giants or heroes) are descended all lords and nobles.

At first it appears that the succession of dwarf, giant, and hero represents the three functions. But dwarfs are characterized as both kings and guardians of treasure, that is, as both first- and third-function beings. Dumézil understands that the society then lacks a second function, yet it is nonetheless a total society. Giants enter in a second-function role but are subdued and disappear. When they are later mentioned as ancestors of the nobility and the knights, this designation might be taken as social criticism on the part of the author. Knights seem to be both second- and third-function representatives: warriors and rescuers of damsels in distress.[57] Then at the end the peasant is introduced, apparently to contrast with nobility and heroes. While this last division is definitely tripartite, its origin need not be traced as far back as Indo-European times, since the social division mentioned reflects the actual state of affairs existing in medieval Europe.[58]

Einar Haugen's notions of binary opposition and mediation seem to be reflected in the *Heldenbuch.* The first part speaks of an opposition between dwarfs and dragons which is mediated by giants. Then the opposition becomes one between dwarfs and giants. It seems that the giants who exhibited characteristics that related them to dwarfs[59] and characteristics that related them to dragons opted in favor of the latter. Thus the mediation was neutralized and a new mediating factor linked to both dwarfs and giants, that is, the hero, entered on the scene. His mediation was final. The tyranny of the giants was overthrown (that they themselves were possibly rehabilitated after their servitude is another way of interpreting the statement that giants became the ancestors of the nobility) and the rescued dwarfs were left to themselves.

In further support of the Haugenian approach, one can cite an Ossetic legend[60] that describes how the Ossets' ancient heroes, the

[57] Donald J. Ward, "The Separate Functions of the Indo-European Divine Twins," in Puhvel, *op. cit.*, pp. 193–202.

[58] Mediaeval European society was actually far more complex; what is important is that it was *viewed* by its members as tripartite. See pp. 32–34, above. See also *Das deutsche Heldenbuch*, p. 764, for bibliographical note. The MSS and early editions indicate that the *Heldenbuch* goes back at least to the fifteenth century, and quite probably it is earlier than that.

[59] Note their common love of treasure (Haugen, "Mythical Structure," p. 865). Dwarfs, dragons, and giants share this feature.

[60] See Dumézil, *L'idéologie tripartie*, pp. 10–11.

Narts, were divided into three families: the Boriatæ, characterized by wealth; the Alægatæ, distinguished by intelligence; and the Æxsærtægkatæ, noted for strength and heroism. This triad, representing the third, first, and second functions respectively, suffers a transformation to binary opposition in a Chechen variant.[61] Here two groups are mentioned, the Njärt and the Orxustoy. The former represent a utopian society identified by the adjectives "pious" and "rich," whereas the latter misuse their "strength" and are represented as a band of marauders.[62] Thus the first and third functions are pitted against the second in a struggle that offers a striking parallel to the dwarf-giant conflict.[63] But what is striking about the approach and what argues for the validity of Haugen's system in this instance is the concreteness of the parallelism. Although no genetic claims are made for the similarities between Ossetic and Germanic versions,[64] a common structure already discernible on the literal level most certainly underlies both. On this level, at least, Haugen appears more convincing.

APPENDIX*

Von den gezwergen.

Es ist auch czů wissen warvmb got die cleinen zwerg vnd die grossen rysen, vnd darnach die held ließ werden. Zů dem ersten ließ er die zwerglin werden vmb des willen, das das lant vnd gebürge gar wiest vnd vngebawen was, vnd vil gůtes von silber vnd gold edel gestein vnd berlin in den bergen was. Darumb machte got die gezwerg gar listig vnd wyse das sie übel vnd gůt gar wol erkanten vnd warzů alle ding gůt waren Sie wisten auch warczů die gestein gůt waren. Etliche steyn die gebent grosse sterck. Etlich machtent die vnsichtber die sie bey in trůgent. Das hieß eyn nebelkap Vnd darumb gab got den zwergen kunst vnd weißheit, darumb so bawten sie hipsche hole berg vnd gab

[61] See Dumézil, *Mythe et épopée* I (Paris, 1968), 478–484.

[62] Boriatæ and Alægatæ are once more subsumed by the generic Narts. Although their functional features remain differentiated, this differentiation is possibly vestigial. The distinctive feature is "force" and it marks the opposing Orxustoy (=Æxsærtægkatæ) who form a Nart subgroup. This analysis corresponds to Haugen's views ("Mythical Structure," p. 860), despite the fact that no neutralization of contrasts occurs. See also Dumézil, *Mythe et épopée* I, 479.

[63] Contrast this set of opposing forces with the "normal" functional war in which the first two functions are allied against the third (see above, *passim*; Dumézil, *L'idéologie tripartie*, pp. 56–57). See also Dumézil, *Destiny of the Warrior*, pp. 58–64, in which the second function is noted for its stand somewhat apart from the rest of society: the warrior and the war-god are characterized by "solitude and liberty."

[64] History provides no basis for assuming anything but a polygenetic correspondence; the major obstacle, viewed structurally, is the lack of neutralization.

* From *Das deutsche Heldenbuch*, ed. Adelbert von Keller.

in adel das sie künig waren vnd herren [1c] als wol als die held. vnd gab in grosse reichtunge. Vnd da nu got die rysen ließ werden. das was darumb das sie sölten die wilden tier vnd die grossen würm erschlagen, das die zwerg dest sicherer werent, vnd das lant gebawen mecht werden. Dar nach über liczel iar da wurden die rysen den zwergen gar vil zů leid thůn. vnd wurden die risen gar böß vnd vngetrü. Darnach beschůff got die starcken held das was da czůmal ein mittel volck vnder der treier hant volck. Vnd ist zu wissen das die helden gar vil iar getrüw vnd byderbe warent. Vnd darumb soltent sie den zwergen zů hilff kumen wyder die vngetrüwen risen, vnd wider die wilden tier vnd würm. Das lant was in den zeiten gancz vngebuwen, Darumb macht got starcke held vnd gab in die natur das ir můt vnd sinn můstent stan auff manheit nach eren vnd auff streit vnd krieg Es waren auch vil künig vnder den zwergen die hetten rysen zů dienern wann sie hetten ruhe lant vnd wieste weld vnd gebürge nach bey iren wonungen ligen. Die held sahen auch an allewegen frawen zucht vnd ere. vnd warent geneigt zů der gerechtigkeit witwen vnd weysen czů beschirmen. Sie theten auch den frawen kein leyt, es [1d] were dann leibs not, vnd kamen frawen allwegen in nöten czů hilf. Vnd begiengen vil manheit durch frawen willen zů schimpf vnd zů ernst. Ist auch zů wissen das die rysen allwegen waren keiser, künig, herczogen, grafen, vnd herren, dienstleüt ritter, vnd knecht, vnd waren alle edel leüt. Vnd was kein held nie kein paur. Vnd da von seind all herren vnd edel leüt kumen.

Approaches to Germanic Mythology*

EDGAR POLOMÉ, *University of Texas*

Any scientific study of ancient mythology is closely dependent on the available source material. For Germanic mythology the main sources are the *Eddas*, which provide a colorful picture of the Germanic pantheon. The so-called older *Edda* or *Poetic Edda*[1] is a collection of poems which acquired its definite shape in Iceland in the thirteenth century, but whose original poems may be much older, some dating as far back as the ninth century. About half of the thirty-odd "lays" deal with events happening in the world of the gods or contain episodes in which the gods play a prominent part. The others are songs extolling the feats of legendary heroes, sometimes with gods and mythical beings appearing in them. Most important for the historian of religion is the *Vǫluspá*—the Prophecy of the Seeress—an impressive survey of world events from the very beginnings till the doom of the gods, which is, however, often claimed to reflect a rather late form of Germanic belief. Also valuable is the *Hávamál*—the Sayings of Hár—

* A preliminary version of this lecture was given at the University of Texas, Austin, on November 13, 1970, to honor Professor Lee M. Hollander.

The first part of the text is essentially an expanded version of the first pages of my contribution, "The Indo-European Component in Germanic Religion," to the volume *Myth and Law among the Indo-Europeans: Studies in Indo-European Comparative Mythology*, ed. Jaan Puhvel (Berkeley, Los Angeles, and London, 1970), incorporating the most accurate analysis of the sources of Germanic religion given by R. Derolez in *De Godsdienst der Germanen* (Roermond and Maaseik, 1959), pp. 38–43. The remainder of the paper is a rebuttal of the critique of Georges Dumézil's work by Ernst A. Philippson in his article "Phänomenologie, vergleichende Mythologie und germanische Religionsgeschichte," *PMLA* 77 (1962), 187–193.

1 Lee M. Hollander has provided a meticulously accurate translation of *The Poetic Edda* (Austin, 1962), reproducing the verse patterns, the rhythm, and the mood of the original. All quotations in this paper are from his translation.

which contains mostly current wisdom in verse but also narrates how Odin acquired his divine knowledge. Other poems, like the Lays of Hymir and of Thrymr, describe Thor's adventures with the giants. The Lays of Vafthrudnir and Alvíss offer samples of mythological knowledge in the rather artificial pattern of competitions in riddle solving. The Lay of Grímnir tells about Odin's appearances in the world of men. Altogether, the older *Edda* is *not* a holy book; it does not contain a systematic survey of Germanic religion or a strict codification of Germanic ethics. The picture of the pantheon it supplies is far from complete, and the text often alludes to myths and gods completely unknown to us. Accordingly, an important part of Germanic mythology remains a closed book. Moreover, part of what we know through the *Edda* is questionable since the text has obviously not always faithfully preserved the wording of the original, and some passages are open to divergent interpretations. The main problem is to determine what is old and genuinely Germanic tradition. In the *Vǫluspá*, to be sure, the poet uses a solemn respectful tone, but in the *Lokasenna* he scoffs shamelessly at the gods:[2] Is the *Edda*, then, merely a modern embodiment of old motifs? The matter is further complicated by the fact that the *Poetic Edda* represents only the tradition of Norway and of its colony Iceland. There is no trace of mythological poetry from important centers like the island of Seeland in Denmark or Uppsala in Sweden, which must have had mythological traditions of their own as witnessed by the free Latin adaptation of Saxo Grammaticus.

Of a quite different nature are the data from the skalds, whose poetry contains numerous mythological allusions, mainly in the kennings, that is, periphrastic expressions used as substitutes for prosaic terms, such as "Odin of the shield" for "warrior" and "Sif of the jewels" for "woman." In several instances the image alludes to a myth, as, for example, "Odin's booty" for the mead of the gods, symbolizing poetry—a direct reference to Odin's robbing the beverage from the giants.

An extensive compilation of mythological material from the skalds was gathered by the Icelandic scholar Snorri Sturluson (1179–1241) and is known under the name of *Prose Edda* or Snorri's *Edda*. It contains a long prologue in medieval Christian style, starting with the Creation, making the Aesir come from Asia, considering Thor as the grandson of Priamus of Troy, and so on. The *Gylfaginning*—the Duping of Gylfi—describes the whole mythology more or less syste-

[2] Style and content lead Franz Rolf Schröder to the conclusion that the *Lokasenna* is the late work of an Icelandic scholar of the twelfth century ("Das Symposium der Lokasenna," *Arkiv för nordisk filologi* 67 [1952], 1–29).

matically under the form of a vision, whereas the *Skáldskaparmál*—the Language of Skaldship—the poetic handbook which completes the work, is a manual for the study of traditional poetic techniques, containing numerous myths to explain the examples of kennings borrowed from various skalds. It shows that Snorri must have had more sources than the still extant mythological poems at his disposal, but the value of the mythological tradition contained in his work is seriously disputed. Snorri's work was considered mainly as *novellistische Darstellung* by E. Mogk,[3] a designation that does not altogether exclude the authenticity of the material but supposes far-reaching personal adaptation of the original subject matter. According to H. Kuhn,[4] Snorri still believed what he was telling, but W. Baetke[5] is probably closer to the truth when he describes Snorri as a typical thirteenth-century scholar with a strong Latin-Christian background who, with his training, could no longer believe in any heathen myths and gods after two centuries of Christianity in Iceland, but who looked at the ancestral traditions with the same eyes as the Western Middle Ages looked at classical antiquity. Accordingly, Snorri's work is useful only as a reference for possible older traditions, which he may not have invented altogether, in spite of erroneous reinterpretations and willful patterning.

In the long-drawn prose stories of the sagas, man is described in speech and action. Though the texts contain more data on cult practice, they refer to creed only insofar as it motivates or influences man's behavior. The genuineness of the heathen tradition reflected by the sagas is strongly disputed;[6] many scholars do not believe in the possibility of an uninterrupted oral tradition from the time of the actual events related until the moment of their recording in a saga. The intervening time lapse of up to four or five centuries was obviously bridged by notations of the facts in annals and other historical writings, whose data were presumably reshaped later into the extant sagas on the model of hagiographic and other medieval narrative literature.

The acceptance or rejection of these views is of capital importance for the validation of the sagas as documents for the study of Germanic

[3] *Novellistische Darstellung mythologischer Stoffe Snorris und seiner Schule*, Folklore Fellows Communications, vol. 51 (Helsinki, 1923).

[4] "Das nordgermanische Heidentum in den ersten christlichen Jahrhunderten," *Zeitschrift für deutsches Altertum* 129 (1942), 133–166.

[5] *Die Götterlehre der Snorra-Edda*, Verhandlungen der Sächsischen Akademie der Wissenschaften, Philologisch-historische Klasse, 97:3 (Berlin, 1952).

[6] Cf., e.g., the dispute about the authenticity of the cultural data in the Hrafnkell saga, as illustrated by Marco Scovazzi, *La Saga di Hrafnkell e il problema delle saghe islandesi* (Arona, 1960), and my comments in *Revue Belge de Philologie et d'Histoire* 41 (1963), 997–999, and *Journal of English and Germanic Philology* 62 (1963), 472–475.

religion. They would indeed hardly provide conclusive evidence if they had been written by Christians only a few centuries after the conversion of the Icelanders. Characteristic in this respect is the change in judgment of W. Baetke: in 1938 he still accepted the sagas as *Quellenzeugnisse für die Religion der Germanen*; in 1952[7] he showed that their representation of heathen gods and heroes strictly conformed with medieval patterns of thought about paganism and was, therefore, practically worthless for the study of Germanic religion. In this position he was obviously going too far, for at least some data in the sagas are confirmed by external evidence, such as archaeological findings, or by comparative study, but Baetke's criticism was a necessary warning for those using as sources for Germanic religion the narratives about the life of the first settlers in Iceland and the Norwegian sagas of the kings describing late pagan days and the conversion period.

As for data in Latin works dealing with Scandinavian medieval history, the *Gesta Danorum* (ca. 1190–1216) deserves special mention. In this extensive work the medieval scholar Saxo Grammaticus spins out the history of Denmark, dealing with mythological material in a euhemeristic way, by picturing the gods as kings and heroes. His data are a useful complement to the Eddic material and sometimes present divergent versions of similar myths.[8] It is extremely dangerous to accept as direct evidence the mythological elements in the heroic epics and the *Märchenliteratur*, and a similar restraint is advisable with modern folklore and Lapp magic. The exaggerated reliance on such sources by an earlier generation of scholars has warned us against overestimating their validity.

In this dismal situation two attitudes are possible: (*a*) resignation to ignorance in view of the fragmentary data; (*b*) efforts to classify the facts in correlation with ethnographic, psychological, folkloric, and other parallels. The first attitude, excluding a synthetic view of the structural unity of Germanic mythology, concentrates on detailed study of the available facts, with a diachronic classification of the data. The second leads to a reexamination of Germanic religion, focused mainly on pattern and structure.

On the basis of the idea that man shapes his gods according to his own being, several new approaches have been attempted in recent years. The first is that of (*a*) the Vienna school of anthropology, which postulates that religious patterns develop in conformity with levels

[7] *Christliches Lehngut in der Sagareligion*, Verhandlungen der Sächsischen Akademie der Wissenschaften, Philologisch-historische Klasse, 98:6 (Berlin, 1952).

[8] E.g., the Baldr myth (see my analysis in "The Indo-European Component in Germanic Religion," pp. 63–82).

of culture. This view is illustrated by various studies of Alois Closs,[9] which led to a reformulation of the theory of H. Güntert about the ethnogenesis of the Germanic people as the result of the mixture of two populations—the "megalithic" pre-Indo-European agriculturalists and the Indo-European invaders of northwestern Europe—and intimated a parallelism between Germanic and Italic religious traditions. The second is (*b*) the typological analysis of Mircea Eliade, based to some extent on the concept of archetype developed by C. G. Jung and applied to religious studies by Karl Kerényi and Erich Neumann. A typical example is the Germanic mother goddess described by Tacitus in chapter 40 of *Germania*:

> These peoples, each one of which when isolated has nothing remarkable, adore Nerthus in common, that is to say Mother Earth. They believe that she intervenes in human affairs and passes from one to another of the tribes in a wagon. On an island in the ocean there is a sacred wood and, in this wood, a cart covered with cloth which is reserved to her, and which only the priest has the right to touch. He divines the moment when the goddess is present in her sanctuary and he accompanies her, with all the marks of devotion, while she goes forward on her cart drawn by cows. These are days of rejoicing and the places that she honors by her visit and from which she accepts hospitality are in celebration. The people in these places do not make wars, nor take up their arms; every iron object is locked up. It is the only period of time when peace and tranquility are known and enjoyed, and it lasts until the moment when the priest returns the goddess to her temple, satisfied with her contact with men. The cart with its cloth and, if one can believe them, the goddess herself, are then bathed in a secluded lake. The slaves who accomplish this ceremony are immediately swallowed up by the same lake. From there comes a mysterious terror, the sacred ignorance of the nature of a secret that is seen only by those who are going to perish.

The Nerthus ritual is the typical celebration of a cosmic event—the advent of spring—complying with Eliade's pattern:

> For a moment, the life of the whole human group is concentrated into a tree or some effigy of vegetation, some symbol intended to represent and consecrate the thing that is happening to the universe: spring. . . . The presence of nature is indicated by a single object (or symbol). It is no pantheist adoration of nature or sense of being at one with it, but a feeling induced by the presence of the symbol (branch, tree or whatever it may be), and stimulated by the performing of the rite (processions, contests, fights, and the rest). The ceremonial is based on a comprehensive notion of the sacredness of all living force as expressed at every level of life, growing, wearing itself out and being regularly regenerated. This

[9] "Die Religion des Semnonenstammes," in W. Koppers, ed., *Die Indogermanen- und Germanenfrage* (Salzburg and Leipzig, 1936), pp. 549–674; "Das Versenkungsopfer," in W. Koppers, R. Heine-Geldern, and J. Haekel, eds., *Kultur und Sprache* (Vienna, 1952), pp. 66–107; "Die Religion der Germanen in ethnologischer Sicht," in F. König, ed., *Christus und die Religionen der Erde* (Vienna, 1952), II, 271–366.

"bio-cosmic sacredness" is personified in many different forms, changing, it would seem, to suit mood or circumstance. . . . What remains, what is basic and lasting, is the "power" of vegetation, which can be felt and manipulated equally well in a branch, an effigy or a mythological figure.[10]

The symbol involved in the Nerthus ritual, revealing to the priest the "power" of vegetation in its mobile shrine—the chariot of the goddess—was presumably the appearance of a definite plant or flower. The whole ritual fits into the characteristic pattern of the great goddess, "goddess—vegetation—sacred animals—priests," since heifers draw the Nerthus chariot and a high priest and slaves attend upon the goddess as she is driven around the fields to effect the irradiating of her power during the ceremonial procession, characterized by general peace (all weapons are locked up; there is joy everywhere: *laeti tunc dies*). Presumably the community as a whole participates in the orgiastic frenzy that sets flowing the sacred energy of life. But the goddess is exhausted by the irradiation of her vital force; to regenerate it and to restore it ritually to her, she must be immersed in a lake with the compensatory human sacrifice of the slaves attending her. The ritual of Nerthus thus appears as a symbolic reactualization of spring, aimed at promoting agrarian fertility through a solemn procession and at regenerating the vital force of mother earth, symbolically, by the immersion of her emblem, and concretely, by the drowning of her attendants.[11] By applying Eliade's approach it is, accordingly, possible to reinterpret a Germanic ritual as the enactment of a scenario sui generis, based on patterns whose variations abound in the most diverse cultures. This method, however, is not particularly productive for the interpretation of myth.

The third approach is (*c*) George Dumézil's new comparative Indo-European mythology, based on the functional tripartition of social life into (1) sovereignty, with its double aspect, juridical and magical; (2) physical force, mainly for military purposes; and (3) fertility, with its correlates of prosperity, health, long life, and so on. This approach is not a subjective interpretation of social facts; it was gradually elaborated on the basis of Indo-Iranian traditions, where the Avestan texts show an original division of society into three classes—farmers, warriors, and priests, symbolized by the plow, the war ax, and the cup—and where numerous testimonies going back to Vedic times attest the original tripartition of Aryan society into *brāhmaṇas* (priests), *kṣatriyas* (military caste) and *vaiśyas* (cattle raisers).[12]

10 *Patterns in Comparative Religion* (Cleveland and New York, 1963), pp. 321–322.

11 E. Polomé, "A propos de la déesse Nerthus," *Latomus* 13 (1954), 167–200.

12 To the data assembled by G. Dumézil in the first chapter of his *L'idéologie tripartie des Indo-Européens*, Collection Latomus, vol. 31 (Brussels, 1958), pp. 7–33,

On the theological level, these three classes are represented by hierarchized functional Vedic gods: (1) sovereignty is exerted in its magical aspect by Varuṇa and in its juridical aspect by Mitra; (2) the god of physical force is Indra, fighting monsters, armed with his *vajra* (thunderbolt); (3) health and wealth are essentially the domain of the twin gods—the Aśvins or Nāsatyas—the antiquity of the system being guaranteed by the appearance of these gods as a group in a treaty signed in the fourteenth century B.C. between an Aryan prince and the Hittite great king. Mentioned as witnesses to the good faith of the Aryans, they embody the functions representing the total social structure. In the Germanic world, the following tripartition would correspond to the Aryan system: (1) Odin would represent the magical aspect of sovereignty and Týr its juridical component; (2) Thor, armed with his hammer, symbolizing the thunderbolt, would embody physical force; (3) Freyr and Freyja would preside over fertility and prosperity.

It is obvious that Dumézil's hypothesis requires two postulates: (1) that Germanic religion is essentially the religion of the Indo-Europeans in its transformation by the Germanic tribes; (2) that the tripartite system survives changes in society; only the functional attributes of the gods, not their names and specific personalities, are of vital importance.

The first assumption is utterly rejected by Karl Helm,[13] who claims that

> Die germanische Religion ist zum kleinsten Teil indogermanische Religion; ihre Grundlage ist die Religion des in den später germanischen Ländern beheimateten und hier vielleicht seit Urzeiten, d.h. schon vor der Bildung des Indogermanentums siedelnden völkischen Subtrates, wie sie sich im Laufe der Jahrhunderte unter den verschiedensten Einflüssen herausgebildet hat.

Helm accordingly emphasizes "Vanic" religion (i.e., the third-function gods of Dumézil) as the pre-Germanic religion of the neolithic farmers and considers, for example, the spread of the cult of Odin as a late development. But if the Vanir and the Aesir reflect the two constituents of the Germanic people in prehistoric times—the neolithic farmers and the Indo-European invaders—the structure of society in those days as assumed on archaeological grounds perfectly

and the discussion by C. Scott Littleton, *The New Comparative Mythology: An Anthropological Assessment of the Theories of Georges Dumézil* (Berkeley and Los Angeles, 1966), esp. pp. 7–19, Emile Benveniste's chapter, "La tripartition des fonctions," in *Le vocabulaire des institutions indo-européennes*, 1 (Paris, 1969), 279–292, is to be added.

[13] "Mythologie auf alten und neuen Wegen," in *Beiträge zur Geschichte der deutschen Sprache und Literatur* 77 (Tübingen, 1955), 347–365.

fits the Indo-European pattern; moreover, the story of the struggle of the Vanir and the Aesir as compared with similar situations after the foundation of Rome reflects a general pattern of conflict and compromise which conforms to Indo-European tradition.

What actually sets Helm and Dumézil in opposition to each other is their basic attitude to the problem of Germanic religion: Helm wants to evaluate the scanty facts from a strictly historical point of view and to reach his conclusions about the individual gods by inductive reasoning; Dumézil has recognized a definite structure as basic to and specific of Indo-European society and, by comparison of the various attested systems, he tries to back up his deductions by referring to the survival of the original tripartition in the most disparate traditions of the Indo-European peoples. As Werner Betz[14] indicates, however, both approaches are useful and even necessary.

As a matter of fact, even those who, like R. Derolez, completely reject Dumézil's views must admit that the structure of Germanic society agreed by and large with his postulated social pattern:

> At the head of every tribe was a king or a group of heads of smaller tribal units; in the latter event, a suitable commander was chosen from among the heads of smaller units in time of war. Various religious elements appeared in the direction of the state: the king was "sacred"; the priests kept order and peace in the "thing" assemblies and punished all crimes. . . . Political power belonged in principle to the "thing"; all important decisions were taken in those assemblies, at which all free men appeared in arms, but among these free men a smaller group of influential families in fact controlled the direction of public affairs, tending to make this situation permanent by isolating themselves from the lower classes and claiming they were born noblemen. Under the free men were the half-free taxpayers and, on the lowest level, the slaves.[15]

As for the Indo-European element versus the non-Indo-European substrate in Germanic religion, it is probable that the Germanic people resulted from the merger of a group of Indo-European conquerors, moving up along the axis Dniepr–Vistula to northwestern Europe, with the neolithic inhabitants of that area. That this merger did not occur without resistance on the part of the first occupants of the territory is likely, and one may presume that after an indecisive series of battles the two groups reached a compromise, since the invaders needed the help of the local population to build up a well-balanced and permanent social structure. Presumably the invaders were mainly youthful warriors, accompanied by a group of priests,

[14] "Die altgermanische Religion," in W. Stammler, ed., *Deutsche Philologie im Aufriss* (Berlin, 1957), III, col. 2476; 2d ed. (1962), III, col. 1558.

[15] *De Godsdienst der Germanen*, pp. 28–29.

who set out to find new territories, in the pattern illustrated by the *ver sacrum* ritual in ancient Italy and apparently also by the Hittite conquest of Asia Minor in the third and second millennia B.C. A nice parallel is provided by the mythical early history of Rome, when the youthful warriors of Romulus made a settlement with the wealthy Sabines to give their emergent nation the necessary, functionally balanced social structure. As a matter of fact, Dumézil has pointedly stressed the parallelism between the initial war between the Romans and Sabines and the war of the Aesir (essentially, the sovereign and warrior gods) and the Vanir (the third-function gods). Both wars may be seen as a kind of diptych of two phases, in which one of the feuding groups prevails provisionally and owes its advantage to its functional specialty: on the one hand, the rich and lusty Vanir corrupt the society of the Aesir from the inside through their women, by sending Gullveig ("gold-drunkenness") to them; on the other, Odin sends his famous spear to create the inescapable magic effect of panic among the adversary. Similarly, the rich Sabines gain the key position of the Romans not by fighting but by buying off Tarpeia with gold or luring her through an irresistible passion for the Sabine chief; Romulus calls on Jupiter Stator to stop the victorious enemy, who suddenly flee in panic, apparently without reason. Both wars end in a compromise that properly integrates the third-function representatives into the new society,[16] a common Indo-European feature that bridges the original gap between the closely associated first and second functions and the third function, and a process also attested in India where the Aśvins achieve full status in the divine society only after a violent conflict ending in reconciliation. It should also be stressed that in the Germanic world close to the Roman Empire an undoubtedly more bellicose type of society prevailed, characterized by the totalitarian system of agriculture described by Caesar (*De Bello Gallico* VI.22) and the predominance of the gods of the first and second function, whereas on the shores of the Baltic a much more peaceful and stable society could safely practice a strictly distributive economy and offer special reverence to the gods of the third function, like the Ingaevones, constituting the amphictyony of Nerthus, or the Naharvali. While instability and insecurity tend to favor a kind of heroic unanimity with focus on the cult of first- and second-function gods, a completely different mood prevails when conditions are less fluid and

[16] Georges Dumézil, *L'héritage indo-européen à Rome* (Paris, 1949), pp. 127–142, reprinted in *La religion romaine archaïque* (Paris, 1966), pp. 78–84 with comments in n. 1, p. 83, on Jan de Vries, "Vǫluspá Str. 21 und 22," *Arkiv för nordisk filologi* 77 (1962), 42–47.

property can safely be transferred from generation to generation. This duality of attitude depending on the state of the community fits perfectly into the Dumézilian system, as he has eloquently shown in his *Mitra-Varuṇa*.[17]

There are also other reasons for assuming Indo-European traditions in Germanic mythology. First, the Germanic religious terminology is by and large Indo-European. Thus, the name of the Aesir, who represent the sovereign gods in the Germanic pantheon, cannot be separated from Indo-Iranian **asura-* 'sovereign god' and Hittite *ḫaššuš* 'king';[18] the Germanic technical term *alu* (*þ*), the word for "beer" in its cultural use, is connected with runic *alu*, used in protective inscriptions intended, for example, to prevent violation of tombs and related to a verbal stem **alw-* 'to protect magically,' which is further related to the Hittite present participle **alwanza* 'being under a spell.'[19]

If Germanic religion represented essentially a survival of the beliefs of the pre-Indo-European substrate, one would expect the technical terminology of the Neolithic religion to survive, but apparently it did not. Besides, it has been shown that the major Germanic gods are reflexes of Indo-European gods and not recent developments. Along this line, a considerable effort has been made to assume the late development of the Odin cult:[20] it is claimed that the spread and division of the Germanic gods preclude the existence of a powerful sovereign god; it is pointed out that he is not attested among the Goths; much stress is laid on the fact that (1) toponyms containing his name are rare in Scandinavia and absent in Iceland; (2) almost no personal names contain the name Odin; (3) the Lapp mythology borrowed from Scandinavia does not show a correspondent to Odin.

---

[17] 2d ed. (Paris, 1948), pp. 152–159; cf. also E. Polomé, "La religion germanique primitive, reflet d'une structure sociale," *Le Flambeau* 37 (1954), 453–454.

[18] Cf. my study, "L'étymologie du terme germanique **ansuz* 'dieu souverain,'" *Études germaniques* 8 (1953), 36–44 (esp. pp. 41 ff.). This etymology remains valid even if the underlying basic concept is not "master of the bonds" (cf. Littleton, *New Comparative Mythology*, pp. 171–172); the etymon would then presumably be the I-E theme I **H_2 en-s-* 'vital power' (OInd. *ásuḥ* 'life, vital strength'; Hitt. *ḫaš(š)-* 'to beget,' cf. *ḫanšatar* = *ḫaššatar* 'engendering, reproduction'), which would compare semantically very neatly with the concept of "life-giving power" underlying the name of Odin (cf. my "Some Comments on *Vǫluspá*, Stanzas 17–18," in E. Polomé, ed., *Old Norse Literature and Mythology* [Austin, 1969], p. 268).

[19] Cf. E. Polomé, "Notes sur le vocabulaire religieux du germanique," *La Nouvelle Clio* 6 (1954), 40–55.

[20] Cf. especially Karl Helm, *Wodan: Ausbreitung und Wanderung seines Kultes* (Giessen, 1946), with the comments of Georges Dumézil, *Les dieux des Germains: Essai sur la formation de la religion scandinave* (Paris, 1959), pp. 47–58 (cf. also Jan de Vries, *Altgermanische Religionsgeschichte*, 2d ed. [Berlin, 1957], II, 46–48, 91–92).

None of these arguments is really cogent. (1) In the *Germania* (chap. 9) Tacitus indicates that Mercurius—the *interpretatio romana* of Odin—was the most venerated among the Germanic gods. (2) In chapter 39 Tacitus describes the ritual of the *deus regnator omnium* among the Semnones, characterized by the sacrifice of a man in fetters in a sacred grove; an Eddic echo of this Odinic sacrifice is provided by the *fjǫturlund* ("fetter grove") in which Helgi is killed with a spear.[21] (3) Anthropological data indicate that quite a few preliterate tribes of small territorial extent and with limited power worshiped powerful gods with universal competence; the limited local power of a chieftain can be transposed mythically as the unlimited power of the cosmic chief. Varuṇa was worshiped in this way by the Vedic tribes, which were similar to the Germanic tribes in social organization. (4) One of the names of Odin is Gautr, and through the localization in Väster- and Östergötland of the place-names containing his name in Sweden, the Scandinavian Odin shows a particular link with the original homeland of the Goths. (5) It stands to reason that Odin's functions as magician and chief made him less likely to be taken over by the Lapps, subjugated or threatened by their Germanic neighbors, the more so because they had a specific magic of their own; the god of weather-changing thunder (Thor), the god of fertility in animals and plants (Freyr), and the god of wind and navigation (Njördr), whose functions were closer to the immediate interests of the Lapps, were certainly better candidates for borrowing. (6) For similar reasons, it is plausible that in its onomastic practices an essentially rural society would have favored gods related to the fertility of the soil and rain-bringing thunder. As a matter of fact, local names with the name of the universally present supreme god are always scarce, and the names of deities with closer local specifications naturally tend to be favored. As for personal names, the fierce god of the *tremendum numinosum* would qualify less than others (similarly, Varuṇa never occurs in Indo-Aryan names). The fact that Odin is the inventor of the runes, according to the *Hávamál*, does not imply that he could not have existed before the runes came to the Germanic North from the northern Alps, where the model for the alphabet was apparently found. As supreme magician, Odin had to

[21] Cf. de Vries, *Altgermanische Religionsgeschichte*, II, 32–34; E. O. G. Turville-Petre, *Myth and Religion of the North: The Religion of Ancient Scandinavia* (London, 1964), pp. 73–74. On the relation with the Helgi episode, cf. in particular Otto Höfler, "Das Opfer in Semnonenhain und die Edda," in H. Schneider, ed., *Edda, Skalden, Saga: Festschrift . . . Felix Genzmer* (Heidelberg, 1952), pp. 1–67. His conclusion that the god in the grove is identified with the tribal ancestor gains special weight in consideration of the position of **Wōđanaz* at the head of genealogies.

add the runes to his domain when they came in. Moreover, as their name shows, the runes are a mere specification of his secret science: Gothic *runa* means 'secret,' 'secret decision,' and is cognate with OIr. *rūn* 'secret,' 'mystery'; the early Finnish loan from Germanic, *runo*, applies to magic songs. So, what Odin originally acquired by hanging on the tree for nine days, starving and thirsting as in a shamanic initiation rite, was a powerful secret lore, of which the runes later on became merely the tool.

Besides, many arguments plead for the antiquity of Odin. (1) His name, reflecting Gmc. **Wōđanaz*, literally means "the master of **wōđ-*," that is, "inspiration," be it poetic or divinatory, as shown by its etymological link with Latin *uātes* "soothsayer, seer" and OIr. *fāith* "poet, seer." (2) As the king of magic he includes among his attributes such particular gifts as ubiquity (he can transport himself everywhere), disguise (he is capable of assuming any shape, often that of an animal, e.g., an eagle after stealing the mead), blinding and paralyzing power, making weapons useless, the distribution of victory; he does not fight himself, in contrast with Thor who fights to eliminate dangers. Odin's technique is the magic "binding" of his enemies, a feature he shares with Varuṇa. (3) His appearance as an old one-eyed man, half-hidden under a hat, also reminds us of Varuṇa, old, bald, weak, hiding under a hat. (4) His mutilation to attain second sight refers to an obscure myth about the loss of his eye, now in the well of Mimir, a loss that enables him to see "far and wide the worlds about," and reminds us of the Greek sage Tiresias who received second sight as compensation for becoming blind.

The link of a mutilation with the acquisition of a specific functional power is particularly significant in the context of the Germanic sovereign gods, as shown by the parallel case of Týr. The story is well known: it had been prophesied that the Fenris-wolf would be a plague to the gods; to subdue him before he grows too big, the gods want to tie him up, but all fetters are broken by him; Odin, then, orders a magic bond from the black elves, but when the gods want to bind the Fenris-wolf with it, he refuses to play their game unless one of them puts a hand in his mouth to guarantee against foul play; Týr volunteers, the wolf is secured, but Týr loses his hand. This episode is a typical example of a heroic pledge to secure a treacherous agreement: the god takes a contractual risk in order to save those of his kind; his sacrifice regularizes the otherwise fraudulent contract; he is willing to pay the price for his functional activity. As the god of law and justice, Týr was naturally expected to stand surety for the gods, whatever the consequences. But there is more to the mutilations of Odin and Týr: they actually represent Indo-European traditions also preserved in the euhemerized myths that constitute the early history of Rome, where they are paralleled by the stories of Horatius Cocles and Mucius Scaevola. The former, who is one-eyed, stops the advance of the Etruscans on the bridge opening the road to the city by his terrible look; neither killed nor wounded by a rain of missiles, he enables the Romans to cut the bridge and saves them from certain defeat. Scaevola penetrates under a disguise into the camp of the Etruscan king Porsenna besieging Rome and attempts to kill him, but kills the king's secretary instead. Caught and brought before Porsenna, Scaevola claims 300 Roman youths are ready to try the same; to convince the king of the truth of this unwarranted affirmation, he puts his right arm into the fire and lets it burn away. The king believes him and starts negotiating.[22]

In view of their functional role in this set of stories, the symmetric mutilations can hardly be fortuitous. Though his mutilation occurred earlier, the one-eyed Horatius Cocles "fascinates" the enemy into paralysis just as does his divine counterpart, the one-eyed Odin in the Germanic world; both Týr and Mucius Scaevola persuade the enemy by a pledge in a deceitful agreement, and each sacrifices a hand to save his group. The difference is essentially that what happens in the "mythical time" in Scandinavia is described as a historical event in Rome, like the struggle of the Aesir and the Vanir in the *Edda* and the Sabine War in Rome.

This does not mean that the Germanic gods have no personality of their own as reflexes of Indo-European functional gods. Actually, they show evident features of adaptation to the Germanic context, namely, a typical slanting of the first-function gods toward the second-function gods. Odin intervenes in wars by producing a paralyzing panic—*herfjǫturr* ('fetters of the army')—which swings the scales, and he does so much oftener than his Vedic homologue Varuṇa; besides, he receives the warriors fallen in combat. Týr presides over combats that are conducted like juridical actions—*vapnadómr* ('decision through the arms')—and the warriors gathered in arms in the "thing" invoke him. This shift is also partly responsible for the downgrading of Thor in the hierarchy, favored by his closeness to the peasants as a result of the fertilizing action of his atmospheric battle to release the rain with his thunderbolt. This is reflected by Adam von Bremen's description

[22] Cf. Georges Dumézil, *Mitra-Varuṇa: Essai sur deux représentations indo-européennes de la Souveraineté*, 2d ed. (Paris, 1948), pp. 163–177; *L'héritage indo-européen à Rome*, pp. 159–169. On the deceitful use of oaths, cf. Benveniste, *Le vocabulaire des institutions indo-européennes*, II, 170–171.

of the function of the two gods in the Uppsala cult: *Wodan, id est furor, bella gerit, hominique ministrat virtutem contra inimicos; Thor praesidet in aera, qui tonitrus et fulmina, ventos imbresque, serena et fruges gubernat.* It also accounts for the insult that Odin throws in Thor's face in the Lay of Hárbardr:

> Gets Othin all earls slain by edge of swords
> but Thor, the breed of thralls.

Here, however, there is a deliberate exaggeration on the part of Odin: actually, Thor patronizes the *karlar* ("free peasants"), as his Lappish name Hora Galles < *Kar(i)las indicates. Moreover, the whole system is further confirmed by the *Rígsþula,* where the whole structure of Germanic society is described in the mythical tale about Heimdallr's progeny.[23] *Thraell* ("the slave") and his descendants remain as alien to the upper classes as the Indian low-caste *śūdras;* they are given ridiculous or scornful names and are left at the bottom of the social ladder:

(st. 11) Whispered and laughed and lay together
Thrall and Thír whole days through.
I ween they were hight Hay-Giver, Howler,
In their hut, happy, they had a brood:

(st. 12) Bastard, Sluggard, Bent-Back and Paunch,
Stumpy, Stinker, Stableboy, Swarthy,
Longshanks and Lout: they laid fences,
put dung on fields, fattened the swine,
herded the goats, and grubbed up peat.

(st. 13) Their daughters were Drudge and Daggle-Tail.
Slattern, Serving-Maid, and Cinder-Wench,
Stout-Leg, Shorty, Stumpy and Dumpy,
Spindleshanks eke, and Sputterer:
thence are sprung the breed of thralls.

Karl, the "free peasant," and his children fulfill the same social function as the Indian *vaiśya*—agricultural producers and craftsmen (one of his sons is called *Smiðr* ["smith"]):

(st. 22) Then gan he [Karl] grow and gain in strength,
tamed the oxen and tempered ploughshares,
timbered houses, and barns for the hay,
fashioned carts, and followed the plough.

(After Karl married Snør ["daughter-in-law"] . . .)

(st. 24) In their homestead, happy, they had a brood,
hight Man and Yeoman, Master, Goodman,

[23] Cf. Georges Dumézil, "La *Rigsþula* et la structure sociale indo-européenne," *Revue d'histoire des religions* 154 (1958), 1–9.

Husbandman, Farmer, Franklin, Croffer,
Bound-Beard, Steep-Beard, Broad, Swain, and Smith.

Next comes Jarl, the "nobleman," indulging in warlike games, like an Indian *kṣatriya*:

(st. 36) Up grew Earl within the hall,
gan bucklers wield and the bowstring fasten,
gan the elmwood bend and arrows shaft;
gan hurl the spear and speed the lance,
gan hunt with hounds, and horse ride,
gan brandish swords and swim in the sea.

His offspring, Konr-ungr, splits from the group and becomes the first *konungr* ("king"), coming out of the warrior class, like the Indian *rājan-*, and acquiring knowledge giving him a magical command over all:

(st. 44) But Kon only could carve runes,
runes lasting ay, life-keeping runes;
to bring forth babies birth-runes he knew,
to dull sword edges and to calm the sea.

(st. 45) Fowls' speech he knew, and quenched fires,
could soothe sorrows and the sick mind heal;
in his arms the strength of eight men had.

These few examples demonstrate that the historical structural approach to Germanic myth may open numerous new stimulating perspectives. Not all of them should be tributary to the Dumézilian "tripartite Indo-European ideology"; his theory is but one aspect of the structural approach. Claude Lévi-Strauss represents another productive way. Internal developments in the Germanic world can be fascinating, as an analysis of the myth of Baldr along these lines has shown.[24]

[24] Cf. Polomé, "The Indo-European Component in Germanic Religion," pp. 63–82.

The Well of Nechtan and "La Gloire Lumineuse"

PATRICK K. FORD, *University of California, Los Angeles*

In his article "Le puits de Nechtan," Georges Dumézil explores the relationship between the myth of Apąm Napā̰t (Vedic Apā́ṃ Nápāt) in the Iranian Avesta and the Irish *dindschenchas* story of Bóand, wife of Nechtan.[1] He establishes a parallel sequence of events in the two traditions, which, according to the "golden rule" of the comparative method, is a requisite for postulating their relationship. Next, he undertakes an examination of the names Nechtan and Nápāt (suggesting **ne(p)ōt-*, **nept-* → Ir. *necht-*; **napāt-*, **napt-*), which in turn raises the issue of Neptūnus (he suggests the name may have arisen through analogical reformation of an earlier name related to **nept-o-no-* [= Ir. Nechtan]). While he draws no conclusion from the etymological kinship he suggests, it is clear that in all three traditions there is a reflex of the paradoxical concept of "fire in water." In the Indo-Iranian and Irish traditions the concept is realized as a potent essence, preserved in a body of water, accessible only to a chosen few, and endowing those elect with extraordinary powers. In this paper I seek to confirm the correspondences that Dumézil has established between the two myths, by identifying that essence with the pagan Irish notion of inspired poetry and its associated wisdom: it was a

[1] *Celtica* 6 (1963), 50–61, reproduced in somewhat revised and expanded form in *Mythe et épopée* III (Paris, 1973), 21–38. The seeds of what is here proposed are to be found in the footnotes to Professor Dumézil's article. Our interests in the material differ, however, and for that reason he was content to leave unexplored the issues examined here. Whatever the problems of Nechtan : Nápāt, the parallels between these two myths permit a further investigation into their significance.

brightly burning essence, as the terms *forosna* and *teinm* suggest, it characterized the elect (*laída*, gl. *tuicsi*), and it was diligently sought by the poets, who knew that its source was in the water.

Let us begin with a summary of the episodes compared by Dumézil. As he explains, Indic and Iranian traditions preserve, respectively, a ritual and a myth of the "Descendant of the Waters." In the *Rig Veda*, Apā́ṃ Nápāt is said to dwell in the waters, emanating a brilliance, surrounded by young maidens—the waters—who purify him. He is the brilliant essence of the waters, who illumines those that honor him. The practical result of this notion of Apā́ṃ Nápāt is that men who go to the rivers to draw water must propitiate their Nápāt. At the sacrifice of soma, when the *adhvaryus* and their companions go to fill their jugs, the *hotar* recites strophes from the hymn of Apā́ṃ Nápāt (*RV*, X, 30), including the following quoted by Dumézil:

> 3. Adhvaryus, go to the waters, to the ocean! Sacrifice to Apā́ṃ Nápāt with the offering! May he give you today the well purified waters . . .
>
> 4. Thou who shinest without fuel amidst the waters, thou whom the priests revere in sacrifices, Apā́ṃ Nápāt, give the sweet waters by which Indra is strengthened for heroism.

Apā́ṃ Nápāt, then, is the essence and the custodian of the force that the essence represents. The brilliance with which he glows, a pure, divine radiation, illumines those that honor him.

In the Iranian Avesta, Apąm Napāṯ exhibits the same paradoxical union of fire and water. The divine essence central to the myth, however, is here represented in the figure of Vᵛarənah (which Dumézil translates "gloire lumineuse"), which comes to distinguish visibly the Iranian princes who were the chosen of God ("Le puits de Nechtan," p. 52 and n. 2).

In *Yašt* XIX, ostensibly dedicated to the Earth, Xᵛarənah is honored by the poet first of all because he belongs to all the classes of divine beings, to the three kings, and so on, and then because he had been the "stake" in a divine battle fought between the Holy Spirit (Spənta Mainyu) and the Evil Spirit (Angra Mainyu). Each of these wished to possess the inaccessible Xᵛarənah. Through the emissaries of these two forces a battle was fought, but Apąm Napāṯ intervened, seizing Xᵛarənah and taking him to the bottom of the mythical lake (or sea), Vourukaša.

Ahura Mazdāh approved this settlement and exhorted men to try to attain the inaccessible Xᵛarənah, guaranteeing to those that succeeded: (1) the gifts of priesthood; (2) power over cattle and pasture; (3) the Vərəthra, the defensive force by which all enemies will be vanquished. The first of the attempts narrated by the text is that by the Turanian Frangrasyan.

Frangrasyan strips and plunges into the lake of Vourukaša, where Apąm Napāt̰ has taken X^{v}arənah, and swims toward him. X^{v}arənah escapes, and his motion of flight discharges from the lake a flow of water known as Haosravah. Frangrasyan's next attempt to seize X^{v}arənah results in a new issue of water, the Vanghazdah; next comes the Awždānvan. At that point, Frangrasyan gives up. In the following four verses, the text eulogizes the river Haētumant and the lake into which it empties, as well as other rivers tributary to the same lake.

The analogous tale from Irish tradition tells how Bóand tested the powers of the well of which her husband Nechtan was custodian.[2] It was the characteristic of the well that whoever should visit it (except for Nechtan and his three cupbearers) would suffer the shattering of his two eyes.[3] When Bóand, through pride, comes to the well, three waves rise up from the well, deprive her of a thigh, a hand, and an eye, and pursue her as far as the sea—henceforth the estuary of the Boyne. In the metrical version, the river is known by fifteen names as it courses the world on its way to paradise and returns to the *síd* whence it came.[4] Dumézil reasons rightly that, since those who approach the well without right suffer a bursting of the eyes, the force embodied in the well must be some kind of deadly ray, a brilliant glittering, or perhaps intense heat; but there is no indication of what that force, essence, or power might be.

In the two traditions (taking the Indic and Iranian sources as ritual and mythic reflexes of the same tradition), we have a mysterious and brilliant essence, embodied in water, protected by a custodian, and with limited right of access. The body of water, as residence of

---

[2] From the prose (Rennes) *Dindschenchas*, ed. and trans. W. Stokes, in *Revue Celtique* 15 (1894), 315.

[3] The importance of the cupbearers is borne out elsewhere in Irish tradition, and it is in this connection that the Neptūnus material is clearly relevant. In "The Second Battle of Moytura" (ed. and trans. W. Stokes, in *Revue Celtique* 12 [1891], 52–130, 306–308), the Túatha dé Danann cupbearers avow that they will bring a great thirst over the Fomorians, and that they will not find a drop of water to drink (§79, 111). In "The First Battle of Moytura" (ed. and trans. J. Frazer, in *Ériu* 8 [1915], 1–63), Eochaid, king of the Fir Bolg, is stricken with an unendurable thirst. When the Túatha dé Danann perceive this, their druids "hide" all the streams and rivers of Ireland from him, and by this ruse they are able finally to kill him (§52–54). M. Ruch ("La capture du devin," *Revue des études latines* 44 [1965], 334–350) says that Neptūnus is the god not only of lakes and fresh waters, but "dieu aussi des eaux jaillissantes dont la vertu est de parer à la sécheresse et au tarissement des sources" (p. 337); in this respect, the legend of the Alban Lake is relevant (see *ibid.*, passim), as well as Dumézil, *Mythe et épopée* III, 39–89.

[4] *The Metrical Dindshenchas*, III, ed. and trans. Edward Gwynn, Todd Lecture Series, X (Dublin, 1913), 27 f.

this potent force, is seen to be the source of other rivers. It is these clear parallels between Indo-Iranian and Irish traditions which allow Dumézil to discuss the relationship of Nápāt and Nechtan and the possible existence of a common notion of "Descendant of the Waters."

What we seek to discover here is the identity of the potent essence, which, in Indo-Iranian tradition, is associated with the three functions (cf. the promises of Ahura Mazdāh ["Le puits de Nechtan," p. 53]) and the practice of poetry. As I suggest at the beginning, Irish tradition knows an essence whose main quality is an illuminating brilliance and whose source is ultimately in the water. It is a quality that characterizes wisdom and the poetic arts, and it is called *imbas forosna* 'wisdom that illuminates'; it is most clearly elucidated in the tales about Finn.

The tales that tell how Finn acquired wisdom are of two types: the first attributes his gift of knowledge to a draught from the Otherworld Well; the second attributes it to contact with the Salmon of Wisdom.[5]

Three versions of the first type are preserved in *Feis Tighe Chonáin* (ed. Maud Joynt [Dublin, 1936]). The first of these tells us that Finn and his companions attempted to enter the open door of the *síd* at Carn Feradaig. The daughters of Bec mac Buain try to prevent their entering by closing the door against them. One of the daughters holds a vessel filled with water from Bec's well which, in the ensuing struggle, spills into the mouths of Finn and his companions, giving them knowledge.[6]

The second version in *Feis Tighe Chonáin* says that Finn drank from each of two wells near Carn Feradaig and, as a result, gained knowledge. In the third, Finn bathes in a lake at Sliab Cuilinn with the result that he loses his strength. In retaliation the *fian* lays siege to the neighboring *síd*. Cuilenn, the lord of the *síd*, comes forth and offers Finn a draught from a golden cup. The liquid restores Finn's original vigor and imparts wisdom to him.

In other tales of the first type, the acquisition of knowledge by a draught of wisdom-giving liquid, the principal motif has been replaced by a secondary development, that of thumb-chewing or thumb-sucking.[7] This latter motif is by no means incidental to the concept

[5] The summaries given here follow T. F. O'Rahilly, *Early Irish History and Mythology* (Dublin, 1946), pp. 326 ff.

[6] In a variant of this version in *Imtheacht an Dá Nónbhar* (O'Rahilly, *op. cit.*, p. 328), there are three daughters (cf. the three cupbearers of Nechtan), each of whom bears a cup of the liquid, called *lionn iomhais* ('liquor, or pool, of wisdom').

[7] O'Rahilly, *op. cit.*, p. 334. As O'Rahilly points out, this motif is undoubtedly related to the divinatory rite described by Cormac in his famous glossary, s.v. *imbas forosna*. It has been translated by Kuno Meyer in *Archaeological Review* 1

of supernatural wisdom; it is secondary only to the tale type just described. In some of the tales of type 1, the acquisition of knowledge occurs in this way: Finn encounters a woman (with a vessel of water, or an empty vessel, the woman "having just distributed drink") at the door of a *síd*. She manages to close the door against Finn, catching his thumb in it. He withdraws the offended member, puts it in his mouth to ease the pain, and upon removing it, begins to chant through his *imbas forosna* 'wisdom that illuminates.'

In the second type, Finn's knowledge is acquired through contact with the Salmon of Wisdom. In the *Macgnimartha Find*[8] the young Finn, called Demne, goes to learn *écse* and *filidecht* ('poetry' and 'the art and practice of a *fili*') from Finn Éces. Finn Éces had been on the Boyne for seven years, watching the salmon of Fec's pool, for it had been prophesied that he would catch and eat that salmon, after which nothing would be unknown to him. The salmon is caught and given to Demne to cook for Finn Éces. In the process Demne burns his finger, puts it into his mouth to ease the pain, and is immediately illumined by the knowledge intended for Finn Éces: "It is that which gave the knowledge to Finn, to wit, whenever he put his thumb into his mouth, and sang through *teinm laída*, then whatever he had been ignorant of would be revealed to him. He learnt the three things that constitute a poet, to wit, *teinm laída* and *imbas forosna* and *dichetul dichennaib*" (Meyer, §18–19).[9]

At first glance this second type appears to emphasize the thumb-in-the-mouth motif as the source of Finn's knowledge. In fact, it accounts

---

(1888), 303, and three times by Whitley Stokes: *Three Irish Glossaries* (London, 1862), p. xxxvi; *Tripartite Life of St. Patrick*, Pt. II, Rolls Series (London, 1887), App. XXXVIII, pp. 569–571; *Transactions of the Philological Society* (1891–1894), p. 157. But precisely what the relationship of Finn's practice is to the ritual described by Cormac is difficult to say. Chewing the raw flesh of a cat or a dog or a pit is not the same as chewing one's own thumb.

[8] "The Boyhood Deeds of Finn," ed. Kuno Meyer (from Laud 610) in *Revue celtique* 5 (1881–82), 195–204; trans, in *Ériu* 1 (1904), 180–190.

[9] There are certainly too many instances of Finn using his *imbas forosna* and *teinm laída* to enumerate here, but I give a few examples: " 'Tis there Finn said, using the incantation called *imbas forosna*: 'A man on the track!' said he. . . . 'Tis then Finn said through *imbas forosna*," etc. (Kuno Meyer, *Fianaigecht*, Todd Lecture Series, XVI [Dublin, 1910], p. 39) ; "Finn put his thumb in his mouth and sang through *teinm laída*, and he said . . ." (*Fianaigecht*, p. xx); "Put thy thumb beneath thy tooth of knowledge and leave us not in ignorance" (Cailte to Finn, *Duanaire Finn*, II, no. xlix, p. 6); "You obtain your power by knowledge and the excellence of your intellect and by chewing of your fingers" (Oscar to Finn, *Duanaire Finn*, II, no. lxii, p. 64). For a discussion of *imbas* (from **imb-uid-t-* 'very great knowledge'), see R. Thurneysen, "*Imbas For•Osndai*," *Zeitschrift für celtische Philologie* 19 (1932), 163–164; N. K. Chadwick, "Imbas Forosnai," *Scottish Gaelic Studies* 4 (1935), 97–135.

for the ritual, the means by which Finn subsequently exercised his powers of great knowledge and divination, not how he originally acquired them. How, then, do we account for the salmon and its special properties?[10]

In the Rennes *Dindshenchas*, the same source in which we find the tale of Bóand and Nechtan's well, is the story of the origin of the river Shannon:

> Sinend daughter of Lodan Lucharglan son of Ler, out of Tír Tairngire . . . went to Connla's Well which is under the sea, to behold it. That is a well at which are the hazels and inspirations (?) of wisdom [translates *cuill 7 imbois na heicsi*], that is, the hazels of the science of poetry, and in the same hour their fruit, and their blossoms and their foliage break forth, and these fall on the well in the same shower, which raises on the water a royal surge of purple. Then the salmon chew the fruit, and the juice of the nuts is apparent on their bellies. And seven streams of wisdom spring forth and turn there again.
>
> Now Sinend went to seek the inspiration [*in imbois*] for she wanted nothing save only wisdom. She went with the stream till she reached *Linn Mná Féile* 'the Pool of the Modest Woman,' that is Brí Ele—and she went ahead on her journey, but the well left its place [*traigis in topur*], and she followed it to the banks of the river *Tarr-cáin* 'Fair-back.' After this it overwhelmed her, so that her back went upwards [*Imasrái(n) iar suide ro tarla a tarr faen fuirri*], and when she had come to the land on this side (of the Shannon) she tasted death. Whence *Sinnan* and *Linn Mná Féile* and *Tarr-cáin*.[11]

According to this legend, obviously analogous and complementary to the Bóand legend, it is the desire for wisdom, not the force of pride, which compels the woman to visit the well. The source of wisdom is in the nuts which are then eaten by the salmon. The details of this otherworldly well differ slightly in the metrical version:

> Connla's Well, loud was its sound,
> was beneath the blue-skirted ocean:
> six streams unequal in fame,
> rise from it, the seventh was Sinann.
>
> The nine hazels of Crimall the sage
> drop their fruits yonder under the well:
> they stand by the power of magic spells
> under a darksome mist of wizardry.

[10] The importance of the fish as a sacred animal has been stressed by Anne Ross in *Pagan Celtic Britain* (London, 1967), pp. 305–351. The association of wells, salmon, and sacred heads lies outside the scope of my paper, though its significance cannot be denied; one thinks immediately of Odin, visiting the otherworldly well of wisdom, presided over by Mimir's Head (Anne Ross [*op. cit.*, pp. 109–110] suggests that this may be Celtic in origin). For a brief summary of the episode of the head of Lomna, Finn's fool, and the salmon, see *ibid.*, p. 121 (ed. in *Fianaigecht*, pp. xix–xx).

[11] *Dindshenchas*, ed. Stokes, p. 457.

. . . . . .

When the cluster of nuts is ripe
they fall down into the well;
they scatter below on the bottom,
and the salmon eat them.[12]

The relationship among the well, the hazel nuts, and the poets is established in a tract cited by R. Thurneysen:

> A *laídh luibenshosach* follows here, which Cormac mac Cuilennain made, concerning the "excellent nuts" which fall from the *Cuill Crimainn* ("C.'s Hazel tree") which stands on the banks of the Segais. Segais is the name of the body of water or of a spring which is among the Fir Breg. . . . Into this spring fell these nuts first of all, then out of the well every seven years or every year into the Boyne river, so that they—filled with *imus* (magical poetic quality)—came to certain persons. These drank the *imus* out of them, so that they then became master poets. And to the value of these nuts Cormac made this song.[13]

Now Segais is the name of the Boyne at its source, the Well of Nechtan, as the *dindshenchas* of Bóand explicitly states.[14] Clearly, the stories of the origin of the Shannon and the Boyne are closely related reflexes of a myth that told how a woman was punished for seeking the "illuminating inspiration" from a body of water guarded by Nechtan. This *imbas forosna* was hidden in the nuts of hazels that grew about the water. It was much sought after by the poets of Ireland (just as the powers of Apā́ṃ Nápāt were sought by the Vedic poets), and it was one of the three things that constituted a poet. Finn, in his role of Finn Éces, Finn the Poet,[15] had watched long on the banks of the Boyne to get at the *imbas*, "for the poets thought that the place where poetry was revealed always was upon the brink of water."[16]

The *imbas*, or 'very great knowledge' (cf. parallel concepts in *druí* from **der-uid-*; Welsh *cyfarwydd, derwydd*), also had the property of illuminating, or kindling. The R.I.A. (Royal Irish Academy) Dictionary gives the following meanings for *forosna*: 'lights up (or 'burns'—as a candle), illumines, kindles, shines.' Two of the three things that constitute a poet, *imbas forosna* and *teinm laída* (through which Finn chanted) were both banished by Saint Patrick, according

---

[12] Gwynn, *op. cit.*, p. 293, ll. 9–16, 21–24.

[13] *Zeitschrift für celtische Philologie* 17 (1927), 268.

[14] Gwynn, *op. cit.*, p. 27, l. 9.

[15] Finn is called "poet" a number of times in the literature: "Fionn fáid(h)" (*fáith* and *fili* are alternative names for the Irish poet-seer) in *Duanaire Finn*, I, no. xxi, p. 57; II, no. xxxvii, p. 3, and no. xlvii, p. 40; "fili" *ibid.*, I, no. xvi, p. 34. For the identification of Finn Éces with Finn himself, see O'Rahilly, *op. cit.*, p. 329 n. 4.

[16] Quoted by Meyer in *Macgnimartha Find* from "Immacallam in dá Thúarad" in *Book of Leinster*, ed. R. I. Best and M. A. O'Brien, p. 186a, ll. 24202–24203.

to Cormac's glossary. O'Rahilly interpreted *teinm* in the latter phrase as the verbal noun of [1]*teinnid* 'cuts, breaks, cracks'; it is often used in the sense of cracking nuts (R.I.A. Contribb. [contributions to the R.I.A. Dictionary]; but cf. [3]*teinnid* 'shines, burns'). *Laéda* (or *laída*) may mean 'pith, marrow' (R.I.A. Contribb., following O'Rahilly). The phrase then may refer to the way in which the poets (or the salmon?) got at the wisdom of the nuts, and this is the way O'Rahilly interprets the phrase (*Early Irish History and Mythology* [Dublin, 1946], pp. 338–339). Native glossators, however, emphasize the sense of illumination: *teinm laeda .i. teinm taithnim 7 teinm tuicsi* . . . (R.I.A. Contribb., s.v. [2]*teinm*) '*teinm laeda*, that is, the shining or burning (reading [3]*teinnid*) of brilliance, radiance, and the shining of the *tuicse*.' *Tuicse* (gen. *tuicsi*) may mean either 'the act of understanding, perceiving,' or 'the chosen, elect,' as in 'God's elect' (R.I.A. Contribb., [1]*tuicse*).

In native Irish tradition, therefore, one of the characteristics of poetry was an illuminating brilliance, which was further interpreted as the shining or the radiance of the elect. In these respects we have close parallels to the brilliant essence associated in Indo-Iranian tradition with Apā́ṃ Nápāt.

The difficulties inherent in the suggestions I have made here are not to be minimized; Irish tradition, like the well of Nechtan, does not readily disburse its mythical essences. But, given the list of correspondences between Irish and Iranian legends, so carefully defined by Dumézil, we are no doubt justified in taking the paradoxical concept of "fire in water" as confirmed in the native Irish treatment of inspired poetry: a potent illuminating wisdom, found in the water, guarded by Nechtan, whose possession endowed the privileged few with extraordinary powers.

Indo-European Structure of the Baltic Pantheon

JAAN PUHVEL, *University of California, Los Angeles*

The new dispensation in Indo-European comparative mythology has yet to make a significant dent in the Baltic area. The ancient traditions of the Old Prussians, Lithuanians, and Latvians are waiting to be rehabilitated from their Mannhardtian putdown as just another installment of rustic European *Wald- und Feldkulte*. It is high time to remind the scholarly community that we are dealing with exceedingly conservative Indo-European social groupings, and not just in the well-recognized linguistic sense. They were rural, to be sure, but no more so than the Germanic or Celtic peoples when first drawn into the light of history, and considerably less volatile at that. The relative lateness of our data is matched by the fact that the Lithuanians were christianized, and merely officially and from the top, only in the late fourteenth and early fifteenth centuries, and that the ecclesiastical authorities in East Prussia had their hands full stamping out heathen practices throughout the sixteenth century. The argument that the Baltic peoples were meek peasants without a hierarchic social structure and attendant ideological underpinnings is patently laid to rest by the expansion of the Grand Duchy of Lithuania to the Black Sea in the fourteenth century and the succession of brilliant rulers from Mindaugas in the thirteenth century, via Gediminas, Algirdas, and Kestutis in the fourteenth to Vytautas in the early fifteenth century. It is equally fatuous to doubt the existence of a well-entrenched and influential indigenous religious establishment, in the light of the description of the "Pagan Pope" in Petrus von Dusburg's *Chronicon*

Prussiae (1326; chap. 5):[1] "Fuit . . . in Nadrowia locus quidam dictus Romow . . . in quo habitabat quidam dictus Criwe, quem colebant pro papa . . . Tante fuit autoritatis, quod . . . a regibus et nobilibus et communi populo in magna reverencia haberetur." (There was in Nadrowia a place by the name of Romow, in which dwelt a certain man called Criwe, whom they honored as pope. So strong was his authority that he was held in great awe by the kings and nobles and the common folk.) Dusburg's reference is to around the year 1260, or to the days of Mindaugas, when secular power ought to have been in ascendancy. Other references to both the Krive institution and the sanctuary at Romowe leave no doubt of a setup fully capable of supporting an ancient priestly tradition not unlike that of the druids or the brahmins and certainly more entrenched than anything attested for the hierarchic divisions of the Germanic peoples, where a priestly class is conspicuously absent.

Of this presumed Baltic body of myth nothing has come down to us by written hieratic tradition, and precious little by the chronographic one. Even in the latter an occasional scrap of myth is incidental to the description of cultic practices. Thus the account of the Lithuanian sojourn, about 1432, of the Bohemian monk Hieronymus Pragensis[2] first speaks of snake worshipers, then of a tribe that kept a perpetual sacred fire that sustained the oracular ministrations of priests. Farther in the interior Hieronymus came upon a tribe that "solem colebat et malleum ferreum rare magnitudinis singulari cultu venerabatur" (worshiped the sun and adored with extraordinary veneration an iron hammer of rare size). The following etiology of the cult was provided by the local priests: "Olim pluribus mensibus non fuisse visum solem, quem rex potentissimus captum reclusisset in carcere munitissimae turris. Signa zodiaci deinde opem tulisse soli ingentique malleo perfregisse turrim solemque liberatum hominibus restituisse, dignum itaque veneratu instrumentum esse, quo mortales lucem recepissent." (Once upon a time the sun had not been seen for several months, because a mighty king had caught it and shut it in the dungeon of a fortress tower. The signs of the zodiac had thereupon come to the sun's help, shattered the tower with a huge hammer, freed the sun and restored it to mankind; therefore, the tool by which mortals had recovered light was deserving of worship.) Hieronymus next chanced upon other tribes that worshiped sacred groves, and he set about chopping them down, including a "quercum vetustissimum et

[1] Cf. the versified German version in Nicolaus von Jeroschin's *Kronike von Pruzinlant* (ca. 1340; ll. 4020 ff.).

[2] Inserted by Enea Silvio Piccolomini, the later Pope Pius II, into chapter 26 of his *Europa* around 1458.

ante omnes arbores religione sacram" (an ancient oak, which in their beliefs was holy above all other trees). His activity generated enough popular resentment for Vitoldus (i.e., Vytautas) to withdraw his missionary's license and hand him his walking papers.

However garbled, we have here a sun myth, and it is also mainly solar tradition that seeps through the principal filter of ancient Baltic mythical lore, namely, the folk songs of Lithuania and especially of Latvia. Ever since W. Mannhardt's study, "Die lettischen Sonnenmythen,"[3] the close of accordances of Lettish solar tradition with the Vedic one have been well known. Just as the twin Aśvins or *Divó nápātā* are rescuers of people from watery distress and become the dual husbands (*pátī*) of the sun-maid Sūryā, even so the Dioscuric *Dieva dēli* save the sun-daughter (Saules meita) from drowning and jointly marry her.[4] But there may be other Indo-European mythic matter as yet undiscovered in the Lettish songs. David Knipe,[5] in discussing the variants of the Indic Suparṇa myth, and especially the Yajurvedic tradition of the birth of poetic meters as Suparṇī's children, mentions the heavenly ascent of Gāyatrī in company with a female goat (*ajā*) and with light (*jyotis*), with the goat winning the soma and Gāyatrī four syllables lost by other meters in previous unsuccessful flights. Knipe (p. 346) recalls not only the Norse mythical goat Heiðrún but also quotes in English a "curious rhyme" from Latvia which he has taken from E. A. Armstrong's book, *The Folklore of Birds* (London, 1958), and which Armstrong had picked up from his "friend Mr. John Millers" (p. 172). In fact we are dealing with a very popular Latvian folk song, attested in many variants in the standard collections.[6] I prefix the Latvian original to the English version:

> Viens gans nomira, citi gani raudāja.
> Cūka raka kapu augstā kalnā.
> Zīle nesa vesti tēvam, mātei,
> Kaza kāpa debesis Dievam sūdzēt,
> Dzenis kala krustu sausā priedē,
> Dzeguze zvanīja līkā bērzā;
> Lielais dundurs sprediķi sacīja.
> Sīki mazi putniņi pātarus skaitīja;
> Vārdiņi ņudzēja smalkajos zariņos.

[3] In *Zeitschrift für Ethnologie* 7 (1875), 73–104, 209–244, 281–330.

[4] For further references cf., e.g., my article in *Studies in Honor of Ants Oras* (Stockholm, 1965), pp. 167–177, and Donald Ward's monograph *The Divine Twins* (Berkeley and Los Angeles, 1968).

[5] "The Heroic Theft: Myths from Ṛgveda IV and the Ancient Near East," *History of Religions* 6 (1967), 328–360.

[6] E.g., *Latwju Dainas Kr. Barona kopojumâ* I.2, pp. 434–435, no. 2692 (Riga, 1922); *Latviešu tautas dziesmas* 1 (Copenhagen, 1952), 344. I owe these references to Professor V. Rūķe-Draviņa.

> One herdsman died, the others cried.
> The Pig dug the grave on a high hill.
> The Tit carried the news to his parents,
> The Goat mounted to heaven to ask forgiveness,
> The Woodpecker carved a cross on a fir tree,
> The Cuckoo tolled in a crooked birch;
> The Gadfly preached the sermon.
> All the birds said the funeral prayers;
> Their words mingled in the tiny twigs.

The strange similarities reside in the mythic combination of goat and bird. In the Suparṇī story it is the goat who brings back the soma-prize from heaven, after various birds have failed; in the Latvian folk song the goat mounts to heaven for the crucial task, whereas the various birds merely officiate at the mundane aspects of the funeral.

In view of such folkloristic manifestations of possible genuine mythic matter we may feel encouraged to approach the chronographic transmission as well with some comparativistic confidence. Hieronymus was exposed successively to snake cult, oracular fire determining whether the sick would live or die, sun worship coupled with a huge hammer fetish, and sacred groves centered on an especially holy ancient oak tree. The *Polish Chronicle* of Jan Długosz from the second half of the fifteenth century also lists the Lithuanian objects of worship as *ignem, fulmen, silvas,* and *aspides,* adding to these the sacrifices to the dead (*Diis patriis*). In addition Długosz essays various *interpretationes romanas*—Vulcanum, Iovem, Dianam, and Aesculapium, respectively—but goes on to say that "Iovem autem in fulmine venerando vulgari suo illum Perkunum, quasi percussorem, appellabant" (in worshiping the thunderbolt they called Jupiter in their own language Perkunus, which would mean 'Striker'). Vestal-type females entertained his perpetual fire and paid with their lives ("capite expiabant") for its extinction. Perkunas as the thunder-god is of course the one long-admitted mainstay of the Baltic pantheon, and the attestations of the name reach back all the way to the thirteenth century: *Perkunovi rekše gromu* 'to Perkun called thunder' in the Old Russian addenda to the translation of the *Chronographia* of Johannes Malalas in 1261 (where Perkunas keeps company with Andaj, Žvoruna called "bitch," and Teljavel', "the smith who fashioned the sun"), and *Perkune* in the *Livländische Reimchronik* of 1290 (l. 1436). Perkunas is not mentioned in the thirteenth-century *Volhynian Chronicle,* but its references to the time of Mindaugas (1252 and 1258) include the same mysterious Andaj and Teljavel' as well as an opaque Nŭnaděj, Diverikŭz (Diviriks), and Mějdějn. The latter is the woodland goddess (Lith. *medainis* 'silvestris') corresponding to the Žemaitic Modeina in Jan Łasicki's *De diis Samogitarum* (ca. 1580), whereas

Diviriks means something like "ruler of the gods" and clearly denotes a high god.

There are only two other Baltic divine names attested before the sixteenth century: the *Collatio Episcopi Warmiensis* (1419), a memorandum to the pope on behalf of the sagging Order of Teutonic Knights, against its Polish-Lithuanian adversaries Wladislaw Jagiello and Vytautas, extols the labors of the conquerors in exterminating "gentes servientes demonibus, colentes Patollum Natrimpe et alia ignominiosa fantasmata" (tribes of devil worshipers, devoted to Patollus Natrimpe and other disgraceful figments), in whose honor the heathens had barbarously shed precious Christian blood.

In the early sixteenth century the material is enriched, and complicated, by the onset of antiquarian quasi history, especially the works of Erasmus Stella of Zwickau and the Dominican friar Simon Grunau from Tolkemit near Frauenburg in East Prussia. Stella's *De Borussiae antiquitatibus* was a fanciful piece of ethnogenesis inspired especially by Jordanes' history of the Goths; it centered on a legendary Alanian chieftain Vidvutus as the unifier and dynastic ancestor of the ancient Borussians. Grunau's *Preussische Chronik* (1517–1521)[7] tells of the Cimbrian Witowudi and his brother Bruteno who came from Sweden and settled on the Vistula in the early sixth century; Witowudi was made king by the local population, and Bruteno became high priest with the title Crywo Cyrwaito, in the service of the three gods Patollo, Patrimpo, and Perkuno, whose idols stood in a thick oak tree in a place called Rickoyto, which became the habitat of Bruteno and his priesthood, the *waidolotten* (*Preuss. Chron.*, I, 62). We subsequently hear a lot more about this divine triad. On Witowudi's banner, Potrimppo's (*sic*, p. 77) depiction is described first as "ein man junger gestalt ane bardt, gekronett mit sangelen und frolich . . . und der gott vom getreide" (a man young in appearance and without beard, crowned with ears of corn and joyful of mien, and the god of grain). The second face was "wie ein zorniger man und mittelmessigk alten sein angesicht wie feuer und gekronet mit flammen, sein bart craus und schwarcz" (the likeness of an angry man of middle age, his face like fire and crowned with flames, his beard curly and black). The third face was that of an "alter mahn mit einem langen groen bardt und seine farbe gantz totlich, war gekronet mit einem weissen tuche wie ein morbant unde sag von unden auff die andern an unde his Patollo mit namen" (old man with a long green beard and a wholly deathlike complexion; he was crowned with a white cloth like a turban and looked up at the others from below; his name was Patollo). The oak in which these three deities were installed (p. 78) "war

[7] Ed. M. Perlbach, 3 vols. (Leipzig, 1876–1896).

stetis grün, winter und sommer," and was divided into three equal parts for the individual idols. Perkuno had his perpetual fire which the *waidlotten* were to maintain on pain of death, Potrumppo (*sic*) had a snake in a jar covered with sheaves of grain and fed with milk by the *waydolottinnen* (priestesses), and Patollo had as his sacred objects skulls of man, horse, and cow. Later on (pp. 94–96) Grunau describes the three gods further, after saying that they were brought in by the Cimbrians and supplanted earlier sun worship. Patollo is called "der obirster abgott der Bruteni," "ein irschrocklicher got," "ein got der todtin." Potrimppo was "ein gott des gluckis in streitten und sust in anderen sachin." Both are said to have been sanguinary in terms of human sacrifice ("uber die mosze Patollo Potrimppo hetten ein wolgefallen in menschin blute"). Perkuno was the oracular thunder-god. Three other gods are then mentioned by Grunau. Wurschayto or Borsskayto was worshiped generally in villages, wherever there was an oak tree; a young fish was sacrificed to him, and he conferred luck in fishing and good health. Fowl were sacrificed to Szwaybrotto, and firstfruits to Curcho. These three are obvious rustic deities, and Curcho is in fact mentioned as early as 1249, in the peace treaty between the Teutonic Knights and the Old Prussians: "Ydolo, quod semel in anno, collectis frugibus, consueverunt confingere et pro deo colere, cui nomen Curche imposuerunt"[8] (An idol which, once a year, after the harvest, they are wont to fashion and worship as a god, and which they have named Curche). But interest centers mainly on the triadic structure of Grunau's Patollo, Perkuno, and Potrimpo. Does it reflect Old Baltic theological realities, or is it a willful piece of Grunau's penchant for structured historical fantasy? Did the cults at historical Romowe and similar sites bear any resemblance to Grunau's Rickoyto? It has been customary, especially since Mannhardt's withering denunciation of Grunau and all his works,[9] to consider him near worthless as a source on Baltic religion. Every detail has been explained away as pseudoscholarly in kind and propagandistic in intent. We read in a relatively recent work that Grunau "invented a Prussian religion similar to the Norse to indicate the close relationship through the Old Prussians between the Germanic and Norse peoples."[10] The idea of the triad supposedly came from Adam of Bremen's description of the idols of Thor, Wodan, and Fricco in the Swedish temple of Ubsola (Uppsala). For Mannhardt, Grunau must have had access to the *Collatio Episcopi Warmiensis* in

[8] See C. Clemen, *Fontes historiae religionum primitivarum, praeindogermanicarum, indogermanicarum minus notarum* (Bonn, 1936), p. 95.

[9] W. Mannhardt, *Letto-preussische Götterlehre* (Riga, 1936), pp. 190–227.

[10] W. C. Jaskiewicz, "A Study in Lithuanian Mythology," *Studi Baltici* 9 (1952), 65–106, esp. 92–93.

order to have known Patollo and Potrimpo (with the *varia lectio* Natrimpe). And so on. At the other extreme from such hypercriticism we find facile identifications of the type "Patollo may with certainty be identified with Óthinn,"[11] which assume genuine historical identity without facing the meaning thereof (genetic, diffused, borrowed, or what?). Or again, genuine Indo-European genetic tripartition is forthwith assumed, without reference to Grunau's controversiality.[12]

In attempting to strike a saner balance in evaluating Grunau's information, we must readily admit that he may have known Adam's *Gesta Hammaburgensis Ecclesiae Pontificum,* either in some manuscript version (it had not yet been printed) or via renarrations of the type contained in Albert Krantz's contemporary *Suetia.* But are the two accounts really that similar? Adam's (*Gest. Hamm.* 4.25–27) Thor is seated in the middle in the temple, with Wodan and Fricco on either side. Thor is the thunder- and weather-god; Wodan is the war-god embodying "Furor"; Fricco bestows peace and pleasure and is equipped with an immense phallus. Wodan is armed, Thor sceptered. When plague and hunger threaten, Thor's idol gets attention; if war is imminent, Wodan's; if weddings impend, then Fricco's. Blood sacrifices with suspension of corpses are mentioned, and so is (in Scholion 138) a large tree next to the temple, of unknown kind, evergreen in winter and summer.

The only real similarities are the triad and the tree. But even here the discrepancies dominate. Adam's taxonomical mystery tree is incidental to the main cultic scene, whereas Grunau's idols are in the tree itself, which is explicitly an oak. Patollo's skulls and Potrimpo's snake jar are not particularly evocative of Odin's armor or of Fricco's overgrown priapus. All told, if Grunau had been a conscious and unscrupulous assimilator out to scandinavianize his data and relying mainly on fantasy, he could have done much better. As his material stands, it is simply not clear why he would have falsified most of it in the form in which it appears.

It is more reasonable to appraise Grunau against the backdrop of both earlier and later specifically Baltic materials. In my estimation the antecedent data do not militate in any significant way against the postulation of the type of pantheon presented by Grunau. The Krive of Romowe, and his counterparts at other cult centers in lower and upper Lithuania, must be thought of as establishment theologians during the thirteenth and fourteenth centuries, and the presence of a stylized triadic Indo-European priestly paganism just prior to the

[11] N. K. Chadwick, *The Beginnings of Russian History* (Cambridge, 1946), p. 91.

[12] R. L. Fisher, Jr., in J. Puhvel, ed., *Myth and Law among the Indo-Europeans* (Berkeley, Los Angeles, and London, 1970), pp. 148–149.

conversion is no more implausible than that of Uppsala at the time of Saint Ansgar's mission. Whether the pantheon had undergone Germanic influences in the course of early history is a moot question. In the absence of other evidence it is sensible to regard the Baltic traditions as essentially indigenous.

Grunau may thus be regarded as the transitional figure between the eyewitness era and the antiquarian one. However distortedly, he transmitted a piece of the pagan establishment which by the sixteenth century was irretrievably lost. His contemporary and later sources were reduced to repetition or to amassing whatever folk religion remained, and it is not surprising that they record a confused and multiplex crew of divinities. It is the difference between Adam of Bremen and an encyclopedist like Snorri in relation to Scandinavian tradition.

The two principal documents are *Episcoporum Prussie Pomesaniensis atque Sambiensis Constitutiones Synodales* (1530) and its contemporary *Der unglaubigen Sudauen ihrer Bockheiligung mit sambt andern Ceremonien, so sie tzu brauchen gepflegeth.* The list continues through the next two centuries: Martin Mosvidius (preface to *Catechism* of 1547), Jan Malecki (*Epistola de sacrificiis et idolatria veterum Borussorum* of 1551, with a new edition in 1563 by his son Hieronymus), Lukas David (*Preussische Chronik* of 1572–1583),[13] Kaspar Henneberger (*Erclerung der Preussischen grössern Landtaffel oder Mappen* of 1576, second edition of 1595; *Kurze und warhafftige Beschreibung zu Preussen* of 1584), Matys Stryjkowski (*Kronika polska, litewska* of 1582), A. Guagnini (*Choreographia Poloniae, Lithuaniae, Livoniae et Prussiae* [Basel, 1582]), Matthäus Waissel (*Chronica alter Preusscher, Eifflendischer und Curlendischer Historien* of 1599), Caspar Schütz (*Historia rerum Prussicarum* of 1599), Jan Łasicki (*De diis Samogitarum* of ca. 1580, printed in Basel in 1615), Coelestin Mislenta (*Manuale Pruthenicum* of 1626), Johannes Behm (*Duae orationes historicae de duplici divinae gratiae fundamento, Regiomonti 1644*), Christian Hartknoch (*Selectae dissertationes historicae de variis rebus Prussicis* of 1679), and Matthias Praetorius (*Deliciae Prussicae oder Preussische Schaubühne* of ca. 1690).

Elements of the earlier attested cults persist, such as snake worship, but it is particularly ram sacrifice that worried the Church. Georg Sabinus, Melanchthon's son-in-law and rector of the University of Königsberg, summed up matters in a distichal epistle to Cardinal Pietro Bembo in the year 1545:

> Namque ferox hominum genus est et agreste sub arcto,
> Notitiam nondum quod pietatis habet:

13 Published in Königsberg in eight volumes in 1812–1817 by G. E. S. Hennig and D. F. Schütz.

Caeruleos instar sed adorat numinis angues
Mactatoque litat sacra nefanda capro.

For there is a savage race of men, a rustic one under the northern star,
Which as yet has no knowledge of true religion:
But it worships as deities bluish snakes
and performs unspeakable rites by slaughtering a ram.

The typical lists contain such divine names as Occopirmus (sky- or star-god), Suaixtix (sun-god), Auschauts (a healer), Autrimpus or Antrimpus (sea-god), Potrimpus (god of rivers and springs), Bardoayts or Perdoytus or Gardoayts (a seafarers' god), Piluitus or Pelwittus or Pilnitis (god or goddess of rich harvests), Pergrubrius (god of the spring), Parcuns or Percunus (thunder- and rain-god), Pecols or Pocols or Pecollos or Pecullus or Poccollus (or whatever spelling; explained variously as "Pluto," "Furiae," "der Hölle und Finsternis Gott," "die fliegenden Geister oder Teuffel," "deus aëriorum spirituum," etc.). Many other names and epithets patently of "lower mythology" crop up in those writers, but the above listing has claim to title as some kind of postconversion underground pantheon. Apart from some expectable traces of sun worship, and a contingent of sea divinities, it is reducible to healing and fertility deities (Auschauts, Potrimpus, Piluitus, Pergrubrius), plus Percunus and Pecullus.

The name of Potrimpus is thus onomastically integrated, not only with Autrimpus or Antrimpus but also with the fifteenth-century Natrimpe. Granting prefix variation, the theonymic element *trimp-* is firmly attested with a watery fertility connotation, no matter what its ultimate root connection (a comparison with Lith. *trẽmpti* 'stamp, tread on' is not by itself enlightening).

The name Pecullus with its many spelling variants has obviously supplanted Patollus. Henneberger (*Kurze und warhafftige Beschreibung*, p. 10) made it official in 1584: "Potollos, den etzliche auch Pocollos oder Pickollos nennen, der ir oberster Gott war . . ." And Praetorius (*Deliciae Prussicae*, chap. 4, par. 4)[14] closes his long list of assorted deities by remarking that "diese alle aber sind nicht gleichberühmt bei deren Scribenten. Doch haben vor allen andern den unstrittigen Vorzug die drey Götter, so sie in der Romove vor allen andern angebetet haben, geheissen Pykullis, Perkunas und Padrimpus" (yet all these are not equally renowned in their sources. Nevertheless, before all others incontestable preference goes to those three whom they have worshiped above all others at Romove, by the names of Pykullis, Perkunas, and Padrimpus). Is this a harking back to Grunau, with Pykullis and Romove substituted for Patollo and Rickoyto? Or did Praetorius know something via different channels? He

[14] Ed. W. Pierson (Berlin, 1871).

was certainly no intentional perpetuator of pseudoreligion, since (*ibid.*, par. 16) he stresses the fine point that in his time neither the Nadravians (in eastern East Prussia) nor the contiguous Žemaitians (in lower Lithuania) any longer worshiped Padrympus by name but had substituted other patent terms for a fertility god (e.g., Waisgautis). Pecullus' name is identical with Lith. *pikùlas* 'devil,' Lettish *pīkals* 'heathen god, evil being,' and connectible with Lith. *pìktas* 'evil, angry,' *pỹkti* 'be wroth.' The etymology of Patollus is much less clear. We may note V. Pisani's adduction of Skt. *pā̆tālam* 'underworld,'[15] while staying mindful of the brittleness of such distant etymology building in a derivational vacuum.

The Indo-European structure of the Baltic pantheon hinges heavily on a correct appreciation and interpretation of Patollus-Pecullus. On the one hand Christian demonology found him exploitable; on the other it did not quite know what to do with him. He was evidently a god of the otherworld, but at the same time he was the leader of the host of the dead in the pagan sky. Thus the various sources have split him into two, typically Malecki, for whom "Pocclus" is "deus inferni ac tenebrarum," and "Poccollus" is "deus aëriorum spirituum." This hesitation helps to piece together the original nature of this "devil." He has one more name, Lith. Vẽlinas or Vélnias or Véls (nowadays 'devil'), which has the cognates *vẽlės* 'phantoms of the dead' and Veliuonà 'ancestral goddess' (cf. "Vielona Deus animarum" in Łasicki). Mosvidius' preface warns against all *welnuwas*, and Theophil Schultz's *Compendium grammaticae Lithuanicae* (1673; p. 24) glosses Welinas with 'Diabolus.' More significantly, C. Szyrwid's *Dictionarium trium linguarum* (Vilnius, 1629) makes the equation "Velnias yra Piktis" ('Velnias is Piktis' [variant of Pikulas]).

At this point the learned tradition can take us no further, but Lithuanian folklore sheds additional light. The data on Velinas have been recently gathered in the folklore archives of Vilnius by M. Gimbutas, who presents them elsewhere in this volume. Gimbutas has found that in the nineteenth century there were still folk beliefs concerning the *vẽlės* battling or hunting, or marching like battalions in the sky. Velinas was one-eyed, prophetic (epithetically Ragius 'Seer'), and terrible in his trickery; he could raise a whirlwind when angered, and he was the god of hanging and the hanged. This dossier is ample enough to permit a typological comparison with the Germanic *Wōđanaz, both the Tvíblindi and the Hangaguđ aspects of Norse tradition and the one-eyed storm spirit who leads the souls of the hanged as "Wutanes her" across the skies in German folklore. Thus

[15] *Ricerche linguistiche* 1 (1950), 272; *Le religioni dei Celti e dei Balto-slavi nell' Europa prescristiana* (Milano, 1950), 86.

Lithuanian folklore strongly indicates that underneath the death-god of Grunau and the devil of Christian demonology lurks a principal divinity of the Baltic pantheon, whose name Pecullus has the same 'rage' meaning as *Wōđanaz, and whose Lithuanian allonym Velinas is best connectible with ON *valr* 'warrior corpses on battlefield,' *Valhǫll*, OIr. *fuil* 'blood,' Lat. *uolnus* 'wound,' and so on. The presence of such a magical, death-oriented high god in close complementarity with the ruling thunder-god seems to be typical of the Germanic (Odin : Thor) and Celtic (Gaulish Esus : Taranis) pantheons. It may be partly an "areal" Indo-European feature, the presence of which I also suspect in the Volos (Veles) : Perun opposition of the Old Russian tradition, although the thorny issue of direct Scandinavian (Varangian) interference (i.e., an Odin : Thor overlay) complicates matters in terms of prehistoric reconstruction. In any event, I would advocate a close study of Volos : Perun in relation to Velinas : Perkunas in the light of what I have proposed above, rather than such panoramic orchestrations across time, space, and root etymology as that recently undertaken by Roman Jakobson.[16]

In summation, then, the Baltic pantheon may well show many traits peculiar to its condition, such as a hypertrophy of rural deities and a scarcity of overt war-gods. Yet we are fully justified in piercing the overlays and trying to discern its ancient tripartite Indo-European structure in terms of the magical sovereign, the warlike thunderer, and the god of peace and fertility. Grunau did not have to lie about Patollo, Perkuno, and Potrimpo; they or their typological peers were all too real to the ideology of the ancient Balts.[17]

16 "The Slavic God Veles and His Indo-European Cognates," in *Studi linguistici in onore di Vittore Pisani* (Brescia, 1969), pp. 579–599.

17 The argument of this paper was further delivered as presidential address at the Third Conference on Baltic Studies held at the University of Toronto, Canada, in May 1972, under the title "The Baltic Pantheon," and is included in *Baltic Literature and Linguistics. Selected Papers of the Third Conference on Baltic Studies*, published by the Association for the Advancement of Baltic Studies (1973). I am grateful for the opportunity to make my results readily accessible to scholars in both comparative religion and Baltic studies.

The Lithuanian God Velnias*

MARIJA GIMBUTAS, *University of California, Los Angeles*

The standard Lithuanian Vélnias,[1] the more ancient Vẽlenas or Vẽlinas which still exists in some dialects and a short form Velas or Véls, is now a term for 'devil.' Some two hundred years ago Velnias was still one of the most important pre-Christian Baltic deities: the god of the dead and of cattle (wealth and fertility). His role in Baltic mythology can be reconstructed by means of historical records and folklore. In the latter, in spite of the pressure of the Church, Velnias's archaic features are abundant and convincing. In the following text the older form Velinas is used.

In the Latvian grammar of the year 1783, by Lange-Stender, Véls is "god of the dead," and Veli (Velli) is "days of the god of the dead." In sixteenth-century sources Velionìs is called "god of the dead" to whom offerings were made during the days of the god of the dead, and there was also a feminine form, Veliuonà.[1] Until the end of the nineteenth century it was believed that *vẽlės* or *vẽlės*, ghosts of heroes, were battling or were pursuing wild game. Clusters of *vẽlės*, like regiments of an army, could be seen in the sky or on earth, between two cemeteries, or marching in formation along their own paths. One could clearly hear the clash of weapons, whistling, hand clapping, the barking of dogs, and laughing. These paths are called "roads of Deivės (or Velės)." The Deivės may have been Baltic battle maidens

*A first version of this study was presented to the Second Conference on Baltic Studies of the Association for the Advancement of Baltic Studies, held at San Jose, California, in November 1970 (see *Second Conference on Baltic Studies. Summary of Proceedings* [Norman, 1971], pp. 118–119). For suggestions and comments I am grateful to Roman Jakobson, Jaan Puhvel, and Norbertas Velius.

1 W. Mannhardt, *Letto-preussische Götterlehre* (Riga, 1936), pp. 357, 359, 387.

leading the dead heroes to the realm of Velinas. The name *Vẽlinas* may be connected with Old Norse *valr* 'battlefield dead' and *Val-hǫll* 'hall of dead warriors.'

The root *vel-* is frequent in Baltic toponymy, especially in names for swamps, peat bogs, pits, meadows, lakes, and rivers. A few examples:

Vẽleno raistas: swamp near Jieznas, central Lithuania
Velenų̃ duobės: pits near Klaipėda
Velenų̃ pelkē: swamp near Klaipėda
Velēnìjos pieva: meadow near Mosėdis, northwestern Lithuania
Vēlỹs: lake near Daugėliškis, northeastern Lithuania
Veliuonà: river near the town of Veliuona

In the files of the Institute of Lithuanian Language and Literature in Vilnius there are nearly 400 names with this root, indicating its importance and deep antiquity. About 40 percent of them belong to the names of swamps. Second in popularity are those of the pastures or meadows, then come those for rivers and lakes. *Vélnio akìs* 'Velinas's eye' is a frequent name for a pond in a forest. The same root is encountered occasionally for hillocks and huge stones. Velinas's garden (*Vélnio darželis*) is a small square or a hillock in the middle of a forest. There are special Velinas's plants growing in ponds and swamps (*vélniaropē, vélniacibulē, vélniadagys*). Dragonflies are called "Velinas's horses."

Velinas's name could not be pronounced for taboo reasons, and instead many other names were used. Many of them designate his abode or visiting places: Raistìnis (one from the swamps, *raĩstas* 'swamp'), Balìnis (*balà* 'bog,' 'marsh'), Kìrnis (*kìrnis* also means 'bog'; this name is mentioned by Jan Łasicki in the sixteenth century), Šilìnis (from šìlas 'pine forest'), Gabìkis (from *gabjauja* 'threshing barn,' *gãbija* 'fire'), Pinčiùkas or Kaũkas (dwarf-sized Velinas's relatives living in cattle sheds or stables). One of the most abundantly used alternative names of Velinas, mentioned in dictionaries since the sixteenth century, is Pìkulas, Pìkis, Pìktis. "Velnias yra Piktis" (Velinas is Piktis), explains Szyrwid in his dictionary of the seventeenth century.[2] 'Zorngott' (god of anger) stands in Mielcke's dictionary of 1800,[3] and 'Höllengott' (god of the underworld) in the dictionary by Kurschat of 1874.[4] There are about 100 place-names in Lithuania having the root *pikt-*. In Lithuanian legends Velinas can raise a whirlwind if he is angered.

---

[2] C. Szyrwid, *Dictionarium trium linguarum* (Vilnius, 1629).

[3] C. G. Mielcke, *Littauisch-deutsches und deutsch-littauisches Wörterbuch*, 1 (1800), 199.

[4] F. Kurschat, *Wörterbuch der litauischen Sprache*, 2 (1874).

Another name used for Velinas is Ragius 'seer,' from the verb *regēti* 'to see,' stressing the aspect of clairvoyance of Velinas. Its female counterpart is Ragana 'seeress,' in present Lithuanian 'witch.' Clairvoyance is among the most eminent characteristics of Velinas, richly preserved in legends.

Velinas's one eye is magic, like the Germanic Odin's (who lost his eye as payment for a drink from the holy spring). From a description of Lithuanian paganism in 1595 by Henneberger we learn that there was a holy spring Golbe near Įsrutis (Insterburg) in Lithuania Minor, to which men came "to become one-eyed," that is, to sacrifice one eye. It was a great honor to be one-eyed, and some one-eyed old men were still living in Henneberger's time.[5] "Velinas's water" exists in the legends of the twentieth century; one can become clairvoyant if one moistens one eye with this water. Clairvoyance in legends is associated with Velinas's participation in dance parties in beautiful palaces, which after a cock's crow become swamps. Velinas constantly mingles with village musicians, or he himself is a musician. The motif of music, dance, and clairvoyance has good analogies in other Indo-European traditions. In the Russian *Igor' Tale* "the seer Boian," performer of gusli, magician, and prophetic poet, was 'grandson of Veles' (*Velesovŭ vnukŭ*); the Old Russian Veles may be a deity cognate in name and kind with Velinas.[6]

The Lithuanian proverbs say "clever as a Velnias." This phrase implies the association of Velinas with wealth and commerce. Velinas helps the poor and good people by stealing things, misleading swindlers, bringing supernatural gifts, completing their labors, or solving instantly their difficult problems. Occasionally he appears as a fiery or crowned snake. A person who received his crown would become clairvoyant and omniscient, would see hidden treasures, and would understand animal language. A Lithuanian goblin Aĩtvaras, a demonic relative of Velinas, appears as a flying fiery snake, or a black crow, a black cat, or a grain-vomiting rooster in a farmer's house. He brings grain, milk products, and money. He is also a treacherous thief, taking things away from people he dislikes and bringing them to others, particularly to those who respect him. If angered, he may destroy all treasures, or burn the house, or cause lice or itching of which it is impossible to rid oneself. Aĩtvaras is hatched from a seven-year old cock's egg kept under the armpit, or from a boar's testicle. Kaukas, who in sixteenth-century and later documents was identified

[5] K. Henneberger, *Erclerung der Preussischen grössern Landtaffel oder Mappen*, 2d ed. (Königsberg, 1595), p. 327. Cf. Mannhardt, *op. cit.*, p. 313

[6] Cf. R. Jakobson, "The Slavic God Veles and His Indo-European Cognates," in *Studi linguistici in onore di Vittore Pisani* (Brescia, 1969), pp. 579–599.

with Velinas, has survived as a mythical being similar to Aĩtvaras. He is imagined in the form of a dwarf, dwelling in houses, grain barns, cattle sheds, and fields, and bringing good and well-being into these dwellings. Kaukas's antiquity is revealed in the use of the root *kauk-* in the names of places, such as Kaukaras (hill), Kaukstyra (river), and so on. In the swampy region of Užnemunė, in southern Lithuania near Dovinė, there are three little hills called "Kaukas's hills," on which it is said priests used to make offerings.[7] There was a class of priests called Kaukučones.[8] In Old Prussian *cawx* meant 'velnias.'[9] In Finnish, Kouko or Kouki, borrowed from the Baltic, means 'devil' or 'bear.'

The expression "the cows of Veli" appears in Latvian mythological songs. Hence the parallel with Old Russian Veles/Volos who is called *skotĭjĭ bogŭ* 'cattle-god.' Stryjkowski's chronicle of 1582, which includes a list of Lithuanian gods of his time, mentions a "god of herds" Goniglis Dziewos in east Lithuanian dialect (from the Lithuanian verb *ganýti* 'to herd,' and noun *ganỹkla* 'pasture'). Horses, bulls, he-goats, and other animals were sacrificed to him on a huge stone, and prayers were said in which he was implored to guard the cattle against wolves and other beasts of prey.[10] The name "god of pasture" was used apparently as a taboo substitution. Even in twentieth-century legends, Velinas has his own herds and has shepherds who take care of the herds. His association with meadows is indicated by some legends in which Velinas rakes and mows grass.

The present Velinas in folklore appears in pastures disguised as a child and plays "to throw a disk" with shepherds. This child, however, is very strong: when he flings the disk, it flies buzzing and howling, and since no one can stop it, it travels for many miles. Velinas is very strong. He lifts up or carries huge stones and builds stone bridges or dams across rivers. Whirlwinds start when he carries stones. If he steps up on a stone, his footprints remain. These, called *Velnio pėdos* 'footprints of Velinas,' are associated with miraculous occurrences. Rainwater falling into the footprints acquires magic properties, and women come to the rock seeking fertility.

In folklore Velinas flirts with and seduces maidens who then give birth to a Velinas's child. From birth this child is exceptionally strong and has an arch (bow) on his stomach. The mother of the child dies if she hears him crying at birth. Such children, who can sit upright soon after birth, are killed by more experienced women.

---

[7] J. Totoraitis, in *Lietuvių Tauta* 1, no. 2 (1908), 184.

[8] Mannhardt, *op. cit.*, pp. 549, 555.

[9] E. Fraenkel, *Litauisches etymologisches Wörterbuch* 1 (Heidelberg, 1962), 230.

[10] M. Stryjkowski, *Kronika polska, litewska* (Königsberg, 1582). Cf. Mannhardt, *op. cit.*, p. 331.

Velinas's connections with pastures and huge rocks are without doubt motifs remaining from prehistoric times, but a larger part of the belief in Velinas centers on him as god of the underworld, constantly in need of human blood. His kingdom is in the depths of swamps and lakes. He lures people into swamps or lakes and drowns them, but his usual means of killing is by hanging. Velinas, the ruler of the world of night and death, is the creator of snakes, toads, frogs, other crawling creatures, black birds, black and killer animals, and rocks. He assumes many forms: snake, black dog, black pig, black horse, goat, huge fish (usually pike or perch), rabbit, strange unnatural bird, drake, small black bug, dwarf, or young man.

Velinas, the punishing god, is greatly feared. Therefore the form he takes is not distinguished from fright-arousing images, hallucinations, and dreams. The true form of Velinas cannot be described, because whoever sees him dies immediately. He is also imagined, however, as riding in a chariot or a sleigh drawn by horses.) In legends and beliefs Velinas dramatically lures humans into the unknown. Appearing in the form of a handsome young man, he invites girls to celebrations, showers them with gifts, and dances through the night. In the morning it is discovered that the girl has hanged herself. Velinas invites handsome young people into grand palaces, where the music is magnificent, but suddenly palace, musicians, and youths all sink into the depths or find themselves in a swamp. People whom Velinas entertains or befriends are found choked or hanged. The fiddle tunes of Velinas are associated with traveling to his kingdom. Even today, villagers and farmers hear the fiddle melody after someone's death. If an individual toys with a rope making a noose for hanging, Velinas finishes the game. Toward evening, near swamps, lakes, and forests, disguised as a person, a drake, or some strange bird, he lures and calls a person into the deep until the person begins to drown. Stuck waist-deep, the victim hears Velinas's echoing laughter. Velinas employs cruel methods of getting offerings; for example, he peels the skin off women in the sauna. In the guise of a snake he approaches at night, tears off the sheets and quilts, throws the person on the floor, and frightens him to death; he also comes as a person or as a heavy load to smother the individual. In the form of a *žaltys* (*Tropidonotus natrix*) he chokes a girl desiring beads and sucks out her blood, or he jumps around the necks of berry pickers and cannot be removed. Evenings he appears as a black dog in the cemeteries. He bites, and the wounds never heal. He may appear as a black pig, shrieking and frightening people to death. As a wolf he tears one apart. Velinas rides a black horse and people move aside, saying, "Let him ride wherever he is riding." On a rainy evening a little goat is found in a swamp or a field. He is wailing: *me-ke-ke*. A farmer catches him and comforts him, saying, "Poor little goat got lost." Then the little goat gets heavier and heavier and finally he kicks the farmer fiercely and darts away laughing. Sometimes when a pike or a perch is caught, it sprouts horns and wings and then, turning into a monster, it disappears. In the water these same fish can tip a boat and sink it. Incarnated in a formidable snake with a red head and a crown, this god is menacing and punishing the living world. For seven years this "king of snakes" lives underground. Then he crawls out of the cave and strikes, and his bite is fatal. No charm can save a human being, an animal, or a plant.

As a snake, his main incarnation, Velinas survived well into the twentieth century. The interplay of life and death, of vitality and poison, of the snake corresponds neatly with the concept of the dynamic, versatile, and unpredictably dangerous god, the dispenser of fertility and wealth, and the ruler of the underworld. In popular tradition the snake is associated with sexual life, and since the element of fertility is essential to the concept of prosperity and happiness, the snake was supposed to ensure the fertility of the soil and the increase of the family. The toad, Lith. *rupūžė*, represents the female aspect of the same symbolism and is the main incarnation of Ragana.

The recognition of Velinas's ancient features in folklore as one of the very important pre-Christian gods fills a gap in the study of Baltic mythology. The Baltic Velinas was no less important than and of similar stature as Veles/Volos in Slavic, Odin and Ull in Old Norse, Varuṇa in Indic, and Hades and Hermes in Greek mythology. Velinas, magician-god of the otherworld, death, and night, and Dievas (<*Deivas), the god of sky and daylight, were high gods having distinct Indo-European origins.

Vṛtrahan—Vərəthragna: India and Iran

STEVEN E. GREENEBAUM,
University of California, Los Angeles

In the Indo-European ideological system, the place of Vṛtra, the dragon slain by Indra in the Vedic tradition, has long been a difficult problem. In India, on the one hand, there is a full-blown mythic structure integrating Vṛtra. It is he who bottles up the earth and it is he with whom the Ādityas cannot cope. It is hard to imagine the birth of Indra, and indeed the entire Indra myth, without the context of Vṛtra. In fact, it may well be said that Indra is born for the purpose of disposing of Vṛtra; and for this act he earns the title Vṛtrahan.

In Iran, however, the story is entirely different. Here Vṛtra does not seem to exist. To be sure, the *epithet* of Indra may be found in Vərəthragna; but in Iran Vərəthragna is a god unto himself and has little to do with the Zarathustrian demon that Indra has become. The conclusion drawn by a number of mythologists who have studied the problem, among them Dumézil and Benveniste, is that in Indo-Iranian tradition the name Vərəthragna/Vṛtrahan (< *Vṛtraghna/Vṛtraghan) existed, but the concept, or figure, of Vṛtra did not.[1] Accordingly, it is further assumed that the Indians either invented a Vṛtra or attached the name to an already existing dragon myth, thereby explaining Indra's epithet. *Vṛtraghan would then be explained as meaning "smasher (ghan) of hostility (Vṛtra)."[2] In India this hostility was personified; in Iran it was not.

---

[1] E. Benveniste and L. Renou, *Vṛtra et Vṛθragna* (= *V et V*) (Paris, 1934); G. Dumézil, *The Destiny of the Warrior* (= *D of W*) (Chicago, 1970), pp. 115–138.

[2] M. Dresden in S. N. Kramer, *Mythologies of the Ancient World* (Chicago, 1961), pp. 350–351.

There are, however, some problems. If this line of reasoning is correct, the Indic myth appears inventive and the Iranian one conservative. Yet, in most other contexts, the reverse would appear to be true. The reforms of Zarathustra revamped the Iranian pantheon and it is clear that, while most of the deities were probably kept in one form or another, many of the characteristics and often the whole tradition behind a god were enormously altered.[3] And yet, as there is no particular creation myth for an "Indra" in Iran and no Vṛtra crisis to require it, it would seem that an impasse has been reached.

It is perhaps possible, however, to support the idea of an Indo-Iranian concept of Vṛtra. Instead of attempting to explain Vṛtra away in India, perhaps he may be found in Iran. If so, the hunt for Vṛtra can begin at only one place: the epithet Vərəthragna.

While Zarathustra includes a god Vərəthragna in his pantheon, the name is used elsewhere. Indeed the epithet is used to apply to heroes of particular prowess,[4] and it is this use that proves interesting. There is, it would appear, one hero to whom the epithet is particularly appropriate: Thraētaona.

The deed for which Thraētaona earns the epithet Vərəthragna is the slaying of Aži Dahāka, the "second man" in the titanic struggle of Yima, Aži Dahāka, and Thraētaona. The struggle itself may be placed well back in Iranian tradition and later it may be found in Firdausi as the struggle of Jamshid, Zohak, and Feridun.[5]

In brief, the myth runs as follows. Yima rules over a golden age which ends when he sins. At that moment the divine Xᵛarənah departs from him (Xᵛarənah[6] is that which a sovereign has which sets him apart; it is perhaps best translated as "divine glory"). Having lost the Xᵛarənah, Yima is easily replaced by the monster Aži Dahāka. In turn, however, Aži Dahāka is defeated and replaced by the hero Thraētaona, who had received the Xᵛarənah from Yima.[7]

The receipt of the Xᵛarənah by Thraētaona is of special note. Aži Dahāka never received it, which makes Thraētaona the legitimate ruler after Yima. Benveniste points out that Thraētaona, besides receiving the Xᵛarənah, obtains the title Vərəthragna for the slaying of Aži Dahāka.[8] Benveniste goes on to show a special relationship between the receipt of the Xᵛarənah and the title Vərəthragna.[9] Later

[3] E.g., see F. Cumont, *The Mysteries of Mithra* (New York, 1956), chap. 1, esp. pp. 4–5.

[4] Dumézil, *D of W*, p. 118.

[5] R. Levy, trans., *Shāh-nāma* (Chicago, 1967), pp. 9–25.

[6] Termed *Farr* by Firdausi; cf. Levy, *Shāh-nāma*, p. 7.

[7] Xᵛarənah also goes to Mithra and Kərəsāspa (*Yašt* 19).

[8] *V et V*, p. 21.

[9] *Ibid.*, pp. 31–32.

Benveniste states that "the relationship of Vṛtrahan to Indra . . . corresponds to that of Vərəthragna and Thraētaona."[10]

In summary: Thraētaona earns the epithet Vərəthragna by slaying Aži Dahāka. The "right" to this title is reinforced by Thraētaona's receipt of the Xᵛarənah. Indeed the comparison may be made that Thraētaona's closeness to the title Vərəthragna parallels Indra's closeness to Vṛtrahan. Thus it might well be argued that, as with Indra, Thraētaona was the prototype of the *Vṛtraghan, and after him great heroes were known by the same title.[11] Vərəthragna, then, would be an epithet made into an "abstract" god when Zarathustra placed "Indra" among the demons.

If this is true, and if Vṛtra is to be found in Iran, Aži Dahāka would seem to be the logical candidate. Additional support for this hypothesis comes from the weapons the gods Indra and Thraētaona use in the battle with their respective antagonists. Indra's weapon for the slaying of Vṛtra was the *vajra.* This is cognate with the *gurz,* the weapon Feridun (Thraētaona) used in his slaying of Zohak (Aži Dahāka).

After the deed, Indra is known as the slayer of Vṛtra; Thraētaona, as the smiter of Aži Dahāka. Both earn the title *Vṛtragh(a)n(a). Indeed the connection of the epithet with both Indra and Thraētaona is similar: while it would seem to revolve primarily around them, it later applies to other heroes as well. Both figures, then, would seem to be prototypical examples of *Vṛtragh(a)n(a), Indra for his slaying of Vṛtra and Thraētaona for his slaying of Aži Dahāka.

Having reviewed the evidence relative to the similarities between the slayers, let us now review that which links the slain. It may be noted that both Aži Dahāka and Vṛtra appear to be three-headed dragons.[12] Also, they may both be seen as outsiders (Vṛtra is neither Deva nor Āditya; Aži Dahāka/Zohak is specifically mentioned as being from a foreign land),[13] and both are slain by gods other than those they attacked (Vṛtra attacks the Ādityas but is slain by Indra who is a Deva; Aži Dahāka attacks Yima but is slain by Thraētaona).[14]

Beyond this there is a linguistic possibility that is most interesting. First, it may be noted that Vṛtra is commonly called Ahi throughout the Vedas. Ahi and Aži are cognates and mean dragon. Second, another not quite so frequent epithet of Vṛtra is Dāsa, which may refer

---

[10] Benveniste also sees a connection between Indra and Trita. Therefore the complete picture, as he sees it, is Vṛtrahan—Indra equals Indra—Trita equals Vərəthragna—Thraētaona (*ibid.*, p. 196).

[11] Dumézil, *D of W*, p. 117.

[12] Aži Dahāka may also be viewed as three-mouthed rather than three-headed.

[13] Levy, *Shāh-nāma*, p. 11.

[14] The implications here concerning the "Kingship in Heaven theme" are being further explored in a paper in progress.

to Vṛtra as the destroyer of all things,[15] but more specifically refers to a non-Indo-European people that the Indic people encountered.[16]

Of interest in this connection is the name Dahāka. The *-ka* may be separated as merely being a productive denominative suffix of vague meaning.[17] We are left then with *Daha*, a word of obscure origin,[18] which would appear in India as *Dasa*. Unfortunately, for our purposes, Vṛtra is never called, to my knowledge, *Ahi Dasa.[19] But these linguistic similarities (*Ahi—Aži, Dasa—Daha, vajra—gurz*), together with the epithets involved (*Vṛtrahan—Vərəthragna*), and the similarity in themes (both Vṛtra and Aži Dahāka are characterized as three-headed dragons who are "outside the system") would seem to indicate that a tradition of the slaying of *Vṛtra Aźhi Dasa was common to Indic and Iranian myths.

The foregoing raises interesting implications, particularly concerning the term Dasa.[20] As noted earlier, both Vṛtra and Aži Dahāka are outsiders; they are not part of the established order. Both may well be styled as the enemy of the gods. The connection of this enemy with the people called in the Vedas Dāsa (a subjugated non-Indo-European people) is most intriguing.

It may be recalled that the interpretation of *Vṛtraghan made by those interpreting the myths in such a way as to see Vṛtra as an Indic invention was that of "smasher of hostility" (see above). It may be seen that this interpretation may be used to bolster the opposite argument.

If *Vṛtra is the *Aźhi of the *Dasa—in other words, if he is the "hostile dragon of the non-Indo-European peoples"—then the epithet of "smasher of hostility" for Indra, and by the same token for Thraē-taona, is both appropriate and revealing.

Might not the Aži Dahāka, the dragon of the Daha, be a mythic representation of the non-Indo-European peoples who were defeated when the Indo-Europeans moved in? Or might it be a reflection of a "revolt" of the conquered peoples? Either way, the dragon would

15 H. H. Wilson, trans., *Rg Veda Sanhita* (London, 1866), p. 87.

16 E.g., *Rig-Veda* I.51.8; I.63.4; and I.32.11, where Vṛtra, Ahi, and Dāsa are mentioned in the same verse.

17 See J. Wackernagel and A. Debrunner, *Altindische Grammatik*, Band II, 2 (Göttingen, 1954), p. 539. My thanks to Professor Jaan Puhvel, of the University of California, Los Angeles, for his aid with the finer points of I-E linguistics.

18 M. Mayrhofer, *A Concise Etymological Sanskrit Dictionary*, II (D-M) (Heidelberg, 1963), 38–39.

19 The connection of Dasa and Daha is not new (see *ibid.*). In fact, *Ahi Dāsa has been proposed before: K. Rönnow, *Trita*, I, 16, is noted by Benveniste in *V et V*, p. 166, and is given a sympathetic ear.

20 I am indebted to Professor C. Scott Littleton, of Occidental College, Los Angeles, with whom I have discussed the Dasa question at length and who has given valuable advice here and throughout the paper.

appear to represent the indigenous population and their hostility to the Indo-European conquest. If it does, what we may have then is a direct mythic reflection or representation of a historical event or series of events, which may shed some light on other problems in Indo-European myth. For example, in Greece a possibly related term may be associated with the defeated pre-Indo-European inhabitants (e.g., Δάαι).[21] But however tantalizing this possibility or others may be, they are beyond the scope of this paper.

Withal, two tentative conclusions may be drawn from the preceding discussion. First, it would appear that among the Indo-Iranians there was indeed a tradition of the slaying of Vṛtra. Second, it would then appear that this slaying was connected with the slaying of an "outside" god, who may have been a representation of the indigenous population conquered when the Indo-Iranian (Indo-European?) peoples settled.

---

21 Mayrhofer, *op. cit.*, pp. 38–39.

Dodona, Dodola, and Daedala

DAVID EVANS, *California State University, Fullerton*

From the earliest reports in Homer the oracle of Zeus at Dodona seems to have been held in particular awe by Greek and Latin authors. Any oracle is bound to be awesome to some degree, but Dodona, with its remote location in inland Epirus, an oak tree that spoke the will of a god, prophetic priests with unwashed feet who slept on the ground, and later priestesses called "Doves," was becoming legendary in its own time. And as with any popular folk legend the sources show some variation in detail and a certain inconsistency. But these ancient sources, when evaluated in the light of comparative Indo-European mythology, are hardly inconsistent at all, and many of Dodona's "legendary" aspects can easily be explained.[1]

In his recent book on Zeus's oracles,[2] Professor Parke has done an admirable job of setting forth the evidence from classical literary sources and archaeology concerning the cult center and the oak-tree oracle at Dodona. He has restricted his research, however, almost entirely to the classical sources concerning Dodona itself and has limited his conclusions mainly to matters having to do with the functioning

1 For reading and discussing earlier drafts of this paper and for making several suggestions which I have incorporated in it, I wish to thank Jaan Puhvel, Marija Gimbutas, Atsuhiko Yoshida, Steven Lattimore, Dan Gershenson, Andrew Cincura, Anne Cohen, and Antoinette Botsford. In particular I would like to thank my colleague Otto Sadovszky for pointing out the Slavic words *duda* and *kozá* and the Latin *iuglans*, which proved to be important points in the argument presented herein, and in general for his most helpful criticism. The majority of the ideas, however, and the direction of this paper are my own unless otherwise indicated, and I take full responsibility for their presentation here.

2 H. W. Parke, *The Oracles of Zeus: Dodona, Olympia, Ammon* (Cambridge, Mass., 1967).

and responses of the oracle and its relationship to other oracle centers in ancient Greece. Since his research in these areas has been exhaustive, this paper should be viewed as a supplement to his book. Here I examine Dodona more in regard to its place in the network of Greek and Indo-European myth and religious custom and dwell sparingly on the oracular responses.

DODONA AND DODOLA

Before discussing the Greek and Latin sources it is well to examine the name Dodona, a word that carries a wealth of meaning. It is related etymologically to a name found today in Serbia as Dodola, in Bulgaria as Djuldjul, in Macedonia as Dudulé, in Lithuania as Du(n)dulis, and so on.[3] These names are given to a participant in a ceremony carried out in the spring or in any time of drought in the Slavic and Baltic regions to ensure rainfall and consequently the fertility of the earth. The Dodola is usually a young virgin girl, although in some instances this person is a young boy. The chosen person is stripped naked, adorned with living plants, and then marched through the village dancing, generally with a retinue of other young girls. In the northwest coastal region of Yugoslavia it has been noted that the participants carry oak branches.[4] As they pass the houses, the women throw buckets of water on the Dodola, often invoking God to send rain.

In many instances, however, a name such as Dodola is not used in the ceremony. Instead one finds in these same regions some such name as Peperuda, Peperuga, or Paparuda. In modern Greece the name is Perperouna, Perperinon, Perperouga, or Parparouna. These are all simply reduplicated alterations, probably because of a speech taboo, of the name of the pagan Slavic thunder-god Perun. In Baltic Lithuania and Latvia he is known as Perkunas and in Albania as Perendi. A similar name is encountered farther afield among the Indo-European peoples. In the Indian Vedic hymns there occurs a Parjanya, god

[3] The etymology was suggested by Roman Jakobson in "Slavic Mythology," in Maria Leach, ed., *Funk and Wagnalls Standard Dictionary of Folklore, Mythology, and Legend* (New York, 1950), II, 1026. Additional references to the Dodola and its various other names are found in Edmund Schneeweis, *Serbokroatische Volkskunde* (Berlin, 1961), Pt. I, pp. 161–164 and pl. 37; Wilhelm Mannhardt, *Wald- und Feldkulte* (Berlin, 1904–1905), I, 329 ff.; Jacob Grimm, *Teutonic Mythology* (New York, 1966), 2, 593–596; Sir James George Frazer, *The Golden Bough*, 3d ed. (London, 1932), I, 272 ff.; Marija Gimbutas, "Ancient Slavic Religion: A Synopsis," in *To Honor Roman Jakobson* (The Hague and Paris, 1967), I, 742–744. For a more modern example see Louis Petroff, "Magical Beliefs and Practices in Old Bulgaria," *Midwest Folklore* 7 (1957), 217–220.

[4] Schneeweis, *op. cit.*, p. 162.

of the storm cloud, and in pagan Scandinavia there was a god Fjörgynn as well as a goddess Fjörgyn, who was said to be the mother of the thunder-god Thor.[5] These names are cognate with the Latin *quercus*, "oak," and Celtic *Hercynia Silva*, an oak forest. The Indo-European roots **perg-* and **perk*^{u}*u-s*, from which the words all derive, have the meanings "to strike" and "oak," respectively.[6] It has even been suggested, quite plausibly, I feel, that the Greek κεραυνός "thun-

---

[5] See especially Jakobson, "Slavic Mythology," p. 1026, and Gimbutas, *op. cit.*, pp. 742–744. The Scandinavian situation is rather complex. The god Fjörgynn is very obscure. In the *Lokasenna*, 26, Frigg, Odin's wife, is called *Fjorgyns maer*, "Fjörgynn's mistress," while Snorri in *Gylfaginning*, 8, and *Skáldskaparmál*, 19, makes her Fjörgynn's daughter. The *Lokasenna*, however, may well represent an alternate tradition to that related by Snorri, one that the poets were trying to discredit by putting it into the mouth of the trickster Loki in his fliting of the gods.

The goddess Fjörgyn is slightly better known. In the *Vǫluspá*, 48, and the *Hárbarðsljóð*, 56, Fjörgyn is said to be the mother of Thor, the thunder-god. Elsewhere Thor's mother is Jörd, "Earth," who is, in fact, called *fjörgyn* by the poets, as Snorri states in the *Skáldskaparmál*, 54. Thor's father is Odin, father of all the gods including even Jörd.

A clear picture begins to emerge. It seems likely that a supreme god, probably a thunder-god called Fjörgynn, was originally matched with an earth-goddess (i.e., Jörd) who came to be called Fjörgyn after him. The offspring of this union was Thor, a god who came to have strong connections with fertility and life giving. As Odin came by popular consensus to assume the role of supreme god, he would have usurped the position of Fjörgynn, and his wife Frigg, that of Fjörgyn-Jörd. Frigg then suffered the misfortune of being branded as a woman of loose morals, consorting not only with Fjörgynn but also with Odin's brothers Vili and Vé. Thus she later came to be equated with Venus (i.e., Aphrodite). Actually it can be seen that all these extramarital affairs of hers are attempts of the poets to reconcile what amount to different versions of the same myth, the union of an earth-goddess with a sky-god. Thus the discrepancy in the accounts of the nature of the relationship between Frigg and Fjörgynn is explainable. As a supreme god and father of all, Fjörgynn would naturally be Frigg's father also, while Frigg can just as easily be matched with him as a representation of a union between earth and heaven. A curious Greek parallel is Persephone, who is usually the daughter of Zeus but in one source is his mistress (see *Orphicorum Fragmenta*, collected by Otto Kern [Berlin, 1922], fr. 210 ff.). Later in this paper I demonstrate that Persephone is cognate with Fjörgyn by the same process of tabooistic alteration and reduplication.

One can schematize the Scandinavian situation of divine couplings as follows:

?
Fjörgynn = Jörd-Fjörgyn
Fjörgynn = Frigg
Odin = Frigg
Odin = Jörd-Fjörgyn
|
Thor

For a discussion of the Scandinavian sources with reference to past scholarship on the subject, see E. O. G. Turville-Petre, *Myth and Religion of the North* (New York, 1964), pp. 96–97, 188–189.

[6] Julius Pokorny, *Indogermanisches etymologisches Wörterbuch* (Bern and München, 1959), I, 819, 822.

derbolt," otherwise of doubtful etymology, is an alteration of a tabooed *Περαυνός, a name for the thunder-god.[7] One should also note the cognate Greek noun *κορύνη*, "a wooden staff or club."

THE NUDIPEDALIA

The Slavic custom of the Dodola has a curious parallel in Roman religion, where there occurs an obscure ritual called the Nudipedalia ("Barefoot") performed to make rain in times of drought. Although not recorded before the first century A.D., it is probably very ancient. Its first notice is in Petronius's *Satyricon*:[8]

> Antea stolatae ibant nudis pedibus in clivum, passis capillis, mentibus puris, et Iovem aquam exorabant. Itaque statim urceatim plovebat, aut tunc aut numquam; et omnes redibant udi tamquam mures.

> In former times the matrons used to go barefoot up a hill with their hair loosened and with pure thoughts, and they would persuade Jupiter to send rain. And so immediately it rained bucketfuls, either then or never, and they all returned soaking wet like rats.

Tertullian also mentions this ceremony:[9]

> Cum stupet caelum et aret annus, Nudipedalia denuntiantur, magistratus purpuras ponunt, fasces retro avertunt, precem indigitant, hostiam instaurant.

> When the sky is struck dumb and the year is dry, the Nudipedalia is announced. The magistrates remove their purple garments, turn their fasces backward, utter a prayer, and perform a sacrifice.

The similarity of the Nudipedalia to the Dodola custom is at this point perhaps somewhat obscure, but both are rain-making ceremonies performed to a sky-god in times of drought, and both involve a procession of women. The motifs of bare feet and the ascent up a hill will shortly be shown to occur in connection with Dodona.

DODONA AND THE GOATSKIN

If Peperuda, and like names, are derived from the name of the Slavic and Baltic thunder-god, then it is likely that Dodola and its cognates, including Dodona, are derived from an alternate name or epithet of the thunder-god, for the two names occur in their variant forms over the same broad area and are in fact interchangeable. Such an epithet

---

[7] J. J. Mikkola, "Slavica II," *Indogermanische Forschungen* 8 (1898), 303–304.

[8] Petronius, *Satyricon*, 44, 18.

[9] Tertullian, *De Jejuniis*, 16. See also his *Apologeticum*, 40, 14. A similar ceremony involving a barefoot procession with prayers to the saints and the Virgin for rain was performed near Liège about the year 1240 or 1244. It would appear to have been a reinterpretation of the Roman Nudipedalia. See Grimm, *Teutonic Mythology*, I, 174–175.

is suggested by another Slavic cognate of Dodona, the word for "bagpipe": *dude* in Slovenia, *duda* in Byelorussia, *dudy* in Bohemia and Moravia, and *duda* in Hungary (borrowed from Slavic). German has the borrowed form *Dudelsack*. This ancient instrument is generally made from a goatskin, and often a goat is depicted on it.[10] Dodola and its cognates then may mean "he/she of the goatskin," in which case Dodona would be the place where the "goatskin" god is worshiped. (Dodona is more likely to have been connected originally with the goatskin than with the bagpipe since this musical instrument is not attested in Greece until several centuries after the first mention of Dodona.) This derivation of the name of Zeus's sanctuary is consistent with what we know of Zeus's close connection with a goatskin in the form of his aegis, a Greek word that itself means "goatskin." Drawing from its Homeric citations, Farnell has described this aegis as "something that can be put around the body as a shield or breastplate and something in which things could be wrapped; it is shaggy and has metal ornament—golden tassels, for instance; above all, it is a most potent and divine battle-charm, which strikes terror into the enemy."[11] The aegis thus is clearly connected with war, although Zeus is not normally a warrior in Greek myth. When he is, however, he uses his weapon, the thunderbolt (κεραυνός), to great effect.

A connection between the goat and a thunder-god is not really unusual among Indo-European peoples. In Rome there was a festival of Jupiter on July 5 at the Caprae Palus, "Marsh of the She-Goat," the very spot where Romulus disappeared from the earth in a violent thunderstorm.[12] The chariot of the Lithuanian thunder-god Perkunas was drawn by a he-goat, and a he-goat's skin was hung on a pole as a rain charm.[13] In Scandinavia two goats are closely connected with Thor, the thunder-god and a great warrior.[14] They draw his chariot and are especially associated with his hammer, which serves both as a thunder weapon and an instrument for hallowing and restoring life, evidently with phallic significance. Zeus's thunderbolt likewise has this double function. It is a weapon that can cause death and destruc-

[10] Anthony Baines, *Bagpipes* (Oxford, 1960), pp. 74–80 and Pls. V, 19; VI, 20, 21; XIV, *d*. The relationship between goats and bagpipes is clear from another Russian word, *kozá*, which has the meanings "goat, litter, tripod, and bagpipe." See Max Vasmer, *Russisches etymologisches Wörterbuch* (Heidelberg, 1953), I, 589–590.

[11] Lewis Richard Farnell, *The Cults of the Greek States* (Oxford, 1896), I, 98.

[12] Plutarch, *Vita Romuli*, 27; Livy, I, 16, 1.

[13] See Gimbutas, *op. cit.*, pp. 742–744. The Ossetes of the Caucasus region erect a similar pole with the skin of a black he-goat by the grave of a man who has been struck by lightning. Prayers are offered to St. Elias who is worshiped as a thunder-god in this region. The Circassians on the Caspian erected a goatskin on a pole and offered prayers on St. Elias's Day. See Grimm, *Teutonic Mythology*, I, 174.

[14] Snorri's *Edda, Gylfaginning*, 43. See also Turville-Petre, *op. cit.*, pp. 81–82.

tion, and it is also the sign of rain that brings life to the earth. There is still a widespread belief in European folklore that a person struck by lightning has healing powers. The goat serves as a link between these constructive and destructive aspects of thunder. It is a well-known symbol of fertility, and its skin is a potent battle charm. This latter function still persists in the Scottish bagpipes, which are used primarily in a martial context and can produce a quite terrifying sound.

The Greek Zeus in general has well-documented associations with the goat, yet there is unfortunately no evidence from ancient literary sources that a goat figured in the cult practices or in the portrayal of Zeus specifically at Dodona. On the other hand, it should be pointed out that very little is in fact known about cult practices there. It is not even certain just how the oracular responses were rendered. All we know is that an oak tree somehow "talked." In any event, among the earliest objects found at the site of Dodona in Epirus are several fifth-century bronzes and possibly one sixth-century bronze of Zeus thundering, along with two sixth-century bronze goats.[15]

MULTIPLE SITES CALLED DODONA

If the name Dodona is derived from the cult name of a thunder-god, this fact would be of the utmost importance in explaining certain seemingly contradictory and confusing statements about Dodona in the ancient sources. There is strong evidence for the existence of one or more places in Greece called Dodona, in addition to the familiar location in Epirus.[16] This evidence goes as far back as the earliest Greek literary source, Homer's *Iliad*. Dodona is mentioned there twice, first in the Catalogue of Ships (II, 748–755):

> *Γουνεὺς δ' ἐκ Κύφου ἦγε δύω καὶ εἴκοσι νῆας·*
> *τῷ δ' Ἐνιῆνες ἕποντο μενεπτόλεμοί τε Περαιβοί,*
> *οἳ περὶ Δωδώνην δυσχείμερον οἰκί' ἔθεντο,*
> *οἵ τ' ἀμφ' ἱμερτὸν Τιταρήσιον ἔργα νέμοντο,*
> *ὅς ῥ' ἐς Πηνειὸν προΐει καλλίρροον ὕδωρ,*
> *οὐδ' ὅ γε Πηνειῷ συμμίσγεται ἀργυροδίνῃ,*
> *ἀλλά τέ μιν καθύπερθεν ἐπιρρέει ἠΰτ' ἔλαιον·*
> *ὅρκου γὰρ δεινοῦ Στυγὸς ὕδατός ἐστιν ἀπορρώξ.*

---

[15] Parke, *op. cit.*, pp. 274–276.

[16] Parke (*ibid.*, pp. 5–6, 38–40) takes note of this evidence but dismisses it as "simply the process of Thessalian nationalism working on a Homeric passage which needed no such hypothesis to explain it" (p. 40). The sources still remain, however, with all their difficulties for those who hold to the single location of Dodona in Epirus. Since we now believe that the name Dodona is connected with a cult object of a god and is not simply a meaningless geographical place-name, the problem warrants reexamination here.

> And Gouneus led twenty-two ships from Kyphos. The Enienes followed him as well as the staunch Perrhaibians, who made their homes by hard-wintered Dodona and who worked the land by lovely Titaressos, which delivers its sweetly flowing water into the Peneios. But it does not mix with the silver-eddying Peneios but flows on top of it like oil, for it is a branch of the Styx, the fearful oath.

This passage occurs in the midst of the cataloguing of the various Thessalian contingents, and furthermore, the Enienes, Perrhaibians, Titaressos, and Peneios are all to be located in Thessaly. This particular Dodona then must be located there also. The exact site is, of course, uncertain, but since it was in the land of the Perrhaibians, it would seem to be somewhat southwest of Mount Olympus.

The other mention of Dodona in the *Iliad* (XVI, 233–235) would seem to indicate another site of that name in or near Achilles' kingdom in Achaea south of Thessaly. In this passage Achilles begins a prayer to Dodonean Zeus, asking him to help Patroclos:

> *Ζεῦ ἄνα, Δωδωναῖε, Πελασγικέ, τηλόθι ναίων,*
> *Δωδώνης μεδέων δυσχειμέρου· ἀμφὶ δὲ Σελλοί*
> *σοὶ ναίουσ' ὑποφῆται ἀνιπτόποδες χαμαιεῦναι.*

> Lord Zeus, Dodonean, Pelasgic, dwelling far off, lord of hard-wintered Dodona; and about you dwell the Selloi, prophets with unwashed feet, sleeping on the ground.

This prayer is obviously a very special one. Achilles has just poured a libation from a goblet from which he is accustomed to pour only to Zeus. Patroclos is Achilles' companion and fellow countryman about to go into battle at the head of the Myrmidons, the best fighters in their kingdom's contingent. The question therefore arises: Why should Achilles invoke a god worshiped in faraway Epirus? The answer is, of course, that he does not, and the evidence is in the Catalogue of Ships, where (II, 681–685) we find that Achilles is the leader of those who dwelt about Pelasgic Argos and those who held Hellas, called Hellenes, as well as various other peoples:

> *νῦν αὖ τοὺς ὅσσοι τὸ Πελασγικὸν Ἄργος ἔναιον·*
> *οἵ τ' Ἄλον οἵ τ' Ἀλόπην οἵ τε Τρηχῖνα νέμοντο,*
> *οἵ τ' εἶχον Φθίην ἠδ' Ἑλλάδα καλλιγύναικα,*
> *Μυρμιδόνες δὲ καλεῦντο καὶ Ἕλληνες καὶ Ἀχαιοί,*
> *τῶν αὖ πεντήκοντα νεῶν ἦν ἀρχὸς Ἀχιλλεύς.*

> Now those who inhabited Pelasgic Argos and who lived at Alos and Alope and Trechis and who held Phthia and Hellas abounding in fair women, who are called Myrmidons and Hellenes and Achaeans, of these and their fifty ships Achilles was the leader.

All the identifiable peoples and places in this passage are located near the mouth of the Spercheios. It is in this region then that we should locate Pelasgic Argos and a site called Dodona where the god is "Pelasgic." For what would be more natural than that Achilles should invoke a powerful local deity of his homeland in this situation? Without becoming involved in the thorny Pelasgian controversy, we can with reasonable certainty state that Zeus's epithet Πελασγικός must in this instance tie him firmly to the area of Achilles' kingdom known as Pelasgic Argos.

The Selloi, with their unwashed feet so reminiscent of the Roman Nudipedalia,[17] also help to locate this Dodona in the area of Achilles' kingdom. Selloi is really an alternate form of Helloi, as the scholiasts on this passage point out, citing Pindar's use of the alternate form. This ancient observation still holds under modern linguistic scrutiny. Helloi, of course, suggests a connection with the Hellenes and Hellas in the kingdom of Achilles. The scholia further call the Helloi a γένος or ἔθνος, a "tribe," although Homer himself would seem to be thinking of them as a priestly group. Possibly, then, they were members of a hereditary priestly clan or caste who looked after the worship of Zeus and interpreted his pronouncements from the oracle at Dodona. The scholia state that the form Helloi is derived from a certain Hellos, an oak cutter to whom the oracle was originally revealed by a dove. Hellos is further described as Θεττάλου, which could in this context mean either "Thessalian" or "son of Thettalos." In either event a connection with Thessaly would seem to be established. It happens that in ancient times there was a region in central Thessaly known as Pelasgiotis. This region is contiguous to Achilles' kingdom, which lay south of it. In the Pelasgiotis was a town of Scotussa where Suidas, a Thessalian historian of the fourth century B.C., located the sanctuary of Zeus called Dodona.[18] He added that the oak was burned down and the worship transferred to the Dodona in Epirus at the bidding of Apollo. This story does not imply, of course, that the sanctuary in Epirus did not already exist when the oak in Thessaly was burned down. Support for Suidas comes from Stephanus of Byzantium, who in commenting on the passage in *Iliad* XVI, 233–235, states flatly that there were two Dodonas, one in Thessaly and one in Thesprotia (Epirus).[19] Scotussa in Thessaly is close enough to the known area of Achilles' kingdom that it could be on its outer limits. This

[17] The relationship was pointed out long ago by A. B. Cook, "Zeus, Jupiter, and the Oak," *Classical Review* 18 (1904), 365 n. 26.

[18] *Fragmente der griechischen Historiker* (Jacoby), 602 fr. 11.

[19] Epaphroditus in his commentary states that there was a town in Thessaly called Βωδώνη, where Zeus was honored. Although tantalizing, this piece of evidence must remain a curiosity pending further information.

location would explain the Homeric phrase *τηλόθι ναίων*, "dwelling far off." Further confirmation of this hypothesis comes from a fragment of Hesiod,[20] who says that there is an oracle of Zeus called Dodona in a region known as Hellopia (cf. Helloi, Hellas, Hellenes) located *ἐπ' ἐσχατιῇ*, which I translate as "at the border":

> *ἔστί τις Ἑλλοπίη πολυλήϊος ἠδ' εὐλείμων*
> *ἀφνειὴ μήλοισι καὶ εἰλιπόδεσσι βόεσσιν·*
> *ἐν δ' ἄνδρες ναίουσι πολύρρηνες πολυβοῦται*
> *πολλοὶ ἀπειρέσιοι φῦλα θνητῶν ἀνθρώπων·*
> *ἔνθα δὲ Δωδώνη τις ἐπ' ἐσχατιῇ πεπόλισται·*
> *τὴν δὲ Ζεὺς ἐφίλησε καὶ ὃν χρηστήριον εἶναι*
> *τίμιον ἀνθρώποις* <
> > *ναῖον δ' ἐν πυθμένι φηγοῦ·*
> *ἔνθεν ἐπιχθόνιοι μαντήϊα πάντα φέρονται.*
> *ὃς δὴ κεῖθι μολὼν θεὸν ἄμβροτον ἐξερεείνῃ*
> *δῶρα φέρων* <*τ'*> *ἔλθῃσι σὺν οἰωνοῖς ἀγαθοῖσιν*

There is a place called Hellopia with many cornfields and goodly meadows, rich in sheep and goats and shambling cattle, and numberless are the races of mortal men, rich in sheep and oxen, which dwell there. A city called Dodona has been founded there at the border, which Zeus loved and [made] his oracle honored among men. . . . And they dwelt [?] in the base of the oak. From there men on earth bring all kinds of prophecies. And so whoever goes there to inquire of the immortal god and comes bearing gifts with good omens . . .

This Dodona then would seem to have been at the most northerly reach of Achilles' kingdom. Hellopia must have been a district of Pelasgic Argos, the area known in historical times as Pelasgiotis, where Pelasgic Zeus was worshiped.

JASON, HERACLES, AND ACHILLES

If we accept the location of a Dodona near Scotussa in the Pelasgiotis and one in the land of the Perrhaibians near Mount Olympus, and if we keep in mind the fact that the name Dodona is cognate with a cult name that is widespread even today in the Balkans, we can better explain some puzzling mythological and literary passages in which Dodona figures. The first is the legend of the Argonauts. Unfortunately the early Greek epics that recounted this legend have not survived, but we do know from as early as Aeschylus that the ship *Argo* had a beam in it taken from the oak at Dodona which would give prophecies on certain crucial occasions.[21] There are numerous reasons for considering this Dodona to be the one near Scotussa. The

[20] Hesiod, fr. 240 (Merkelbach and West).
[21] Aeschylus, fr. 20 (Nauck).

very name Argo is, of course, reminiscent of Pelasgic Argos. Furthermore, the ship sets sail from nearby Pagasae. Jason is associated with the city of Iolcos, and the Argonauts are often referred to as Minyae. All this suggests that the legend arose in Thessaly. There is no connection with Epirus at all.

But there may even be a much deeper connection between the legend of the Argonauts and Dodona. Jason, in fulfillment of a prophecy, appeared to Pelias with one foot bare. One explanation is that Jason, as he came down from Cheiron's cave after a heavy rain, noticed an old woman standing at the bank of the river Anauros afraid to cross. Jason carried her over but lost a sandal in the mud. On the other side the woman revealed herself as Hera and promised to favor him for his kindness.[22] Jason's bare foot is strikingly reminiscent of the Selloi with their unwashed feet. Jason then in an older version of the legend may have been a priest of Zeus and Hera at the Thessalian Dodona, one of the Selloi. The oracular beam in the *Argo* would then be most appropriate.

Another legend concerning Dodona which might better fit the Thessalian location is the account of Heracles' death given in Sophocles' *Trachiniae*. Heracles mentions a prophecy from the oracle and speaks of the Selloi there.[23] Admittedly this passage could be based on Homer, but it is a fact that the play is set in Thessaly, so that the Thessalian location for Dodona would seem more appropriate here. There is evidently some confusion in Sophocles' mind, however, since in another passage he mentions two doves as the means of prophecy.[24] Doves, as we shall see, are more closely linked with the location in Epirus although not without other attestation in Thessaly. But the confusion is perhaps not surprising when we consider that the oracle in Thessaly near Scotussa was no longer extant in Sophocles' own time, surviving only in legend, whereas the site in Epirus was well known and still functioning. Sophocles clearly has Epirus in mind, but the Dodona of the original legend may have been the one in Thessaly.

Now let us return to Achilles. We have already seen that he prays to the god of Dodona and that there is a sanctuary of this name on the remote northern edge of his kingdom. But there are many other connections between this hero and Dodona. Philostratus the Elder writes that Achilles was worshiped as a god by the Thessalians, who sent embassies to offer sacrifices at his tomb on instructions from Dodona.[25] This custom fell into disuse at a very early period but was revived in altered form in a time of famine (cf. the Dodola custom and

[22] Apollonius Rhodius, III, 66 ff.

[23] Sophocles, *Trachiniae*, 1164 ff.

[24] *Ibid.*, 171–172.

[25] Philostratus, *Heroicus*, 20, 25.

Nudipedalia for rainmaking) and continued up to the time of Xerxes' invasion. It is also known from a very late source that Achilles was worshiped in Epirus under the name Aspetos, "Unutterable,"[26] obviously an example of speech taboo. Possibly this worship had been transferred to Epirus at the time when the Thessalian Dodona cult was transferred there.

Achilles has further mythological connections with the thunder-god. In *Iliad* XVIII, 204, he is given the aegis by Athena. He appears wrapped in it, wearing no armor, and with a golden cloud above him and a flame leading down to his head. He stands outside the wall before the ditch and shouts three times like a battle trumpet (σάλπιγξ, v. 219), frightening the entire Trojan army and causing it to retreat in panic. Obviously he is to be identified here with Zeus.[27]

In another myth we find Achilles dressed as a woman at the court of Lykomedes in order to escape service at Troy. He is found out when he shows an unusual interest in some armor that is left in the women's chambers. This motif has a parallel in Scandinavian mythology where the thunder-god Thor goes to the court of the giant Thrym in the guise of the goddess Freyja. When his hammer, which had been stolen, is placed on his knees, he grasps it, reveals his identity, and kills the giants.[28] Georges Dumézil points out an Indic parallel in the *Mahābhārata*.[29] The warrior Arjuna, whom Dumézil interprets as the epic euhemerization of the storm-god Indra, undergoes a metamorphosis into a eunuch and becomes an instructor in song and dance. Dumézil also cites passages where Indra himself and his warrior troop, the Maruts, display effeminate traits. Delcourt has noted similar transvestism in Theseus and Heracles in Greek myth.[30]

But Achilles may also, like Jason, have a close connection with the Selloi. Achilles has a vulnerable heel, which was the result of his having been held there by his mother Thetis, who was bathing him in the Styx to confer immortality. This "unwashed" heel can be seen as the equivalent of the unwashed feet of the Selloi and Jason's foot without the sandal, which he lost while fording a river.[31]

26 Plutarch, *Vita Pyrrhi*, 1.

27 Vian states that Achilles is here identified with Athena, but since Achilles is a male figure, he seems to me to be acting more like Zeus (see Francis Vian, "La fonction guerrière dans la mythologie grecque," in *Problèmes de la guerre dans la Grèce ancienne*, ed. Jean-Pierre Vernant [Paris, 1968], p. 66).

28 See the Lay of Thrymr in the *Poetic Edda*.

29 Georges Dumézil, *Mythe et épopée* I (Paris, 1968), pp. 72–73.

30 Marie Delcourt, *Hermaphrodite* (Paris, 1958), chap. 1 *passim*.

31 It is not known whether the individual Selloi kept one foot or both feet unwashed. The adjective ἀνιπτόποδες is ambiguous, but from the comparative evidence adduced here and in the following pages it seems likely that only one foot was left unwashed.

Both Achilles and Jason are raised by the centaur Cheiron. And just as Jason is the leader of a special warrior band, the Argonauts or Minyae, so Achilles is the leader of the fierce Myrmidons. Association with a warrior band is a characteristic of Indo-European deities and heroes of the second function, as explained by Georges Dumézil, and finds its prime example in the Indic storm-god Indra and his warrior band, the Maruts.[32] But while Achilles is most closely associated with the Myrmidons, his kingdom actually seems to be composed of representatives of all three functions. For in *Iliad* II, 684, it is stated that he brought with him to Troy the Myrmidons, Hellenes, and Achaeans. The Myrmidons are, of course, par excellence second-function warriors, while the Hellenes can be interpreted as representatives of the first function through the connection of their name with the priestly Selloi. The Achaeans are the people of the third function responsible for health and sustenance, for Ἀχαία is an epithet for the earth-goddess Demeter, and ἀχαιά is given by Philetas as the equivalent of ἔριθος, "day laborer" or "hired servant."[33] Achilles then is a typical Indo-European ruler, closely associated with the thunder-god, leading a people who are divided into three social classes of priests, warriors, and food producers, although to what extent this tripartite division still carried meaning for Achilles, much less for Homer, must remain conjectural. Since all three classes seem to engage in combat, my guess would be that the distinction of functions had become blurred in the legend of the Trojan War and survived more in their names than in their social roles.

THE DAEDALA

We have thus far located three sites called Dodona and have taken a new look at certain legends related to them. There is no certain evidence that there were any other sites so named, although possibly some of the sources that suggest a Thessalian location refer to a site other than that near Scotussa. This could be merely speculation. There remains, however, one extremely important Greek religious observance that shows a close connection with the cult of Zeus at the various places called Dodona and with the Slavic Dodola customs. This observance, the celebration of the Daedala at Plataea in Boeotia,[34] was a ceremony held about every four years in which a wooden

[32] For a brief exposition of Dumézil's views see his *L'idéologie tripartie des Indo-Européens*, Collection Latomus, vol. 31 (Brussels, 1958). See also C. Scott Littleton, *The New Comparative Mythology* (Berkeley and Los Angeles, 1966; 2d ed., 1973).

[33] Philetas in *Collectanea Alexandrina* (J. U. Powell), p. 90.

[34] Pausanias, IX, 3, 1–9. See also Eusebius, *Praeparatio Evangelica*, III, 1–2, whose source is Plutarch's lost treatise, *De Daedalis Plataeensibus*.

image of the bride of Zeus was carved from an oak tree chosen by ravens from a sacred grove. The image, decked out in bridal ornaments, was drawn to the banks of the river Asopus and back to town attended by a large procession. Every sixty years, in a celebration called the Great Daedala, the fifteen images that had accumulated were drawn on wagons to the Asopus in a procession and then taken to the top of Mount Kithairon and burned after sacrifices to Zeus and Hera. Pausanias, one of the chief sources of information on the Daedala, adds that in early times there was an oracle of the Kithaironian nymphs called Sphragidion in a cave about fifteen stades below the altar on Kithairon's peak. There is an etiological legend connected with the rite. Hera and Zeus had quarreled, and Zeus planned to make her jealous in order to win her back. According to Pausanias the local despot Kithairon told Zeus to make a wooden image of Plataea, daughter of the river Asopus. The image, decked out like a bride, was called a *daidalon,* "work of art." Plutarch, following a slightly different tradition, states that the image was called Daidale and was made on the orders of Alalkomeneus. In any event, it was intended that Zeus should marry this "bride." As the log was being carried in the bridal procession, Hera saw it and rushed at it, tearing off the ornaments. Thereupon she realized that it was a ruse and was reconciled with Zeus.

The connections with Dodona are striking, particularly the oak tree and the presence of an oracle. But just as important, the procession with the tree decked out like a bride is remarkably reminiscent of the modern custom of the Dodola and the ancient Roman Nudipedalia celebrated on hilltops. Even the very name Daedala would seem to be cognate with Dodola and Dodona.[35] The etiological legend undoubtedly arose as the significance of the name Daedala became lost and in order to reconcile the existence of her as Zeus's bride with Hera, the generally acknowledged bride of Zeus in historical times.

Possibly a further connection with Dodona is the curious account given by Thucydides of the escape from Plataea.[36] The men of that city kept their right feet bare while escaping, allegedly to keep from slipping in the mud. But then there is no logical reason why they should not have kept both feet bare. Possibly, therefore, the bare foot was a custom familiar from the Daedala ceremony, since a comparable practice is found among the Selloi of Dodona. Perhaps the escaping citizens were treading on ground sacred to Zeus and Hera and felt it

---

[35] In a future paper I hope to examine the meaning of the word δαίδαλος and the famous craftsman of that name.

[36] Thucydides, III, 22, 2. I am grateful to Steven Lattimore for calling my attention to this passage.

necessary to remove a sandal, although more likely they believed that this act gave them the protection of the gods in their daring undertaking, because it was borrowed from local religious cult practice.[37]

DODONA AND THE UNDERWORLD

We have thus far noticed several motifs that occur frequently in connection with places called Dodona and with related rituals involving a Dodola or Daedala. These are a connection with rain and a marriage of the sky- or thunder-god with his bride, including a procession in which the bride is decked out in a special wedding costume and is carried about or escorted. One also finds an oracle and priests or celebrants with bare or unwashed feet. Finally, the oak tree seems to stand at the very center of things as a link between sky and earth and between god and man. The oak is the tree that is struck by the thunderbolt, the tree that Zeus takes as his bride, the tree that is sacrificed on the top of a mountain to Zeus and Hera, and the tree through which Zeus speaks to men.

We have still hardly discussed the most famous site called Dodona, located in Epirus; it is the only place so named that continued as a religious center into historical times. Certain practices connected with this site shed further light on the motifs already discussed. It is well known, from both literary and archaeological sources, that Zeus's wife at Dodona in Epirus was considered to be Dione and that Zeus bore the cult epithet there of Naïos. Furthermore, there were celebrations in Zeus's honor called the Naia, about which little is known. Naïos and Naia would seem to be related to the verb νάω, "to flow," and to the naiads, for Hyginus states that the nymphs called Dodonides are called by others naiads.[38] Some kind of connection with water is therefore indicated. This would not be surprising, since we have already mentioned the relationship of Dodona to Slavic and Roman rain-making ceremonies. Possibly the Naia contained a ceremony for rainmaking and consequent fertility. If so, it would be quite likely that the Naia displayed some similarities to the Daedala and Dodola rituals.[39]

The name Dione is interesting, for it is a feminine form of Zeus, bearing the same suffix as Dodona. The -n- suffix is extremely common for divine names among many branches of the Indo-European peoples, especially the Italic. In fact, Dione has an almost exact parallel

37 This region has another curious connection with feet, for Mount Kithairon is the place where the infant Oedipus was exposed with his feet bound and pierced.

38 Hyginus, *Fabellae*, 182, 1–2.

39 A. B. Cook compares the Daedala to the Naia at Dodona but fails to see the possible etymological connection ("Zeus, Jupiter, and the Oak," *Classical Review* 17 [1903], 181).

in the Latin Diana, who was worshiped in a grove at Nemi which contained a sacred tree, quite likely an oak.

Zeus has a further interesting connection with water at his cult center at Dodona in Epirus, not so much a connection with rain and its fertilizing of the earth as with underground water and the world of the dead. We are told by Ephorus that the oracle there, in almost all its responses, commanded sacrifice to Acheloos.[40] People took this name as a designation for water in general and not simply for the river in Acarnania, for Ephorus adds that Greeks were accustomed to call water "Acheloos" in oaths, prayers, and sacrifices. We know little about Acheloos, but the river was obviously of considerable importance in early Greek mythology. It seems to have rivaled Okeanos as a sort of "father of waters." Homer, at least, probably held that view, as Achilles is made to speak the following lines in *Iliad* XXI, 193–197:[41]

ἀλλ' οὐκ ἔστι Διὶ Κρονίωνι μάχεσθαι,
τῷ οὐδὲ κρείων Ἀχελώιος ἰσοφαρίζει,
ουδὲ βαθυρρείταο μέγα σθένος Ὠκεανοῖο,
ἐξ οὗ περ πάντες ποταμοὶ καὶ πᾶσα θάλασσα
καὶ πᾶσαι κρῆναι καὶ φρείατα μακρὰ νάουσιν·

But it is not possible to do battle with Zeus, son of Kronos, with whom neither Lord Acheloos contends nor the great might of deep-flowing Okeanos, from whom all rivers and the whole sea and all springs and great wells flow.

Line 195 ("nor . . . Okeanos") was omitted by Zenodotus, and Pausanias appears to have used this reading also.[42] Acheloos, then, is in this tradition the source of all water and would probably have been thought of as an underground river.

The name Acheloos is quite similar to that of one of the well-known underground rivers, Acheron, a name that is cognate with Baltic and Slavic words for pond or lake (Lithuanian *ẽžeras, ažeras*; Old Prussian *assaran*; Old Church Slavonic *jezero*).[43] The problem in equating the names Acheron and Acheloos, however, lies in the fact that Ρ and Λ are two quite distinct sounds in Greek. Still, some kind of connection

[40] Ephorus in *Fragmente der griechischen Historiker* (Jacoby), p. 70, fr. 20. See Parke, *op. cit.*, pp. 153–156, and Macrobius, V, 18, 2–12.

[41] It has been proposed that the names Achilles and Acheloos are cognate (see Hermann Usener, *Götternamen* [Frankfurt am Main, 1948], pp. 14–15). I find the evidence unconvincing, and besides, Achilles nowhere displays the characteristics of a euhemerized river-god. Indeed, in the passage quoted here, he engages in combat with a river-god.

[42] Pausanias, VIII, 38, 10.

[43] Hjalmar Frisk, *Griechisches etymologisches Wörterbuch* (Heidelberg, 1960), I, 200.

between the two names is indicated by the word ἀχερωΐς, "white poplar," found in *Iliad* XIII, 389, and XVI, 482, for which Eustathius and some manuscripts give the alternate reading ἀχελωΐς. Pausanias states that this tree was brought to Olympia from Epirus by Heracles, who saw it growing there on the banks of the Acheron.[44] The tree's wood was used for sacrifices at Olympia, where the altar was made of the ashes of the thighs of sacrificial animals cemented with water from the river Alpheus, which is "the dearest river of all to Olympian Zeus."[45] This local river probably fulfilled the same function as Acheloos did in the rest of Greece and at Dodona. It is the oath, that which is "binding." Its use in the construction of the altar is therefore most appropriate. A. B. Cook has furthermore convincingly demonstrated that the white poplar at Olympia was a substitute for the oak, probably because it was more common there than the oak.[46] The *Etymologicum Magnum* indicates that Heracles brought the tree up from the underground Acheron, for it states that he saw it growing there while on his way to get Kerberos. It adds that Aristotle called the tree αἴγειρος (cf. αἴξ, "goat"), normally the name for the black poplar.[47] Cook believes that this latter name is connected with Egeria (or Aegeria), the local nymph of the grove at Nemi where the sanctuary of Diana was located.[48]

If we posit some connection between Acheron and Acheloos, a number of facts become clear. First, we notice that Ἀχελώϊος (or Ἀχελῷος) appears to be an adjectival formation, perhaps derived from a phrase such as Ἀχελώϊον ὕδωρ, "water of Ache(r/l)on." We note further that the Acheron, rather than the Styx, is sometimes described as the river that one must cross to reach the world of the dead. The Styx is, of course, the great oath of the gods. It has just been mentioned that the Greeks swore oaths by Acheloos. Possibly we can state then that the Styx and the Acheron-Acheloos represent alternate traditions of the same mythic concept. The Styx is generally the most important Greek underworld river, but around Dodona it is likely that the Acheron assumed greater importance. For the source of the Acheron (as well as the source of the Acheloos) is only a few miles from Dodona in Epirus. On the Acheron near its confluence with the Cocytus and the Pyriphlegethon was a famous oracle of the dead

44 Pausanias, V, 14, 2. 45 *Ibid.*, V, 13, 8.

46 Cook, "Zeus, Jupiter, and the Oak," *Classical Review* 17 [1903], 273.

47 *Etymologicum Magnum*, ed. T. Gaisford (Lipsiae, 1816), Ἀχερωΐς.

48 A. B. Cook, "The European Sky God," *Folk-Lore* 16 (1905), 283. Dumézil connects Egeria with the verb *egerere*, "let out, discharge," making her a goddess of childbirth, but this is impossible in view of the alternate spelling Aegeria, so that Cook's hypothesis must remain more plausible (see Georges Dumézil, *La religion romaine archaïque* [Paris, 1966], p. 397).

(Nekyomanteion), probably the same one that Odysseus consulted.[49] Circe, in describing it to Odysseus, gives prominence to Acheron while mentioning the Styx only by way of saying that the Cocytus is a branch of it.[50] Undoubtedly this oracle of the dead maintained a close association with nearby Dodona. In fact, Odysseus is twice made to report in his lies that he had consulted Dodona rather than the Nekyomanteion.[51]

There is further evidence that the other Dodonean oracles had some underworld connections, for the fragment of Hesiod cited previously for the Thessalian Dodona seems to state that Zeus dwelt ἐν πυθμένι φηγοῦ, "in the base of the oak."[52] The next line adds to this feeling: ἔνθεν ἐπιχθόνιοι μαντήϊα πάντα φέρονται ("From there men on earth bring all kinds of prophecies"). The ἐπιχθόνιοι are possibly meant to be contrasted with the god dwelling in the base of the oak. Of course, the very fact that the oracle came from an oak with roots deep in the ground is significant in this respect. The other Dodona near Mount Olympus, we recall, was connected by Homer with the river Titaressos, which he called a branch of the Styx.[53] A late source, Servius, states that a fountain flowed from the roots of the oak at Dodona in Epirus and that the priestesses there interpreted its murmurings as the oracular responses of the gods.[54] Other late sources also mention remarkable springs at this Dodona.[55]

Acheloos as a river-god also seems to have strong underworld connections. A myth of this god's fight with Heracles over the hand of Deianeira[56] tells that in the struggle Acheloos changes shape into a snake and a bull, but Heracles vanquishes him and breaks off one of his horns. The Naiads or, according to Ovid, Diana (Dione?) picks it up and fills it with fruits and flowers so that it becomes the horn of plenty. The river-god's shape changing, the snake and the bull, and the horn of plenty (cf. Ploutos) are all definitely chthonian. Deianeira, of course, turns out to be the instrument of Heracles' death in a story that we have already seen to have connections with Dodona. Other tales about Heracles had him capture the underworld dog Kerberos or even fight with and wound Hades himself.[57] Significantly, this last myth is told by Dione herself in her only appearance in Homer! These

---

49 N. G. L. Hammond, *Epirus* (Oxford, 1967), pp. 65–66.

50 Homer, *Odyssey*, X, 513–514.

51 *Ibid.*, XIV, 327–330; XIX, 296–299.

52 Hesiod, fr. 240 (Merkelbach and West).

53 Homer, *Iliad*, II, 751–755.

54 Servius, on *Aeneid*, III, 466.

55 Mela, II, 43; Pliny the Elder, II, 228; Solinus, 72; *Etymologicum Magnum*, ed. T. Gaisford, ἀναπαυόμενον ὕδωρ.

56 Sophocles, *Trachiniae*, 9 ff., 555 ff.; Ovid, *Metamorphoses*, IX, 1 ff.

57 Homer, *Iliad*, V, 395–402. Joseph Fontenrose, *Python* (Berkeley and Los Angeles, 1959), pp. 321–364, treats these myths as part of a much larger complex of related myths.

myths all seem to point to an older myth in which Heracles offended an underworld deity (Acheloos-Hades) by taking something from him (Deianeira and possibly also the white poplar tree, ἀχερωΐς, and the dog Kerberos) and wounding the god in the process. For this offense Heracles had to suffer, and Deianeira became the instrument for punishing him. That some such older myth existed is indicated by the connection of the stories of Heracles with two different sites called Dodona, one in Thessaly and, through Acheloos, one in Epirus.[58] Thus the myth probably goes back to a very early time.

If Hades bears a certain similarity to Acheloos, a problem arises, for Hades also has many similarities to Zeus. In fact, Hades and Zeus do not seem to have been clearly differentiated in very early times. The name Hades, although undoubtedly old, does not appear in the very earliest times as the exclusive name for a distinct god of the underworld. Instead, as early as Homer we find this god called Zeus Katachthonios, Zeus Eubouleus, Zeus Bouleus, Zeus Chthonios, and Zeus Trophonios.[59] The name Hades may originally have been an epithet that became a name only later, as the functions of the sky-god and ruler of the dead in the underworld became more and more distinct. For Hades himself is well known to have possessed no cult in Greece under that name except in Elis,[60] whereas worship of an underworld Zeus was fairly common in Greece.

The female counterpart of Zeus Katachthonios was Persephone, also known as Pherrephatta and in Italy as Proserpina. I propose that these names are all formed in the same way as the Slavic and Baltic Peperuda, Peperuga, Paparuda, and so on, and as the modern Greek Perperouna, Perperinon, Perperouga, and Parparouna. They are simply reduplicated forms of the name of the Indo-European thunder-god, altered because of a speech taboo. Persephone is the bride of the underground thunder-god and bears an altered feminine version of his tabooed name, just as in the world above Dione is the feminine of the sky-god Zeus. Such alteration would be appropriate for a goddess who is characterized as ἐπαινή, "dreadful."[61] Not only is Persephone

---

[58] In this regard it is worth mentioning that there was another river Acheloos, which flowed from Mount Lycaeum in Arcadia, where sacrifices were made to Zeus. See Pausanias, VIII, 38, 10.

[59] For Zeus Katachthonios see Homer, *Iliad*, IX, 457, and Pausanias, II, 2, 8. For the other names see Farnell, *op. cit.*, I, 38–41 and notes.

[60] Pausanias, VI, 25, 2.

[61] Cf. Homer, *Iliad*, IX, 457; Ζεύς τε καταχθόνιος καὶ ἐπαινὴ Περσεφόνεια ("Underground Zeus and dreadful Persephone"). There is absolutely no way by which the form Persephone can produce Pherrephatta and Proserpina except by a process of deliberate alteration. This difficulty, combined with the fact that no other satisfactory etymology has ever been given for Persephone, serves to make plausible the view presented here.

etymologically related to Peperuda, and so on, but their functions also are more or less the same. In the Homeric Hymn to Demeter, Persephone is carried underground by Hades, an act that causes a drought on earth. Only when she is released does the land become fertile again. It will be recalled that in the ancient Daedala ceremony the images are led to the river Asopus and back to Plataea. Petroff reports that in Bulgaria the Peperuda was often thrown into a pool of water or a stream and then rescued. He adds that the retinue of girls would throw objects into the pools or streams "with the purpose of drowning the evil power which prevented the rain."[62] The bodies of water must represent the underworld and be the equivalent of Hades in the myth of the rape of Persephone. These rituals, whether consciously or unconsciously, are reenacting a myth of the release of the sky-god's bride from the underworld so that she can be fertilized by the sky-god.

If Hades (as Zeus Katachthonios) and Persephone are both related through their names to Indo-European sky- or thunder-gods, one might wonder how the Greeks managed to connect them with the underworld. This is not so difficult to understand as it might at first appear, for it has already been shown that the oak tree provides a connecting link between the sky and the underworld and that Zeus dwells in the oak. Zeus lives not only above ground but also in the ground. Hades' rape of Persephone can be viewed as a sort of Hieros Gamos in reverse. During the period of the year when Persephone is with Hades the fruit of the earth is held back and is contained in roots and seeds that lie hidden underground. In order to release the fruit of the earth Persephone, who symbolizes it, must be brought

---

Martin P. Nilsson (*Geschichte der griechischen Religion* [Munich, 1967], I, 474) approaches the problem from a quite different direction. He believes that this goddess was a pre-Hellenic chthonian deity whose name the invading Greeks found difficult to pronounce. Thus it comes out in a variety of spellings and pronunciations. I cannot support this view because of Persephone's similarities in myth to the Daedala and Peperuda customs with their obvious Indo-European connections, although it is quite possible that there has been some later syncretism of Persephone with pre-Hellenic goddesses of the earth in Greece.

Of course, there is no Greek thunder-god whose name corresponds to Perun, Perkunas, Parjanya, Fjörgynn, etc., and becomes, when altered, Persephone, Pherrephatta, Proserpina, etc. We know only of the *κεραυνός* and *κορύνη* in Greek, which seem to be altered forms of this name but altered in a quite different manner from Persephone, etc. It would seem that this Indo-European name of the thunder-god was completely lost among the Greek-speaking peoples and survives only in altered form as a name for the female counterpart of the god in his underworld aspect. Perhaps closest to the original form of the name, but likewise the name of a female figure, is the nymph Herkyna (cf. Celtic *Hercynia Silva*), a playmate and virtual double of Kore (Persephone) at Lebadeia in Boeotia, after whom an underground stream is named. See Pausanias, IX, 39, 2.

62 Petroff, *op. cit.*, p. 218.

back above ground. This would seem to be the meaning behind such ceremonies as the Dodola and the Daedala. The attention is thereby shifted from the underworld to the sky and world above, from Zeus Katachthonios to Zeus the sky-god. Thus in a sense Zeus too is brought back above ground. In myths Zeus and Hades are generally quite separate. Their similarities are best seen in cult names. Persephone is likewise never actually the bride of the sky-god Zeus except in one source,[63] although her mother Demeter, with whom she is often equated, is Zeus's bride.

THE MOTIF OF THE BLEMISHED FOOT

It is appropriate now to turn to Scandinavia to a myth told in Snorri's *Gylfaginning* (26–31). This long narrative begins with the thunder-god Thor traveling on a journey with his goats and the god Loki. They stop at the house of a farmer, who has a son Thjálfi and a daughter Röskva. Thor slaughters the goats and has them skinned and cooked. Then he tells the family to eat and to throw the bones on the skins, which he has spread out. Thjálfi, however, breaks one of the thighbones in order to get at the marrow. In the morning Thor consecrates the goatskins with his hammer, and the goats return to life. But one of them is lame in a hind leg. Thor threatens to kill the whole household but is persuaded to grant mercy and take Thjálfi and Röskva as his servants.

This myth contains a number of motifs in common with those already associated with Dodona, but the context is quite different. We see the goats and a thunder-god and, most important, the goat's lame thigh. The latter is comparable to the blemished feet of the Selloi, the participants in the Nudipedalia, Jason, Achilles, and especially the altar at Olympia. For it will be recalled that this altar was made from the ashes of the thighs of victims, cemented with the water of Alpheus. On it was burned the white poplar, ἀχερωΐς. In all these contexts the person or animal with the blemished foot gains the protection of the sky-god or -goddess and a certain sort of "immortality." But he also knows he is mortal. His bare foot in direct contact with the earth below or another visible blemish on his foot is proof of his mortality. His immortality is more in the form of a closeness to the god, brought about by performing something that the average person does not do. It is the result of a sort of divine patronage. The heroes, of course, perform superhuman or great warlike deeds; the Selloi and the participants in the Nudipedalia are interceding between the god and the people, interpreting oracular responses or producing rain; and the goats are under the protection of the god yet furnish food,

[63] *Orphicorum Fragmenta*, fr. 210 ff.

milk, and warm skins for man. The blemished foot, then, is a sign of both immortality and mortality, a mark of an "oath" binding its wearer to the earth, signifying that the world below has its claim too. Yet while wearing this mark, a person gains a kind of superhuman power and intimacy with the god above.

This symbolism is still felt in the Dodola ceremony, for, as Schneeweis reports, around Boljevac in Yugoslavia on the day before the ceremony the people remove the wooden cross from the grave of an unknown dead person and bind it to the right foot of the rain-maiden (i.e., the Dodola). They lead her to the river and submerge the cross, which has been weighted down with a stone. On the day of the procession the cross is supposed to float.[64] Here we see a perfect example of the ancient symbolism still operating in a modern folk context. The girl, who is about to become temporarily "immortal," is still tied to the earth, in this instance actually tied to the grave.

The motif of a bare or blemished foot as a sign of immortality occurs in other ancient contexts. In Roman legend Caeculus of Praeneste, one of Turnus's Latin allies, led a band of primitive warriors, some of whom were armed only with slings while others wore skullcaps of wolfskin and had nothing on their left feet.[65] Here is a very close parallel to the Irish sky-god Lug, who before the second battle of Mag Tured walked around the Túatha dé Danann on one foot with one eye closed, reciting a poem.[66] For Caeculus's name is the diminutive of Latin *caecus*, "blind," cognate with Gothic *haihs* and Celtic *caech*, both meaning "blind in one eye."

There is a somewhat confused reference to a statue of Athena at Teuthis in Arcadia, which depicts the goddess as wounded and with a purple bandage on her thigh. The explanatory legend is that a local hero, Teuthis, wounded the goddess, who was disguised at the time

---

[64] Schneeweis, *op. cit.*, p. 162, reports that the role of the rain-maiden (Dodola) is often performed by a gypsy girl, taking this as evidence that the custom is gradually dying out. This fact, however, may be simply an indication that the role is an extremely awesome one, which only an "outsider," someone "special," is willing to undertake. Petroff, *op. cit.*, p. 218, reports that in Bulgaria the Peperuda is usually an orphan. In Greece the Pyrperouna is likewise usually an orphan. See Grimm, *Teutonic Mythology*, 2, 594. A motif of the blemished foot much like the Yugoslavian one was reported in eleventh-century Germany by Burchard of Worms. In a rain-making ceremony "a little girl, completely undressed and led outside the town, had to dig up henbane with the little finger of her right hand and tie it to the little toe of her right foot. She was then solemnly conducted by the other maidens to the nearest river and splashed with water." The name of the ceremony or of the maiden is not given, but the ceremony is undoubtedly related to the Dodola and is strong evidence that such a custom was known to the ancient Germans. *Ibid.*, 2, 593.

[65] Virgil, *Aeneid*, VII, 678–690.

[66] See Jan de Vries, *Keltische Religion* (Stuttgart, 1961), p. 54.

and had angered him, and in return was visited by a wasting disease and a famine in his town. An oracle from Dodona instructed the inhabitants to make the statue, and the disease and the famine were lifted.[67] The story of Teuthis wounding the goddess may be a late rationalization, but it is noteworthy that the god of Dodona is responsible for lifting a famine and that the means by which it is lifted is a statue with a wounded thigh.[68]

MOTIFS OF SLEEPING ON THE GROUND AND PROPHETIC DOVES

In addition to having unwashed feet, it will be recalled, the Selloi sleep on the ground. This custom also has some parallels outside Greece. Gellius records that the Roman Flamen Dialis slept on a bed whose feet were smeared with a thin layer of mud and that he was not allowed to sleep three successive nights away from the bed, nor was anyone else allowed to sleep on it.[69] And in pagan Prussia, where oak trees were said to be oracular and to serve as the homes of gods, the priest of the god Potrimpo was required to sleep on the ground for three nights before sacrificing to the god.[70] The purpose of this practice may have been to enable the priests to get close to the source of occult wisdom in the lower world where the roots of the tree penetrated. Possibly these priests made a spiritual descent there in their dreams.

At Dodona in Epirus there is a tradition of prophecy by the sound of doves in the oak as well as from the tree itself, and the prophets there were priestesses called Peleiades, "Doves," rather than the Selloi of the Dodona in Thessaly. These priestesses have come under considerable discussion by scholars from antiquity to modern times,

---

67 Parke, *op. cit.*, p. 150; Pausanias, VIII, 28, 4; Polemo in *Fragmenta Historicorum Graecorum* (Müller), III, fr. 24.

68 It is remarkable how many Greek heroes had a blemished foot. Oedipus, who also became blind and was a prophet, has already been mentioned, and we should recall Odysseus's scarred thigh. The Thracian Lykourgos (cf. λύκος, "wolf"), son of Dryas, "Oak," was said to have had only one foot (see Ovid, *Ibis*, 346; Hyginus, *Fabellae*, 132). He is thus reminiscent of Caeculus's army and Lug.

The whole problem of "monosandalism" is reviewed by A. Brelich in "Les Monosandales," *La Nouvelle Clio* 7–9, pt. 2 (1955–1957), 469–484; he concludes that the phenomenon is linked to initiation rites and the summoning of chaotic powers. It occurs in the preinitiate state, which is a kind of Chaos, a preliminary condition of the cosmos. He points out (p. 478) that monosandalism occurs often in sepulchral art. Frazer (*op. cit.*, III, 310–313) also deals with the problem. He believes that monosandalism is connected with unbinding and ridding of restraints in order to entangle an enemy. I cannot entirely agree with these writers in the emphases of their conclusions, for their interpretations ignore the real significance of monosandalism, which is the body's direct contact with the earth through the bare foot.

69 Gellius, X, 15, 14.

70 Frazer, *op. cit.*, II, 248.

with most of the confusion being caused by the name Peleiades. Does it mean "doves" or "old women"? Actually, it can have either meaning, for the name is derived from the Indo-European root **pel*, meaning "gray."[71] In some languages this root came to be applied to the dove from its color. Thus in Greek we have πέλεια, "dove," and πελιός or πολιός, "gray." Latin *pullus* means both "chicken" and "dusky," while *palumbus* means "dove." In Greek, πολιός was frequently used to designate old people. The Greeks around Dodona were probably aware of these linguistic connections in choosing the old women to be interpreters of doves. These prophetic women, the Peleiades, therefore can be seen to be simply extensions of the original prophetic doves.

It would appear that the number of old women was three.[72] The number of doves, of course, must have varied, but the usual number given by ancient writers is two. Sophocles speaks of two doves,[73] while both Herodotus and Servius mention one, which was originally part of a pair.[74] In any event, there can be no doubt that doves were involved in the working of the oracle at Dodona in Epirus, even if their precise role is somewhat obscure.[75] Parke has gathered ample evidence to support this view,[76] and one cannot agree with Nilsson, who attributes the tradition of doves to Herodotus's invention.[77]

Doves are frequently encountered elsewhere as oracular birds. Colombet gives evidence for the existence of dove oracles in ancient Gaul and posits a further connection of these oracles with underground water.[78] But the birds one finds in connection with the god need not necessarily be doves. Zeus is often depicted with an eagle, and Hades often has two ravens or eagles. Ravens chose the oak for the Daedala at Plataea. And in pagan Scandinavia it was two ravens, whose names mean "Thought" and "Mind," who flew every day over the earth and reported back to Odin.[79] In kennings these birds are called hawks, cuckoos, gulls, and the like. The identity of the sky-god's

---

71 Pokorny, *op. cit.*, pp. 804–805.

72 Strabo, VII, 7, 10; *Epitome*, 7, fr. la (Loeb).

73 Sophocles, *Trachiniae*, 169 ff.

74 Herodotus, II, 55; Servius, on *Aeneid* III, 466.

75 Zeus himself could take the form of a dove. In this form he appeared to the maiden Phthia at the town of Aigium (cf. αἴξ, "goat"), and coins of that town depict Zeus as an infant suckled by a goat between two tree stumps with an eagle hovering above (see Cook, "Zeus, Jupiter, and the Oak," *Classical Review* 17 [1903], 186). It should be noted that this maiden's name is the same as that of Achilles' homeland.

76 Parke, *op. cit.*, chaps. 3, 4.

77 Nilsson, *op. cit.*, I, 424.

78 Albert Colombet, "Les divinités aux oiseaux en Gaule et le dieu aux colombes d'Alésia," in *Mélanges d'archéologie et d'histoire offerts à Charles Picard* (Paris, 1949), I, 224–240.

79 Turville-Petre, *op. cit.*, pp. 57–59.

bird or birds then is not especially important; any dark bird will do. In the same way the identity of his tree is not particularly significant. Oaks seem to be preferred, but any large tree can serve the purpose. Suffice it to say that at the places called Dodona the tree was the oak and the bird was the dove.

The doves at Dodona probably had a special connection with Dione. Doves are usually associated in Greek myth with Aphrodite, and Homer tells us that Dione was the mother of Aphrodite.[80] It is quite likely, then, that Aphrodite took over the doves from Dione. For by Servius's time, if not much earlier, Dodona was considered to be a sanctuary of Jupiter and Venus,[81] which would be an *interpretatio Romana* for Zeus and Aphrodite. Pausanias reports that prayers were recited there to Zeus and the Earth.[82]

It is quite likely that there existed a Mycenaean dove goddess, if Palmer's interpretation of *pe-re-*82* on the Pylos tablet Tn 316 as Πελείᾳ is correct.[83] Here Peleia is mentioned in a context with Iphimedeia and Diwia. Iphimedeia, like Aphrodite, obviously has a fertility function, and Diwia, like Dione, is a feminine name formed from the name of Zeus. Zeus and Hera, however, are named in the same inscription along with a mysterious Di-ri-mi-jo, son of Zeus. It would seem then that in this early period at Pylos there was considerable variety in the character of Zeus's female counterpart. Probably in later times Peleia, Iphimedeia, and Diwia coalesced into Aphrodite in most of Greece, while Dione and the doves remained behind at Dodona in Epirus to represent the more archaic tradition. Dione then would have been equated by outsiders not with Hera but with Aphrodite-Venus, as in fact happened.

DODONA AND AENEID VI

Such an equation of Dione and Aphrodite-Venus through their common attribute of doves may have facilitated a possible literary bor-

---

80 Homer, *Iliad*, V, 370–371.

81 Servius, on *Aeneid* III, 466. Servius may here be recalling yet another ancient site called Dodona, for he states that it is located in Aetolia. This would bring us close to the river Acheloos, which we have seen to be closely connected with Dodona. The method of divination mentioned by Servius, from the murmurings of a sacred fountain, is not the usual one known in Epirus. Furthermore, we have the curious account given by Scholiast C on Pindar, *Pythian* IV, 133, that the Aetolians were shod on only one foot "because they were so warlike," διὰ τὸ πολεμικώτατοι εἶναι. The main problem in positing another Dodona in Aetolia, however, is that Servius is a very late source.

82 Pausanias, X, 12, 10.

83 Leonard R. Palmer, *The Interpretation of Mycenaean Greek Texts* (Oxford, 1963), pp. 261 ff. Other suggestions have been advanced which seem less satisfactory (see Lydia Baumbach, *Studies in Mycenaean Inscriptions and Dialect, 1953–1964* [Rome, 1968], p. 212).

rowing by Virgil from a lost epic dealing with Dodona. In *Aeneid* VI occur many of the motifs discussed in this paper in connection with Dodona. The oracle at Cumae belongs to the god Apollo, but the motifs are more appropriate to Dodonean Zeus. Apollo here may well be a substitution to make this episode conform with his role in the rest of the poem. The substantiating evidence is considerable. Apollo's female divine counterpart at Cumae is Diana (Trivia), whose name, as we have already seen, was formed in the same way as Dione's and whose cult in an oak forest is reminiscent of Dodona (v. 13 and *passim*). The temple was built by Daedalus (v. 14), a name that naturally reminds us of the Daedala and the probable cognate Dodona.

In a curious passage (vv. 74–76) Aeneas asks the prophetic sibyl to speak to him directly rather than through leaves. Earlier in the poem (III, 441–452) it is explained that the sibyl is accustomed to write the prophecies on leaves, which she sorts out in her cave. But sometimes a gust of wind blows them away, and the consultants must go away disappointed. Interestingly, writing also figured in the functioning of the oracle at Dodona in Epirus. Some 150 lead tablets containing written inquiries and dating from about 500 to 250 B.C. have been recovered from the site.[84] No responses of the oracle have been found, but if these were written, they would have presumably been carried away from the site by consultants.[85] The method described by Virgil may then represent the means of response at Dodona immediately preceding the use of lead tablets. The use of leaves for delivering responses would be most appropriate for Dodona, as it was the sound of rustling leaves which was said by some to be the voice of the god.[86] Probably the use of leaves was abandoned in favor of lead tablets for the very reason found in the *Aeneid*, that leaves could easily be blown away. Our knowledge of the lead tablets helps to date Virgil's presumed source before 500 B.C.

Proceeding in *Aeneid* VI, we notice that Aeneas is led to the golden bough by two doves, the birds of his mother Venus (vv. 190–193). Of course, for Venus we can substitute Dione at Dodona.[87] The tree is described as an oak (v. 209, *ilice*). The golden bough itself does not occur as a motif in connection with Dodona, but it is interesting that Virgil notes the rustling of the golden leaves in the breeze (v. 209)[88] and the doves settling in the tree (v. 203). The motif of golden foliage

---

84 Parke, *op. cit.*, pp. 100–101.

85 *Ibid.*, pp. 110–111.

86 Ovid suggests this means of prophecy for an oak sprung from the seed of Dodona in *Metamorphoses*, VII, 614 ff. See also the late Byzantine Suidas under the entry Δωδώνη.

87 Cf. Virgil, *Aeneid*, III, 19, *Dionaeae matri*.

88 Cf. *ibid.*, III, 442, *Averna sonantia silvis*. Bronze oak leaves and acorns have, however, been found at the site of Dodona in Epirus (see Parke, *op. cit.*, p. 32 n. 21).

does appear, however, in Scandinavia; there was a grove with such foliage in Asgard called Glasir, which stood before the doors of Valhöll, the realm of dead warriors.[89] Aeneas's descent into the underworld could be modeled after a descent made at the oracle of the dead on the Acheron near Dodona. But preparatory to Aeneas's descent is the funeral of Misenus, presided over by a priest with the curious name of Corynaeus (v. 228). This name means "of the staff," and in Virgil's original source it may have been not a personal name but the name of a type of priest.[90] In any event, the word *κορύνη*, "staff, club," has already been shown to be cognate with *κεραυνός*, "thunderbolt," which is probably a tabooistic alteration of the Indo-European thunder-god's name. Thus it is likely that the original of Corynaeus had some connection with Zeus. Another hint that Virgil's tale is related to Dodona and Epirus is the fact that the swamp of Avernus is said to be an overflow of the Acheron (v. 107). We know, in fact, that the region of the Acheron near the oracle of the dead was swampy and unhealthy in ancient times and remains so today.[91]

There can be little doubt, then, that the imagery of *Aeneid* VI comes from Dodona and the oracle of the dead in Epirus. Virgil must have transferred imagery from Zeus and Dione in Epirus to Apollo and Diana in Italy in order to make his poem more consistent in respect to Apollo's preeminent role. The doves of Dodona he assigned to Aeneas's mother Venus (Aphrodite), who also had this attribute in myth. The question that arises is that of Virgil's source. Possibly there was a lost Greek epic about the adventures of Aeneas, for there is an actual tradition that he visited Dodona.[92] But I am more inclined to think that the source is a lost epic that told an alternate version of the return of Odysseus, in which that hero consulted both the oracle of the dead on the Acheron and the oracle at Dodona. That such a version once existed has already been suggested by Woodhouse.[93] We know, in fact, that Virgil did draw much of his material from earlier Greek epic sources now lost, and Woodhouse's plausible

89 Snorri, *Skáldskaparmál*, 32, "Glasir stands with golden leaves before the halls of Sigtyr."

90 The pagan Prussians also seem to have had a "staff priest." Peter von Dusburg, writing in 1326 of the Prussians of the preceding century, states that there was a man called Criwe at the town of Romow who was a sort of "pope" over all the peoples of Prussia and Lithuania. This name may be connected with a Prussian word *kriwule*, which means a "crooked staff" (see Wilhelm Mannhardt, *Letto-preussische Götterlehre* [Riga, 1936], pp. 88, 94–97).

91 Hammond, *op. cit.*, pp. 64–69.

92 Dionysius Halicarnassensis, *Antiquitates Romanae*, I, 51, and I, 55, 4; Servius, on *Aeneid* III, 256 (quoting Varro). See Parke, *op. cit.*, pp. 147–148.

93 W. J. Woodhouse, *The Composition of Homer's Odyssey* (Oxford, 1930), chaps. 17, 18.

hypothesis would clear up some of the inconsistencies in the *Odyssey*. Odysseus does allude to a visit to Dodona in the *Odyssey*, but only in his lies.[94]

THE INDO-EUROPEAN SKY-GOD

The evidence adduced thus far gives a fairly consistent picture of Zeus at the various places called Dodona. He is above all the god of the sky or, more precisely, of the weather. He possesses the thunderbolt and can send rain. The power to send thunder and make rain would seem to have been the oldest aspect of his Dodonean cult, and it is the most widespread in related myths and rites throughout the Indo-European world. It can be seen especially in Zeus's cult name Naïos in Epirus and in the rites of the Dodola and Nudipedalia. Closely related to this aspect of the god is his fertilizing of the earth by means of rain, which is best seen in the related ritual of the Daedala. In all events, Zeus is coupled with his bride, either Hera as in Thessaly and Boeotia or Dione as in Epirus. The oak tree is the link between the sky and the earth, for it stretches to the sky and penetrates into the earth. The thunderbolt and the rain must be viewed primarily as symbolic of the act of fertilization. In fact, the oak tree may be seen as symbolic of the god's sexual organs, for in Greek a certain kind of chestnut is called *διοσβάλανος*, "acorn of Zeus," while the Latin equivalent is the similarly formed *iuglans*. We know, of course, that *βάλανος* is normally "acorn" in Greek. The specialized term "acorn of Zeus/Jupiter" probably came to be applied to the chestnut (in Latin the walnut) when it became no longer necessary for the early Greek and Italic peoples to depend on acorns for nourishment. The symbolism of "nuts" still survives, of course, in colloquial English usage. Further evidence of this symbolism comes again from *Aeneid* VI, where the sibyl mentions the "fruits," *fetus*, growing on the golden bough (v. 141). Aeneas must offer the bough to the queen of the underworld (v. 636), who is called *Iuno inferna*, "Juno of the lower world" (v. 138). It should also be recalled that in some parts of Yugoslavia the participants in the Dodola ceremony carry oak branches. This offering must represent the bringing of the sky-god's power of fertility to the god's bride, who has been trapped below the earth.

Since the oak penetrates the earth and is an extension of the sky-god himself, it is not illogical that the sky-god should be thought of as dwelling in the oak. This belief certainly prevailed in pagan Prussia and may be hinted at by Hesiod in the phrase, *ναῖον δ' ἐν πυθμένι φηγοῦ*, "and they dwelt [?] in the base of the oak." If the god dwells

[94] Homer, *Odyssey*, XIV, 327 ff.; XIX, 296 ff.

in the tree, then any sound that comes from the tree may be considered the voice of the god. Thus the tree becomes oracular. The tree penetrates to the underground waters which spring from Acheloos or the ocean. These waters are at the source of occult wisdom in the underworld. Thus in his most ancient conception in Greece, Zeus is simultaneously a sky-god and an underworld god.

The Greek Dodonas find parallels in various parts of the Indo-European world in the Prussian oak oracles, the Gallic dove oracles, and especially in pagan Sweden in Uppsala.[95] The temple there is described by Adam of Bremen around 1070 as "totally adorned with gold," a phrase reminding us of the temple of Apollo and Diana near Cumae with its *aurea tecta*, "golden ceiling."[96] The temple at Uppsala was dedicated to the worship of three gods, of whom the chief was Thor, who "rules in the sky and governs thunder, lightning, the winds, rain, fair weather, and produce of the soil." The others were Wodan, who "makes wars and gives man bravery in the face of enemies," and Fricco (Freyr or possibly Frigg), a priapus figure who "distributes pleasure among men." Adam adds, "If there is danger of pestilence or famine, sacrifice is offered to the idol of Thor; if of war, to Wodan; if marriage is to be celebrated, they offer to Fricco." In Greece we see all these functions assumed by Zeus, sometimes in alliance with his bride, Hera or Dione. A marginal note to Adam's description adds that next to the temple at Uppsala was an enormous evergreen tree and a well. The scene is strikingly like our picture of Dodona. The tree and the well at Uppsala are almost certainly representations of the Scandinavian cosmic tree Yggdrasill and the well of fate Urdarbrunnr, the source of wisdom where Odin has pledged his eye.[97] This well is comparable to the Greek underground Styx or Acheloos, both of which were "oaths."

The Indo-European parallels to Dodona then are clear and undeniable, both in the symbolism of the oak tree and in the related rituals and myths. Yet while it has these parallels, Dodona is very much a Greek phenomenon, and one cannot agree with Nilsson, who believes that Dodona was originally a non-Greek oracle, a foreign cult taken over by the Greeks and therefore unreliable as a basis for drawing a picture of the Greek Zeus.[98] Quite to the contrary, we see that there were at least three places called Dodona in Greece along with the closely related ritual of the Daedala on the very border of Attica. One could not ask for a cult that was more "Greek." Furthermore, Dodona is closely involved with several of the most important

---

95 Turville-Petre, *op. cit.*, pp. 244–246.

96 Virgil, *Aeneid*, VI, 13.

97 Turville-Petre, *op. cit.*, pp. 279–280.

98 Nilsson, *op. cit.*, I, 427.

Greek legendary heroes—Jason, Achilles, and Heracles—and quite possibly with Odysseus as well. Dodona thus stands at the center of the Greek conception of Zeus and represents perhaps the earliest form of this conception.[99]

CONCLUSIONS

In this paper I present a number of new interpretations, operating under the assumption that certain hitherto obscure or unexplainable data could be elucidated by comparison with similar data from other Indo-European-speaking peoples. The similarities are taken as evidence that the data represent separate traditions, which all stem from a common Proto-Indo-European original tradition. I have concentrated my efforts on explaining ancient Greek material, particularly the traditions concerned with Dodona. Normally such material is explained in terms of other Greek data only or as the result of diffusion from other Mediterranean cultures. Thus my approach is a fairly unusual one, placing the data in an unaccustomed frame of reference.

Since I cover so broad a range of material, it will be helpful to summarize my ideas. Each of the eleven major ideas is discussed at some length in a subsection.

1. The name Dodona is related to a similar set of names, Dodola, and so on, still found in Slavic and Baltic regions for a character in a rain-making ceremony. Another set of names for the same participant, Peperuda, and so on, represents a reduplicated alteration of the name of the Slavic and Baltic thunder-god, Perun and Perkunas, a name that also occurs in cognate form among other Indo-European-speaking peoples with meanings such as "oak" and "to strike" and may be related to Greek words for "thunderbolt" and "staff, club."
2. The Roman Nudipedalia custom shares several motifs with the Dodola custom and Dodona.
3. The name Dodona is derived from a cult name of Zeus meaning "goatskin."

[99] This whole motif complex has a remarkable parallel in the modern Christmas customs of the Germanic area. A sky-god (Santa Claus) descends in fire (through the chimney) to the evergreen tree (sometimes having metallic ornamentation), and abundance results from his visit (gifts). Other motifs are the stockings hung on the mantlepiece, one for each member of the family, so reminiscent of the feet of the Selloi; the yule log, recalling the Daedala; and the mistletoe hung up in the house, which Frazer has taken to be the golden bough of the *Aeneid*. These customs, all occurring together as they do, must be derived from an Indo-European fertility ritual performed in times of drought or barrenness similar to the Dodola, Daedala, and Nudipedalia.

4. There is ancient Greek evidence for the existence of at least three sites called Dodona, the historical one in Epirus, one in Thessaly, and possibly one near Mount Olympus.
5. The legends of Jason and the Argonauts, the death of Heracles, and the career of Achilles are all connected with the Thessalian Dodona. All three heroes seem to be euhemerized versions of Zeus, and Jason and Achilles may even have been priests of Zeus at Dodona in earlier legends.
6. The Daedala celebration at Plataea in honor of Zeus and Hera combines several features found also in connection with Dodona and the Nudipedalia and Dodola customs. The name Daedala is probably cognate with Dodona and Dodola.
7. The oracle of Zeus at Dodona in Epirus has a connection with underground water and in particular with the river Acheloos, which appears to be related to the Acheron. This connection is probably concerned with Zeus's aspect as an underworld god. His underworld bride is Persephone, whose name, it is suggested, is formed in the same manner as Peperuda, and so on.
8. The motif of a bare or blemished foot, found in several of the legends and customs here discussed, is explained as a sign of invincibility or temporary immortality. Several other examples of it are offered from various Indo-European-speaking peoples.
9. Motifs of priests sleeping on the ground and prophetic doves met in connection with Dodona are discussed and compared with similar data from other Indo-European-speaking peoples.
10. It is suggested that the imagery of Book VI of Virgil's *Aeneid* is drawn from Dodona and the oracle of the dead in Epirus and that Virgil was familiar with a lost Greek epic about Aeneas or Odysseus which recounted visits to these places.
11. The ancient Greek conception of Zeus at the various places called Dodona and in the Daedala custom is paralleled by similar concepts of a sky- or thunder-god held by other Indo-European-speaking peoples.

APPENDIX ON MELAMPOUS

Parke has discussed the possible connection of the seer Melampous, ancestor of the priests of Zeus at Olympia, with Dodona and especially the Selloi through the meaning of the name Melampous, "Black Foot."[100] He further points out the motifs of the oak and prophecy through the speech of birds that occur in connection with Melam-

[100] Parke, *op. cit.*, pp. 164–173. A connection between Melampous and the Selloi was proposed earlier by Willy Borgeaud, "Le Déluge, Delphes, et les Anthestéries," *Museum Helveticum* 4 (1947), 225.

pous. But Parke is unaware of further connections with Dodona. Pliny the Elder states that the plant hellebore was discovered by the prophet Melampous and named *melampodion* after him.[101] Others, Pliny says, claim that it was discovered by a herdsman named Melampous, who noticed that his she-goats were purged after eating the plant. Melampous gave the milk of these goats to the daughters of Proitos and cured them of madness. As a reward Melampous received one-third of Proitos's kingdom of Argos, while his brother Bias received another third.[102] Proitos retained the remaining third, and Melampous and Bias were married to his two surviving daughters. Finally, Pliny adds that a dead scorpion can be revived if smeared with white hellebore.[103]

Hellebore, of course, immediately suggests the Selloi (Helloi), and the plant's name could easily mean "food of the Selloi" or even "drink of the Selloi" (the meaning of βρω- being basically 'to ingest'; cf. Lithuanian *gìrtas* 'drunk'). The plant was well known as a violent purgative effective in curing epilepsy and "madness," among other ailments.[104] As I have suggested earlier, the Prussian priests of Potrimpo may have made a spiritual descent to the underworld in dreams while sleeping out on the ground, and the same may also have been true of the Selloi, hellebore being ingested in order to restore them to sanity. The use of the plant to revive scorpions is most interesting, for the scorpion has a symbolic connection with the goat. Pliny mentions a plant called *tragos*, "goat," which is also called *scorpion*.[105] While I would not at this point venture so far as to equate scorpions with goats, I would point out Thor's revival of his goats and the purging of Melampous's goats with hellebore.[106] Possibly a lost myth stated that hellebore could revive goats. Another lost myth is hinted at by the English name for *helleborus niger*, "bear's-foot." Such a myth might be a variant of the story of Thor's revival of his goats.[107]

Melampous, then, has much in common with the Selloi and is associated with several motifs already discussed in connection with Dodona, particularly the goat. It should be added that Melampous

---

101 Pliny the Elder, XXV, 47.

102 Herodotus, IX, 34; Apollodorus, *Bibliotheca*, I, 9, 12, and II, 2, 2; Diodorus Siculus, IV, 68; Pausanias, II, 18, 4. Apollodorus attributes the legend to Hesiod.

103 Pliny the Elder, XXV, 122. Cf. Theophrastus, *Historia Plantarum* IX, 18, 2.

104 *Ibid.*, 59–60.

105 *Ibid.*, XXVII, 142.

106 Both black and white hellebore were used during historical times as purgatives for goats and other domesticated animals. See Theophrastus, *Historia Plantarum* IX, 10, 1–4.

107 The myth of Thor's revival of his goats is vaguely related to an international folktale type (see Antti Aarne and Stith Thompson, *The Types of the Folktale*, FF Communications, no. 184 [Helsinki, 1964], Type 750B, pp. 255–256). C. W. von Sydow has discussed this type in "Tors Färd till Utgård," *Danske Studier* (1910), pp. 91 ff.

was buried at Aigosthena (cf. αἴξ, "goat"), where he had a sanctuary and an annual festival.[108] He is obviously a representative of Dumézil's first function through his priestly activities. His brother Bias, whose name means "Violence," can be interpreted as a figure of the second or warrior function, both through his name and through his further connection with cattle raiding.[109] He is almost certainly the same Bias who was a companion of Nestor at Troy, for Nestor was brother-in-law to Melampous's brother Bias.[110] Proitos and his daughters represent the third or fertility function. Proitos, twin brother of Akrisios, is associated with the land of Argos, while Melampous and Bias are, in a sense, invading foreigners. The reconciliation of these three functions is symbolized in Greek legend by the marriages of Melampous and Bias to the daughters of Proitos and the triple division of the kingdom. This pattern fits perfectly into the structure of the Indo-European myth of the "War of the Functions" found in Rome, India, Scandinavia, and Ireland.[111]

---

108 Pausanias, I, 44, 5.

109 Homer, *Odyssey*, XV, 225 ff.; Apollodorus, *Bibliotheca*, I, 96 ff.

110 Homer, *Iliad*, IV, 296.

111 Georges Dumézil summarizes his own scholarship and that of others dealing with this mythic structure in *Mythe et épopée* I (Paris, 1968).

Germanic Warg: The Outlaw as Werwolf*

MARY R. GERSTEIN, *University of California, Los Angeles*

Beginning with Jacob Grimm, German legal scholars of the nineteenth and earlier twentieth centuries were in general agreement that *warg* (ON *vargr* 'wolf, outlaw,' OE *wearg* 'monster, outlaw,' ML *wargus* 'outlaw')[1] was the standard Gmc. term for "outlaw" or "peaceless man" and that its basic meaning was "der Würger, der Wolf [the strangler, the wolf]."[2] Unfortunately, Grimm and his followers did not hold fast to the etymologically correct primacy of the strangulation meaning, and they interpreted the wolf aspect as metaphor rather than as actual identity of man and animal.[3] *Warg*, they said,

* The following linguistic abbreviations are used throughout this paper: E=English; F=French; G=German; Gk.=Greek; Gmc.=Germanic; Go.=Gothic; I-E=Indo-European; L=Latin; MHG=Middle High German; ML=Medieval Latin; NHG=New High German; OE=Old English; OF=Old French; OFr.=Old Frisian; OHG=Old High German; OI=Old Irish; ON=Old Norse-Icelandic; OS=Old Saxon; OWall.=Old Walloon; P-I-E=Proto-Indo-European; Sk.=Sanskrit.

[1] Direct impetus for this paper came from an article by G. von Unruh, "*Wargus:* Friedlosigkeit und magisch-kultische Vorstellungen bei den Germanen," *Zeitschrift der Savigny-Stiftung für Rechtsgeschichte, Germanistische Abteilung* 74 (1957), 1 40, which is still stimulating and valuable for its references, although confused and inaccurate. Von Unruh's most important contribution is the emphasis on the connection between *warg* and disease. Adalbert Erler's "Friedlosigkeit und Werwolfsglaube," *Paideuma* 1, no. 7 (1940), does not live up to its title. The best article on Gmc. outlawry is still F. Kauffmann's "Mythologische Zeugnisse aus römischen Inschriften," *Beiträge zur Geschichte der deutschen Sprache und Literatur* 18 (1894), 157–194.

[2] Heinrich Brunner, *Deutsche Rechtsgeschichte*, 2d ed. (Leipzig, 1906), I, 234 (hereafter cited as Brunner).

[3] W. E. Wilda, for example, states that *warg* is "die Bezeichnung des Friedlosen aber auch der Name des Wolfes, so dass beide Begriffe: das friedlose, von Allen verfolgte Thier und der in gleicher Lage sich befindende Mensch fast ineinander

meant "wolf" because the outlaw, like the wolf, lived in the forest and might be killed with impunity by anyone.[4] Grimm seems to have based his explanation on those of late medieval sources, such as this pronouncement from thirteenth-century Anglo-Norman law:[5]

> qe des adunc le tiegne lem pur lou e est criable Wolvesheved pur ceo qe lou est beste haie de tote gent; e des adunc list a chescun del occire al foer de lou.
>
> (that henceforth he be held to be a wolf and is to be proclaimed "wolf's-head" because the wolf is a beast hated by everyone; and henceforth it is up to everyone to kill him for the price of a wolf.)

Although the proclamation of "wolf's-head" may have been taken literally enough in England to give rise to the custom of bringing the heads of wolves and outlaws to the shire authorities to receive the same bounty for each, there seems to be no trace of sacred or magical meaning in men's minds by this time.[6] The outlaw is treated like a wolf because he acts like one. As a legal reality, outlawry in the European Middle Ages was the weapon of a central authority. Its main purpose was to force a man to appear in court, and, if actually carried out as a sentence, it differed little from banishment or exile. This function of outlawry is reflected in the use of *warg* in the earliest Gmc. law codes, which in general show few traces of outlawry as punishment for crimes, but rather bear witness to the efforts of the emerging monarchy to substitute monetary payments for blood feuds. These facts, coupled with the total lack of any mention of outlawry among the ancient Gmc. peoples in the standard classical sources,[7] have led modern scholars not only to reject the claim that *warg* was an ancient term for outlaw, but also to reject the idea of outlawry as the foundation of the Gmc. legal system.[8]

There is substantial evidence, however, that the type of outlawry

---

flossen [i.e., because both outlaw and wolf were called *warg* and were in the same situation, the concepts nearly merged]" (*Das Strafrecht der Germanen* [1842; repr. Scientia Aalen, 1960], p. 280).

4 Jakob Grimm, *Deutsche Rechtsalterthümer* (Göttingen, 1854), p. 733.

5 *Mirror of Justices*, ed. W. J. Whittaker, Publications of the Selden Society, 7 (London, 1895), p. 125. Quoted (vaguely) in Brunner, I, 235.

6 The notion that the expression comes from the actual wearing of a wolf mask in medieval times is without basis, although maintained by R. Eisler, *Man into Wolf* (London, n.d.), p. 144, and by M. Eliade, "Les Daces et les loups," *Numen* 6 (1959), 15–34, esp. 18.

7 The most important passages are Tacitus, *Germania* 12 and 21, where the penal system is described and where there is mention of a system of composition, even for homicide related to feud, but—no mention of outlawry.

8 See especially J. Goebel, *Felony and Misdemeanor* (New York, 1937); F. Ström, *On the Sacral Origin of the Germanic Death Penalties* (Stockholm, 1942).

designated by *warg* in Gmc.[9] is ancient, although its original legal function is no longer clear even in the earliest law codes. The earliest Gmc. text, Wulfila's fourth-century translation of the Bible into his native Gothic, shows *warg* as a well-established legal term. In Mark 10:33, "*gawargjand* ina dauþau" is the expression for the condemnation of Christ, who is later "reckoned with the kinless" at the time of his execution.[10] *Warg* occurs in three other forms in Wulfila: Romans 8:1 "Ni waiht þannu nu *wargiþos* þaim in Xristau Jesu" (There is no condemnation to those who are in Jesus Christ); 2 Corinthians 7:3 "ni du *gawargeinai* qiþa" (I do not say this in condemnation); 2 Timothy 3:2 *launawargos* translates "ungrateful" (ἀχάριστοι) and would mean literally *warg* of reward. He who breaks the obligation to render gratitude for services rendered is equivalent to an oath breaker. This last passage refers to the dreadful times to come before the end of the world and the Last Judgment. This context is strikingly similar to that of the *vargǫld*, an age of monstrous crimes before the fall of the gods in the ON *Vǫluspá*:

Broeđr muno beriaz ok at bǫnom verđaz
muno systrungar sifiom spilla;
hart er í heimi, hórdómr mikill,
skeggǫld, skalmǫld, skildir ro klofnir,
vindǫld, *vargǫld*, áđr verǫld steypiz;
mun engi mađr ǫđrom þyrma. (*Vsp.* 45)

(Brother shall strike brother and both fall,
Sister's sons slay each other,
Evil be on earth, an Age of Whoredom,
Of sharp sword-play and shields' clashing,
A Wind-Age, a Wolf [*warg*]-Age, till the world ruins:
No man to another shall mercy show.)
(Auden's trans.)

Clearly, more is involved than an ordinary "condemnation"; Christ is reckoned among the kinless and suffers the fate of a *warg*, dies as a *warg*. The use of *warg* in Gothic agrees with the use of *warg* in continental Gmc. and ON legal codes, as well as in OE, OS, and ON poetry. Careful textual analysis shows—in partial vindication of the older legal historians and in total disagreement with current trends—that the proclamation of *warg* originally was a magico-legal pro-

[9] I am deliberately isolating *warg* from the host of Gmc. outlawry terms, all of which must be investigated individually before a composite view of Gmc. legal institutions can again be attempted.

[10] Mark 15:28, "jah miþ unsibjaim rahniþs was." For the term *unsibjaim* as an item of petrified legal vocabulary, see S. P. Schwartz, "Comparative Legal Reconstruction in Germanic," in *Myth and Law among the Indo-Europeans*, ed. Jaan Puhvel (Berkeley, Los Angeles, and London, 1970), 39–53.

nouncement which transformed the criminal into a werwolf worthy of strangulation. It will become evident, I hope, that the attributes that the outlaw of later medieval literary tradition, such as Robin Hood, Gamlyn, or Grettir, retained as outer form—wolfish nature, shape-changing (by disguise), and the fate of hanging—are in reality survivals of essential features of an outlaw tradition so ancient as to be not merely Gmc. but I-E: that of the monstrous criminal, the outlaw as werwolf.

The outlaw as werwolf may be traced back to the earliest extant I-E legal records, to fragments of Hittite law which are perhaps as early as 1600 B.C.: "If anyone elopes with a woman and afterwards a rescuer follows them, if two men or three men die, there shall be no compensation. 'Thou art become a wolf' [zi-ik-wa UR.BAR.RA ki-ša-at]."[11] The pronouncement in this text has been compared with the earliest known occurrence of the term *warg* in a Gmc. legal document, the *Lex Salica,* where the phrase "wargus sit," "he shall be a *warg,*" is used of a grave robber. Clearly, the *LS* expression represents in the third person the formula rendered by direct address in the Hittite text. The criminal, by means of oral pronouncement, is legally changed into a werwolf. Hittite also offers direct etymological as well as thematic connections with Gmc. *warg.* Puhvel has shown[12] that Hittite *ḫurkel,* basically a legal term denoting sexual abominations (sodomy and incest), derives from the same P-I-E root as Gmc. *warg* (**wargaz*), from P-I-E **Ḫwergh-,* with the basic lexical meaning of 'strangle.' The crime of *ḫurkel* renders the community unclean. It denotes a sexual crime so monstrous that it is literally a "hanging matter."[13] The Hittite LÚ.MEŠ *ḫurkilaš* 'men of *ḫurkel,*' demonic beings whose tasks include capturing a wolf and strangling a serpent, "in the sense of 'men of strangulation' are paralleled by ON *vargr,* OE *wearg,* OHG *warg* 'robber, criminal.' "[14] The felicitous neutrality of Puhvel's 'man of strangulation' is immediately evident: it includes both active and passive meanings. The *warg* is a strangler who deserves to be strangled. The Gmc. *warg,* however, like the Hittite 'man of *ḫurkel,*' is not

[11] Ernst Neufeld, *The Hittite Laws* (London, 1951), p. 11, par, 37, text I. In a note to this text (p. 153), Neufeld takes "Thou art [*sic*] a wolf" to be a scribal addition. J. Friedrich, *Die hethitischen Gesetze* (Leiden, 1959), p. 26, par. 37. F. Imparati, *Le leggi ittite* (Rome, 1964), p. 221, has "ti sei comportato come un animale da preda," which is not nearly strong enough. She quotes R. Haase, "Bemerkungen zu einigen Paragraphen der hethitischen Gesetzestexte," *Archiv Orientální* 26 (1958), pp. 28–35, who (p. 34) makes a comparison between this text and the *Lex Salica* formula which is discussed below.

[12] Jaan Puhvel, "Hittite *ḫurkis* and *ḫurkel,*" *Die Sprache* 17 (1971), 42–45. I am much indebted to Professor Puhvel for this reference.

[13] *Ibid.*, p. 44.

[14] *Ibid.*

merely "der den Strang verdient," he who deserves the noose;[15] he is a werwolf, a demonic shapechanger whose criminality pollutes the community.

WARG IN CONTINENTAL GMC. LEGAL DOCUMENTS

The earliest recorded Gmc. legal evidence for *warg* as a form of outlawry is in the above-mentioned sixth-century *Lex Salica* (55, 2):

> Si quis corpus iam sepultum effoderit aut expoliaverit, *wargus* sit, hoc est expulsus de eodem pago, usquedum cum parentibus defuncti convenerit, ut et ipsi parentes rogati sint pro eo, ut liceat infra patriam esse. Et quicumque ei antea panem aut hospitalem dederit, etiam si uxor eius hoc fecerit, DC denariis . . . culpabilis iudicetur.

> (If anyone disinters or despoils a buried body, let him be a *warg*, that is, expelled from this territory, until it is arranged with the kin of the deceased that they be asked on his [the criminal's] behalf that he be allowed within the land. And whosoever gives him food or shelter before this, even if it be his own wife, shall be fined . . . 600 denarii.)

In this passage, being a *warg* is defined as expulsion from a given territory; it is a temporary state that is ended by means of a settlement with the injured party. But it is important to note that this definition is a later addition to the text and that the term *warg* occurs only in this passage. Clearly, the context is crucial here: the man who desecrates a grave is proclaimed a werwolf. The association of werwolf with grave robbing undoubtedly accounts for the preservation of the rare term *warg* in the same context in the *Lex Ripuaria* (85, 2) and for the fact that the same passage finds its way from one of these codes into the laws of Henry I of England, in a section dealing with crimes against the dead:

> Et si quis corpus in terra vel noffo vel petra sub pyramide vel structura qualibet positum, sceleratus infamacionibus effodere vel exspoliare presumpserit, *wargus* habeatur.

> (And if anyone dares to disinter or despoil a corpse placed in the ground or in a coffin or in stone under a monument or any sort of structure, he shall be held *warg*, a criminal for his infamous deeds.)[16]

The act of despoiling a corpse is that of the wolf, eater of carrion. It is also an ancient and universal belief that the shape-changing wer-

[15] Cf. the excellent article by Hans Kuhn, "Gaut," in *Festschrift für Jost Trier*, ed. B. von Wiese and K. H. Borck (Meisenheim am Glan, 1954), pp. 417–433.

[16] B. Thorpe, *Ancient Laws and Statutes of England*, I, 591. The text is probably corrupt (the *sceleratus infamacionibus* is strangely placed and problematic) but the proclamation of *warg* is clear.

wolf can converse with the dead and gain their treasure.[17] These traits are particularly well developed among the Gmc. outlaws in Icelandic tradition, especially in the person of Grettir, who desecrates graves, despoils corpses, and wrestles with monstrous supernatural enemies.

That the idea of a ravening wolf is implicit in the word *warg* is shown by the only other occurrence of a form based on *warg* in the *Lex Salica*; in *LS* 66, which deals with a man who steals a slave, the slave is taken "trans mare," and the expression used for the criminal act of abduction is "qui eum plagiavit hoc est *uuargauerit*." Since the verb **wargare* is used as a synonym for *plagiare* 'kidnap,' it would seem not to be a strict legal term here, but rather a verb that expresses the act of the werwolf. This use of *warg* is paralleled by the reference to indigenous bandits in a letter from Sidonius to Lupus of Troyes:

> Commendo supplicium baiulorum pro nova necessitudine vetustam necessitatem, qui in Arvernam regionem longum iter his quippe temporibus emensi casso labore venerunt. Namque unam feminam de affectibus suis quam forte *Vargorum* (hoc enim nomine indigenas latrunculos nuncupant) superventus abstraxerat, isto deductam ante aliquot annos isticque distractam cum non falso indicio comperissent. (Loeb ed., II, 258 ff.)

> (I commend to you in virtue of our new relationship an old trouble of the suppliant bearers of this letter. Having travelled to the Arvernian country, a long journey in days such as these, they got no profit for their pains. They had discovered from reliable information that a kinswoman, who had been abducted in a raid of *Vargi* (for so they call the local brigands), had been brought here a number of years ago and sold on the spot.)
>
> (Loeb trans.)

Thus, there is evidence for *warg* as a legal term for a type of outlaw and as a popular term for those who act like ravening wolves.

In a capitulary of Charlemagne (*Capitulare Saxonicum*) dated 28 October 897, the word *wargida* occurs three times in one paragraph as a legal term contrasting with *districtio*:

> Hoc etiam statuerunt ut qualiscumque causa infra patriam cum propriis vicinantibus pacificata fuerit, ibi solito more ipsi pagenses solidos duodecim pro *districtione* recipiant et pro *wargida*, quae iuxta consuetudinem eorum solebant facere, hoc concessum habeant.
>
> (*Monumenta Germaniae Historica* sec. 8, ser. 2, vol. 1, p. 71)

> (It was also decided that for whatever case which might be settled in their own region among their own neighbors, they should receive according to

[17] The concept of the werwolf-sorcerer who robs graves is apparently worldwide. According to William Morgan, *Human Wolves among the Navaho* (New Haven, 1936), pp. 9–12, the Navaho, who have a highly developed lore concerning witches and werwolves, believe in magicians who dig up corpses, eat the flesh, and steal their jewelry.

custom twelve *soldi* for the *districtio* and for the *wargida* which they used to make according to their custom, this should be granted.)

Since *districtio* would be a fine or a banishment of some sort, *wargida*, characterized as an ancient Saxon custom, must be the penalty for an unatonable crime. The *MGH* editor glosses *wargida* as *condemnatio*, the death penalty. This would agree with the corresponding Go. **wargiþa* in Wulfila, but one must be more precise: the condemnation involves a pronouncement of outlawry which carries with it the punishment of death, as with Go. "*gawargjand* ina dauþau," lit. to "be-*warg* to death."

These are the only known occurrences of *warg* in continental Gmc. laws. I have not found *warg* at all in OE law, and only twice in Anglo-Norman law, once in Henry I and once in a fourteenth-century text.[18]

WARG IN OLD NORSE-ICELANDIC LEGAL TEXTS

Examination of the two major ON legal documents, the Icelandic *Grágás* and the Norwegian *Gulaþingslov*, shows that the term *varg* survives in ON as a *terminus technicus* for the outlaw guilty of especially serious crimes.

Grágás

In the *Vígsloði*, the section of the *Grágás* dealing with homicide, one finds *morðvarg* 'murder-*warg*' (par. 47) as a term for a particular subclass of outlaw, under the general heading of *skógar maðr* ("woodman'), whose compensation is fixed at a higher rate than usual.[19] As opposed to *víg*, homicide, *morð* implies killing furtively, by unmanly means such as magic or poison, as well as the attempt to conceal the crime. It is the crime of a skulking werwolf.

Vígsloði 113, the section known as the *Trigþamál*, contains three variations on a formulaic curse for those who break oaths and treaties:

1. hann scal sva viþa *varg* heita, sem viþast er veröld bygd . . . vera hvarvetna raekr ok rekinn um allan heim, hvar sem hann verþr staþinn a hverio dögri.

   (he shall be called *warg* as far as the world is inhabited . . . he shall wander subject to pursuit day and night, wherever he goes.)

---

[18] Cf. H. Bateson, ed., *Borough Customs* (London, 1904–1906), I, 75. In a text dated 1356, in a garbled spelling, the expression "*warg*-tree" (Wahztrew) is used for the local hanging tree. "*Warg*-tree" for gallows is common in ON and is found in OS and OE poetry as well.

[19] The *morðvarg* is grouped with those guilty of murder during the *Alþing* (assembly), the arsonist, and the slave or debtor who kills his master or a member of his master's family.

2. þa scal sa rekinn vera fra guþi oc allri guþs cristni, sva viþa, sem menn *varga* reka, kristnir menn kirkior sökia, heiþnir menn hof blota . . .

(he shall be pursued by God and all God's Christians as far as men hunt *wargs*, Christian men go to church, heathen men make sacrifices . . .)

2*a*. (MS variant) Þa scal hann sva viþa *vargr* raekr oc rekinn sem menn viþaz *varga* reka.

(he shall be outcast as *warg* and hunted as far as *wargs* are hunted.)

Each of these three variants is important. (1) and (2*a*) are closer to oral formulaic style, particularly with restoration of initial *v* in *raekr, rekinn*, and *reka*; (2) is more typical of later medieval written style with its accretion of comparisons and examples. (1) is especially important because it preserves the oral pronouncement of outlawry, "vargr *heita*" (cf. the *Lex Salica* "wargus sit"). In ON, the word *varg* is ambiguous; it can mean 'wolf' as well as 'werwolf/outlaw.' It is misleading to translate *vargr* in (1) as 'exile' and *varga* in (2) as 'wolves,' as did the *Grágás* editors in the parallel Latin text. If *varga* is taken to mean 'outlaws' as well as 'wolves,' then one has a division of living beings into basic categories according to their social function, as is common in OE and ON gnomic verse:[20] Christian men attend church; heathens make sacrifices; outlaws are hunted.

The two types of beings classified as *warg* in the *Vígsloði*, murderers and oath breakers, correspond to the creatures guilty of monstrous crimes, the *meinsvara* and *morðvarga* who are the prey of the monsters Nidhöggr and Fenrir in the ON *Vǫluspá* (39):

Sá hon þar vađa þunga strauma
menn meinsvara ok morđvarga,
ok þannz annars glepr eyrarúno;
þar saug Níđhǫggr nái framgengna,
sleit vargr vera—vitođ er enn, eđa hvat?

(Men wade there, tormented by the stream,
Vile murderers, men forsworn,
And artful seducers of other men's wives:
Nidhogg sucks blood from the bodies of the dead,
The wolf rends them. Well, would you know more?)
(Auden's trans.)

The *vargr* of the last line is clearly Fenrir, the werwolf/outlaw of the ON pantheon. *Varg* rends *varg*; the word 'wolf' is not strong enough, nor is it accurate in this context.

That *varg* is a term for outlaw is further shown by the use of the

[20] For example, "cyning sceal rice healdan" (the king shall rule), OE *Maxims*, II, 1*a*; or "the dragon shall . . . guard the mound," *Maxims*, II, 26–27; or, as in *Cotton Gnomes*, 115*a*, 54–59, "*wearh* sceal hangian" (the *warg* shall hang).

term *vargdropi*, lit. '*varg*-drop' for the offspring of an outlaw (*skógarmaðr*) in the section of the *Grágás* known as the *Arfa-þattr*, inheritance law. It is a technical term, a sort of legal insult, along with *hornung* (offspring of a woman and a freed slave) and *baesing* (offspring of a female outlaw), for a particular category of person not entitled to inherit:

> Þat barn er oc eigi arfgengt, er sa maþr getr er secr er orþinn scogarmadr, þoat hann geti viþ sinni kono sialfs. Sa maþr heitir *vargdropi*.
>
> (*Grágás*, I, 178)

> (That child also may not inherit who is the offspring of an outlaw, even if begotten on his own wife. This man is called a *vargdropi*.)

Again, the text stresses that the man shall be *called* "*varg*-drop"; the idea of a legally binding oral pronouncement is clear. And again, there is an ON literary parallel: in *Sigrdrífomál* 35 one finds the expression "varom vargdropa," combining the idea of outlawry with oath breaking as well as bastardy:

> Þat raeð ek þér it tíunda, at þú trúir aldri várom vargdropa . . .

> (This I counsel tenth: never trust the oath of an outlaw's offspring . . .)

Gulaþingslov

In the *Gulaþingslov*, the term *varg* is also rare and highly specialized; it occurs as a technical term for an outlaw not known to be such, *úvísavargr* (e.g., *Gul.* 144) and as a term for a man outlawed for arson (*Gul.* 98): "þa er hann útlagr oc úheilagr oc heitir *brennuvargr*" (he shall be outlawed and deprived of all rights and shall be called "fire-*varg*"). Again, the verb *heitir*, indicating oral pronouncement, is found linked with *vargr*, whereas the *Gulaþing* cover term for outlaw, *útlagr*, depends on the concept of written law and central authority.

I conclude from the sparse but consistent ON legal evidence that *varg* as it occurs in the earliest written ON codes is an item of petrified legal vocabulary, retained in expressions involving oral pronouncement of outcast status for especially odious crimes, such as arson, oath breaking, and secret slaying. The fact that it is almost exclusively found in compounds (*morðvargr, úvísavargr, brennuvargr, vargdropi*) indicates that such highly specialized terms are less subject to loss or replacement than the single ambiguous word *varg*, which can mean 'wolf' as well as 'outlaw' in ON. It seems, however, that *varg* nearly always conveys a '*wer*wolf' meaning, even when used to designate the animal. It is significant that in *Gul.* 94, the law that "bears and wolves are outlawed everywhere," the wording is "bjorn oc *ulfr* scal hvervetna utlagr vaera."

WARG IN LITERARY TEXTS

1. *Christ and Odin*

I have stressed that Wulfila rendered the condemnation of Christ as "gawargjand ina dauþau." Christ was "be-*warg*ed" to death, hanged on the cross. The analogy between the crucified Christ and the hanged criminal neither begins nor ends with Wulfila, of course. Earlier Christian writers saw the death of Christ as an antitype to that of Absalom (2 Samuel 18:9–17): both are hanged and stabbed with spears. This mode of death is identical in form with the symbolic death of the Gmc. god Wodan/Odin, who hangs in the world tree, pierced by a spear. There can be no doubt that the iconographical identity of Christ and Odin, the fact that both undergo symbolic death as accursed outlaw, as *warg*, paved the way for the conversion of the Gmc. peoples to Christianity. In the pagan North, the complex of ideas belonging to *warg*—werwolf, shape-changing, outlawry, and hanging—remain with the Gmc. deities, Odin, Loki, and Fenrir; in the South, the fusion of Christian belief and pagan tradition allows the old Gmc. term *warg* to survive as the appellation of various dread enemies of God in the "Christian" poetry of England and the Continent. Such various creatures as Grendel, Judas, Antichrist, and the Devil all receive the name of *warg*.[21]

This fusion of Christianity and Gmc. belief is particularly well represented by the language and imagery of the early ninth-century OS poem *Hêliand* ("The Savior"), where the suffering and death of Christ are described in recurring clusters and series of phrases in which the cross occurs in epic variation with pagan modes of punishment. The series 5334 ff. is representative:

5334: *galgon rihtun* 'erect a gallows'
5336: *bôm an berge* 'tree on the mountain'
5337: *quelidun an krûcie* 'tortured on the cross'
5340: *bittra bendi* 'bitter bonds' (referring to the *nails* that pierce Christ)

Despite references to crucifixion and nailing, it is the binding of Christ which is stressed almost incessantly in the *Hêliand*; for example,

4929: *lido-bendiun* 'limb-bonds'
4930: *fitereun* 'fetters'
5356: *an simon haftan* 'held by the rope'

[21] Cf. von Unruh, "*Wargus*," for several references. Antichrist is called *warg* in *Muspilli*, 39.

Thus, in a similar variation, Christ is *an kruci* (on the cross), but the thieves hanging with him are (5564 ff.)

> an them waragtrewe werkô te lône
> lêđaro dâdiô . . .
>
> (on the *warg*-tree as a reward
> for their evil deeds)

This wording is similar to that of an OE gnomic verse (*Cotton Gnomes* 115*a*, 54–59):

> Ā sceal snotor hycgean
> ymb þysse worulde gewinn;
> *wearh* hangian
> faegere ongildan þaet hē
> aēr fâcen dyde
> manna cynne.
>
> (The wise man will constantly
> ponder this world's strife;
> the *warg* will hang,
> properly pay for his previous deeds
> against mankind.)

The taboo word *warg*, never explicitly used for Christ in the *Hêliand*, is the appellation of Judas, the archoutcast:

> that he imu selbon thô simon warhta
> hneg thô an heru-sêl an henginna
> *warag* an wurgil endi wîti gekôs. (5166–5168)
>
> (that he worked the rope for himself
> hung on the sword-rope hanging
> *warg* in the noose and chose his punishment.)

The word *heru-sêl* deserves careful attention. *Heru-* is cognate with Go. *hairus*, ON *hjorr*, and OE *heoru*, all meaning 'sword.' In OS, it is attested only as a bound morpheme, the first component of a compound, as also *Hêliand* 5326, where *heru-bendiun*, 'sword-bonds,' refers to Christ's fetters. Both the OE and ON forms also occur almost exclusively in compounds and are classified as "poetic" words. OS and OE show several parallel compounds; for example,

> OS *heru-drôrag* 'bloody with sword wounds'
> OE *heoru-dreorig* "
>
> OS *heru-grim* 'sword-grim'
> OE *heoru-grim* "

The word is particularly important because of its association with binding and with *warg*: the one time Grendel is explicitly called *warg* (*Beowulf* 1267), the expression is *heorowearh*, lit. 'sword-*warg*.' Perhaps the meaning of the line in the OE "Dream of the Rood" in which *warg* occurs, "heton me *heora wergas* hebben," is, then, "they made me bear 'sword-*wargs*.' " Used in connection with *warg*, the 'creature of strangulation,' the word *heru/heoru* seems to indicate the original dual nature of the *warg*'s punishment: he was hanged and stabbed.

The Judas passage consists almost entirely of Gmc. legal terms, particularly those meaning "bind, strangle"; besides *hneg* and *henginna*, one has

5166: *simo* 'rope' < I-E *sei- 'bind'
5167: *sêl (heru-sel)* 'rope'
5168: *warag*: *wurgil* 'noose' < I-E *wergh- 'strangle'
(= *wer- 'bind' + suffix)

That these words are part of a deep-rooted Gmc. legal vocabulary is shown by a strikingly similar word cluster in ON, in a passage dealing with the oath breaker as *varg* (*Sigrdrífomál* 23):

þat raeđ ek þér annat, at þú eiđ né sverir
nema þann er sađr séi;
grimmar símar ganga at trygđrofi,
armr er vára vargr.

(Secondly, I advise you not to swear an oath
unless it is true;
grim bonds follow breach of contract
accursed is the *varg* of vows.)

Here, the same I-E roots are represented:

simar (*simi*) 'bonds' < I-E *sei- 'bind'
sverir (*sveria*) 'swear' < I-E *(s)wer- 'bind'
vargr < I-E *wergh- 'strangle'
var 'vow' < I-E *wer- 'bind'

H. Wagner, in his analysis of the legal terminology of this passage,[22] noted that ON *simi* and its cognate OI *sin* 'sling' are also more distantly related to ON *seiðr* 'magic,' that is, that which binds magically. Wagner has called attention to an important Celtic parallel to the bonds that bind the Gmc. breaker of vows: the collar (*sin*) of Morand Mac Main, the mythical Irish lawgiver, which tightens about the neck of the guilty man and chokes the life out of him. Another I-E analogy is the Vedic god Varuṇa, who binds the liar and outlaw with slings and whose name may be analyzed as the I-E root *wer- 'bind' + embodiment suffix. The wide distribution of binding as a legal con-

[22] Heinrich Wagner, "Studies in the Origins of Early Celtic Civilisation," *Zeitschrift für celtische Philologie* 31 (1970), 1–58, esp. pp. 2 ff.

cept shows that the idea of a serious crime being a breaking of one's ties with society is extremely ancient in I-E cultures, and that the *warg* as the bond breaker who is bound and strangled is part of an archaic legal and religious *Wortfeld.*

In ON mythology, the deity who corresponds in name and function to Varuṇa, the goddess Var, personification of oath and punisher of oath breakers, remains a shadowy figure, mentioned only by Snorri (*Gylfaginning* 34). The binder god of the ON pantheon is, of course, Odin, lord of the hanged and gallows burden, patron of outcasts and leader of the *berserkir*, frenzied, shape-changing warriors, Odin, who binds his foes with battle fetters and with *seiðr*. Odin differs ideologically from other binder gods in his essential amorality: he delights in strife between kinsmen and urges men to break their vows. The strangled *warg* belongs to him more from a sense of "like seeking like" than in punishment. His very name indicates his nature; Adam of Bremen's "Wodan, id est furor"[23] stands fast (despite H. Wagner's spirited attack):[24] Odin is the embodiment of every form of frenzy (Gmc. **Wōðanaz* is the I-E root **wat*- 'ecstatic' + embodiment suffix), from the insane bloodlust that characterized the werwolf warriors who dedicated themselves to him,[25] to erotic and poetic madness.

The putrefying corpse of a *varg* on the gallows is the emblem of Odin's power and the sign of his presence:

> Miǫk er auđkent, þeim er til Óđins koma
> salkynni at siá:
> *vargr* hangir fyr vestan dyrr,
> ok drúpir ǫrn yfir. (*Grímnismál* 10)
>
> (Odin's hall is easy to recognize:
> a *varg* hangs before the western door,
> an eagle droops above.)

The gallows is "*warg*-tree" in OE, ON, and OS. The "wind-cold *warg*-tree" of *Hamðismál* 17 corresponds to the above description of Odin's hall:

> Fram lágo brautir
> fundo vástígo
> ok systur son sáran
> á meiđi,
> *vargtré* vindkǫld
> vestan boeiar.

[23] Adam of Bremen, *Gesta Hammaburgensis Ecclesiae Pontificum*, Bk. LV, par. 26.

[24] Wagner, *op. cit.*, pp. 46 ff.

[25] Not only the *berserkir*, but also fanatical warriors of continental Gmc. tribes, who were clearly worshiping a *Wōđanaz, a god who was the essence of frenzy, as early as the first century B.C.

(Further they went on their fateful way,
and they saw their sister's son hanging on the gallows,
on the wind-cold *warg*-tree west of the fortress.)

Odin himself hangs nine nights on the gallows tree:

Veit ek, at ek hekk	(I know that I hung
vindga meiđi á	on the wind-swept gallows tree
naetr allar níu,	nine full nights
geiri undađr	wounded with a spear
ok gefinn Óđni	and given to Odin
sjálfr sjálfum mér	myself to myself
á þeim meiđi,	on that tree/gallows
er mangi veit	of which no man knows
hvers hann af rótum renn. (*Hávamál* 138)	from what roots it rises.)

Thus, of the three shape-changing ON divinities—Odin, Loki, and Fenrir—Odin is the most complete *warg* figure: he is both magical binder and bound/hanged himself. It seems likely that Loki, Odin, and Fenrir are all facets of the same outlaw deity, with Loki and Fenrir representing the negative aspects of the binder wolf-god. Certainly, Loki and Fenrir are so closely related and their binding is so similar that Fenrir must be regarded as Loki *í trolls hami* (in monster shape), as F. Ström has convincingly argued.[26] The frenzy of the *warg* Fenrir makes him a danger to gods and men; he must be bound, even if it costs the hand of the god of justice, Týr, that is, even if it means swearing a false oath, which is the act of a *warg*, itself deserving the punishment of binding. Although Týr is not bound or outlawed for his deception, he is henceforth known as "Wolf-joint." The god of oaths bears the visible mark of the vile werwolf, and justice is fatally compromised.

Dumézil has discovered a striking analogue to the ON binding of Fenrir: a late Iranian version of the binding and riding of Ahriman by the hero Taxmoruw.[27] By means of a trick, the demon breaks loose and swallows Taxmoruw; only by pretending to be interested in pederasty can the hero's brother retrieve his body from the demon's belly. In analogy to Týr's loss of his hand, the brother's arm—the one that entered the demon's anus—becomes silvery white and stinking, and the brother voluntarily exiles himself so that others will not become polluted. This version offers insight into aspects of the myth which may have been intentionally suppressed in the late ON version of Snorri. This is an almost incredible accumulation of motifs connected with the *warg*: wolf, binding, outcast, as well as disease and sexual perversion. These last two aspects are, as will be seen in the

26 F. Ström, *Loki: ein mythologisches Problem* (Göteborg, 1956).
27 See Dumézil's paper in this volume.

discussion of other monstrous *wargs* in Gmc. poetry and mythology, essential traits of the *warg*.

2. *Monsters and Diseases*

It should be obvious by this time that the true prototype of the Gmc. outlaw is not Robin Hood or Gisli, but Grendel. This monster and parent of monsters, exiled with the kin of Cain, this fen dweller, is not only expressly called a *warg* (*heorowearh, Beowulf* 1267), but is the offspring of a female *warg* (*grundwyrgenne, Beowulf* 1518). In the lines that conjure forth the shapes of Grendel and his mother in their dreadful domain (1345–1360), the two monsters are clearly shape-changers: one of them had *idese onlicnaes*, "the form of a woman," the other "walked outcast in man's likeness" (*weres waestmum*). Surprisingly, Lehmann states in his discussion of Gmc. legal terminology in the ON *Edda*: "The position of the Gmc. outlaw was so remote from the *Beowulf* author's Christian conception that he must be refashioned as a monster, the *wearh* Grendel."[28] Lehmann rightly compares this "Christian" use of *warg* with that in the pagan passage from *Helgakviða Hundingsbana* II, 33, in which the werwolf-outlaw feeds, like Fenrir, on human corpses:

> Þá vaeri þér hefnt Helga dauđa
> ef þú vaerir *vargr* á viđom úti
> auđs andvani ok allz gamans
> hefđir eigi mat, nema á hraeom spryngir.
>
> (That would be revenge for Helgi's death,
> if you were a *warg* in the wilderness,
> robbed of wealth and well-being,
> gorged with the flesh of corpses.)

In fact, far from being remote, the idea of being cast out as a hideous beast, the most terrible punishment known to Gmc. society, is still current and immediate enough to provide an essential thematic link between Christian theology and pagan ideology, as in the OE Genesis, where "Caines cynne" ('the kin of Cain') are a "*wergum* folce" (l. 1250), just as the *warg* Grendel is of the "kin of Cain." It is interesting that the example of *varg* was taken from the Helgi poems, for there seems to be a connection between the fertility-bringing sea king Helgi, who causes grain to grow and whose ship is protected by iron against witches, and the legendary kings of the Anglo-Saxon royal genealogies as presented in *Beowulf* (and in Aethelweard and in Wil-

[28] Winfred P. Lehmann, "Germanic Legal Terminology and Situations in the *Edda*," in *Old Norse Literature and Mythology: A Symposium* (Austin, 1969), pp. 227–242.

liam of Malmesbury),[29] where one has a sequence of rulers whose names seem to mean "Sheaf," "Shield," and "Barley." Despite other etymologies, the most likely meaning for Beowulf is "Barley-wolf."[30] Beowulf, the archetypal solitary warrior-hero, fights the archetypal outlaw figures, the *wargs* Grendel and his mother. There is also a much closer ON parallel: the same struggle of Beowulf against monster mother and son occurs—down to such minute details as the monster's loss of an arm, bloodstained water, and a term for a weapon which is a *hapax legomenon* in both OE and ON (OE *haeft-mece*, ON *hefti-sax*)—in the ON saga of the outlaw Grettir, who also robs graves and battles other demonic beings.[31]

Surely this creature Grendel, *warg* and son of a female *warg*, fen-haunting shapechanger and parent of monsters, bears a strong resemblance to the great *varg* Fenrir, offspring of Loki (a notorious shapechanger whose sex is doubtful) and parent of monsters, one of whom will devour the sun in monster shape (*Vǫluspá* 40). Both are clearly outlaws, both are *wargs*, both are the offspring of *wargs*. In the OE epic, one has a hero with a name meaning "Barley-wolf" who must fight the monsters. And in the Helgi songs one has a hero who is associated with grain and who is protected by iron against witches. And the struggle of Beowulf is clearly part of ON tradition, since the later outlaw figure, Grettir, inherits the epic fight in his saga. Yet the *Beowulf* is too early to have been influenced by the Norse invasion of England, and there is no evidence that the Scandinavians had access to the *Beowulf*. Both versions must go back to an ancient common tradition, ultimately mythological. The similarity between Grendel and Fenrir is striking evidence of such a tradition, but here one is fortunate enough to have continental Gmc. evidence as well: the various agricultural beliefs and practices related to the *Roggenwolf* 'rye-wolf,' subject of Mannhardt's famous study.[32] Mannhardt himself called attention to the similarities between Fenrir and the *Roggenwolf*. The *Roggenwolf* lurks as werwolf in the grainfield and strangles unwary peasants (*Roggenwolf*, 46); children are warned that he will rend them if they go into the field, "Im Korne sitzt der Wolf und zerreisst euch" (*Roggenwolf*, 8). In one instance the *Roggenwolf* is

[29] See Kenneth Sisam, "Anglo-Saxon Royal Genealogies," *Proceedings of the British Academy* 39 (1953), 287–346.

[30] For other etymologies, see R. W. Chambers, *Beowulf* (Cambridge, 1959), pp. 87 ff.

[31] The parallels have been the subject of much dispute. For a discussion of the problems and for literature, see *ibid.*, pp. 48 ff.

[32] Wilhelm Mannhardt, *Roggenwolf und Roggenhund: Beitrag zur germanischen Sittenkunde* (Danzig, 1865).

confused with the *Pilwiz*, a sorcerer who spirits grain away (*Roggenwolf*, 43).[33] Particularly important with regard to Fenrir is that the *Roggenwolf* must be bound: there are harvest customs where the last sheaf is called "Wolf" and treated as the embodiment of the demon, sometimes even shaped like a wolf. There is even the association of iron with capturing the wolf, as in a children's song recorded in several versions by Mannhardt, where the *Roggenwolf* is caught between two iron stakes (*Roggenwolf*, 33):

> De bösen Wülfe sünt gefangen
> Twischen twên îsern Stangen.

Like Grendel and Fenrir, the *Roggenwolf* is seen as the offspring of a monster mother, the *Roggenmutter* or *Kornmutter*. Mannhardt noted that the *Kornmutter* has iron breasts, and that the ON Angrboda, mother of many monsters and in one myth Loki's wife and mother of Fenrir, sits in "Ironwood" (*Roggenwolf*, 46). Mannhardt was, however, content to make these comparisons, while refusing to make any claims for the identity of Fenrir and the *Roggenwolf*. It is, of course, difficult to compare motifs woven into a complex mythology with no surviving ritual, preserved in ON texts, with remnants of German agricultural customs collected in the nineteenth century, but the correspondences are very real and important, and, as I hope to show, are founded on deep-rooted agricultural mythology. The key to the inter-relationship of werwolf/*warg* as outlaw and as agricultural demon is the identity of the *Roggenwolf*.

Oddly enough, Mannhardt never positively identified the *Roggenwolf*, but he defined it in vague terms as "ein Wesen, . . . das im Getreide seinen beständigen Aufenthalt hat, . . . vom Korn sich nährt, kurzum in irgend einer notwendigen und engen Beziehung zum Saatfelde steht" (*Roggenwolf*, 10), "a being that dwells in the grain . . . eats the grain, in short, which has some kind of necessary and intimate relationship with the grainfield." He comes very close to a definition when he mentions *Wolf* and *Wolfszahn* as names for ergot, as well as for excrescences on trees, but treats these as metaphorical terms for the traces left by the abstract demonic being (*Roggenwolf*, 17). Yet, all of Mannhardt's painstakingly collected data are doomed to remain a chaotic mass of seemingly interminable and intolerably quaint agricultural sayings, unless the *Roggenwolf* is concretely identified as

---

[33] In Roman tradition, the werwolf-sorcerer spirits corn away to other fields; cf. Vergil, *Eclogues* VIII, 95 ff., where Moeris transforms himself by means of herbs, then engages in three typical werwolf activities: he lurks in the woods, calls forth spirits from the grave, and charms the crops.

ergot, the actual grain disease itself, as well as the mythological projection. Ergot has no visible origin, springs from no known roots, destroys the grain, and yet is phallic in appearance and actually increases the volume and weight of the harvest.[34] The appearance and nature of the disease suggested an animal as symbolic embodiment and mythological projection: the wolf. The overwhelming dependence upon rye as a cereal grain in the Gmc. areas, combined with the propensity of rye to ergot infection, would account for the enormous mythological importance of the *Roggenwolf*.

It might seem that, in discussing the monsters Grendel and Fenrir and in connecting them with the continental Gmc. *Roggenwolf*, the basic focus on Gmc. *warg* has been lost. Yet this is not the case. Grendel and Fenrir are explicitly *wargs*, and the word *warg* itself has a range of disease meanings in Gmc.; for example,

OHG *warch* 'pus'
MHG *warc* 'pus'
OE *weargbraede* 'skin disease'
OHG *uuurgida* 'bruise'
uuarahga 'putridity'
uuorahc 'sanies'

MHG *warc* is used in *Iwein* 4924 instead of the expected *getwerc*, 'dwarf':

sî treip ein *warc* der sî sluoc	(a *warc* was driving them before him
mit sîner geiselruten	striking them with a whip
daz sî über al bluoten.	so that they bled all over.)

Warc is usually regarded as a short form of *getwerc* (which can mean 'swelling, knot in wood,' as well as 'dwarf'), but the word *warc* may have been deliberately substituted because of its more sinister connotations and because of its more vivid disease associations: the *warc* is striking his victims and leaving bloody, running wounds. This idea of bloody, running sores is borne out by the use of *warch* to describe the horrible disease that afflicted King Herod in Priester Wernher (4967 ff. and 4981 ff.):

Herodes begunde siechen	(Herod began to be so ill
daz uf den bette ziechen	that bloody pus dripped on the
swebet blut v *warch*	bed coverings
diu sucht diu wart also starch	the sickness became so great
daz er gar fulen began.	that he began to rot.
. . . .	. . . .
Mit den nageln zart er die hut	with his nails he tore at his skin
er was vil armeklichen lut . . .	he screamed pitiably . . .

[34] The classic account of ergot is Rudolf Kobert, "Zur Geschichte des Mutterkorns," *Historische Studien aus dem Pharmakologischen Institute der Universität Dorpat* [now Tartu] 1 (1889), 1–47.

er brach sich allenthalben
uzzen unt innen
do entwichen im die sinne.
michel wart sin unzucht
do dewanch in oh diu tobesucht
daz er armer v unreine
ab einem hohen staine
sih selben erualte
da nam in der tieuel ze gewalte.

he was decaying completely
outwardly and inwardly
he then lost his senses.
his delirium grew very strong
and his frenzy drove him
to cast himself down from a high cliff,
the poor unclean wretch,
then the devil took him for his own.

A few lines later (5025 ff.) the moral is stated:

> Also muz es allen den *ergen*
> die got wellent widersten
> unt siner ordenunge.
>
> (This is the fate of all depraved creatures
> who wish to rebel against God
> and his order.)

Because Herod's misdeeds have placed him beyond the pale of humanity, he is visited with the visible sign of his inward corruption: a monstrous, itching, pussy, bloody skin ailment that drives him mad. The term *arg* is important here; it has in this Christian context the meaning of moral depravity.

A remarkable OHG parallel is the disease description in the *Gospel Harmony* of Tatian (92, 2), where a word based on *warg* is used:

domine miserere filio meo . . . lunaticus est et Spiritus adpraehendit eum, allidet et spumat et stridet dentibus et arescit et male patitur, nam saepe cadet in ignem et crebro in aquam et subito clamat et dissipat eum et vix descedit dilanians eum.

trohtin milti mînemo suno . . . mânôdseoh ist, inti *uoruuergit* geist fâhit inan inti cnusit inti scûmit inti gisgrimmôt zenin inti dorrêt inti ubel druœt, mittiu her ofto fellit in fiur inti ofto in uuazzer, inti sliumo ruofit inti zibrichit inan inti cûmo aruuîzit slîzanti inan.

> (Lord have mercy on my son, for he is a lunatic and possessed by an evil spirit. He strikes out at things, froths at the mouth and gnashes his teeth and is consumed and suffers greatly, for he often falls into fire and water and he cries out suddenly and he is growing weak, for this torment scarcely ever leaves him.)

The Latin "Spiritus adpraehendit eum" ("He is possessed by an evil spirit") is rendered by two expressions in OHG: "*uoruuergit*/geist fâhit inan." What is undoubtedly a description of an epileptic fit is transformed in OHG into a comparison with the actions of a *warg*, a frenzied werwolf.

In the MHG epic *Eneide* of Heinrich von Veldeke, the great underworld dog Cerberus is a diseased *warg* (3265–3267):

Cerberus der arge	(Cerberus the *arg*
und alle sine *warge*	and all the *wargs*
die an hem hiengen.	who follow him.)

Cerberus is a hideous monster who emits intense heat and a pestilential stench from nose and ears. His coat is very rough and it is covered with live serpents which hiss and writhe. Large quantities of hot, sour, stinking foam drip from his jaws. Cerberus is, of course, a devil figure; the devil in dog or wolf shape is a commonplace of later literature, as are his traits of blackness and pestilential odor. But the characteristics of frenzied, diseased *warg* connect him with pagan belief, with the ON Fenrir and with the *Roggenwolf*. The physical symptoms of Cerberus's illness (*Eneide* 3198 ff.) are very similar to those described in Priester Wernher and in Tatian, if one omits the serpents: insane frenzy, intense heat, stench, slavering, rough skin, putridity. And again, as in Priester Wernher, one has the association of *arg* with *warg*.

Another term for disease is used of Cerberus: he is called "des dûveles galle." MHG *galle* 'gall,' like OE *gealla*, signified a sore, or skin abrasion or swelling on plants and animals, caused by disease. In the MHG epic *Parzival* of Wolfram von Eschenbach (7590 ff.), Sigune uses similar disease terminology in cursing Parzival:

gunerter lip, verfluochet man	(dishonored, accursed man
ir truogt den eiterwolves zan . . .	you bear the tooth-mark of the pus-wolf . . .
da diu galle in der triuwe	since the gall-apple has so recently
an iu bekleip so niuwe . . .	infected your moral fibre . . .
ir lebt und sit an saelden tot.	you live and yet are spiritually dead.)

Although Parzival is not physically afflicted, his moral outlawry and diseased spiritual state is described in terms of physical symptoms. (It is significant that Cundrie, who also curses Parzival, has the outward appearance of a monster—rough snout, bear's-ears—and is inwardly pure.) The term *eiterwolves zan* may be compared with the phrase in the *Servatiuslegende* (3220 ff.):[35]

im durchbrast diu gelwe hut	(his yellow skin burst,
warc unt *eiter* dar uz ran	*warc* and *eiter* ran out
liepliche farwe er gewan.	he regained his fair complexion)

Warc and *eiter* both mean 'pus,' but *warc* of course also means werwolf. A hypothetical **eiterwarc* would correspond to the *eiterwolf* of *Parzival*. The expression "eiterwolves zan" is close to a modern German term for ergot of rye, *Wolfszahn*. It seems likely that *wolf* is a

[35] Edited by J. Haupt in *Zeitschrift für deutsches Altertum* 5 (1845); see p. 172 for quotation.

substitute for *warg* in both these expressions, cf. the OE medical term *weargbraede*, which stands for a number of ugly, festering skin diseases. Shortly after *eiterwolves zan*, another disease image occurs: "*diu galle* in der triuwe." It was noted that Cerberus, the *warg*, is called "des dûveles galle" (*Eneide* 3271). This appellation is evidently based on an underlying association of the devil-wolf with disease: *galle* is quite literally a monstrous swelling; *warg*, a bloody, festering disease. The association of *warg* with *galle* may provide a clue to the identity of the mysterious herb *wergulu* in the OE "Nigun wyrta galdor" ("Nine Herbs Charm"):

> Þis is sēo wyrt, đe *Wergulu* hātte,
> Đās onsaende seolh ofer sǣs hrygc
> ondan āttres ōpres tō bōte.
>
> (This is the plant that is named *Wergulu*,
> This the seal sent forth over the high sea
> as a cure for the wrath of another venom.)

Wergulu, if analyzed as **warg-galle*, would compare with the attested OE *wirgung-galere* 'sorcerer.' The sorcerer would cause the disease, the *warg*, by incantation, OE *galdor*. It is a doctrine of Gmc. medicine that witches or sorcerers cause disease in plants, animals, and men by incantation or by shooting disease projectiles (elf-shot).[36] One may compare the use of the word *marentakken* for mistletoe in Dutch and Low German;[37] the word means 'witch-twig': the growth of mistletoe was supposed to be caused by witches riding the branches. The use of *marentakken* as a term for a mysterious, parasitic growth corresponds to the use of the word *wolf* in Germany and the Low Countries to refer to similar growths on trees or swellings on animals. For example, *wolf* alone can mean rust, runners on plants, swellings on trees, a cattle disease (swelling on the back), coarse cloth, a harmful plant or insect, and ergot. *Wölfen* means to lop the dead branches from trees. In compounds, one has *Wolfsgebärde* as a disease name, *Wolfsgeschwulst* 'tumor,' and *Wolfszahn* 'ergot.' The fact that this use of *wolf* corresponds to the use of *warg* in the older languages, cf. OHG *warch*, MHG *warc*, OE *weargbraede*, all having to do with a

[36] Cf. especially the OE charm "Wiđ fǣrstice" ("Against a sudden stitch"):

> This to remedy shot of gods, this to remedy shot of elves,
> This to remedy shot of witch: I will help you.
> Flee there * * * to the mountaintop! . . .

[37] F. Detter's brilliant treatment of the weapon used to slay Baldr provides this important clue as to why mistletoe could have been substituted for a different parasitic plant in the myth as given in Snorri and in the *Vǫluspá* ("Der Baldrmythus," *Beiträge zur Geschichte der deutschen Sprache* 19 [1894], 495–516). In my dissertation I have attempted to show that the original weapon was ergot.

roughness, a bloody festering and swelling of the surface of the skin, suggests that the *wolf* terms are substitutions for an earlier *warg*. The reference to *eiterwolves zan* in *Parzival* seems clearly to be a euphemism for "*warg*'s tooth." *Warg* is rare in MHG except as a term for a coarse, brutal creature (this is the dictionary definition), yet the connotation of disease is still very strong in *Iwein*, where the creature strikes his victims, leaving open, bloody wounds, and in *Eneide*, all aspects of *warg* are fully developed in the slavering, diseased devil-wolf, Cerberus. The *warg* is the causative agent and concrete embodiment of disease, just as the *Roggenwolf* is the supernatural cause and visible grain disease, ergot.

The fact that the diseased *warg* Cerberus is called *arg* is particularly interesting for two reasons: *arg* is associated with *warg* in at least two other relevant texts, and the word *ergot* is still without an established etymology. First, the term used for King Herod and his like, who are afflicted with a disease whose symptoms are blood and with *warch*, a disease that drives Herod insane, is "those who are *arg* (die *ergen*)." Also, in a Scandinavian wolf charm, *varg* is rhymed with *arg*:[38]

Kallar du mig *varg*	(Call me *varg*
så blir jag dig *arg*	and I'll be *arg*.
Kallar du mig af gull	Call me golden,
blir jag dig hull.	I'll be beholden.)

The term *arg*, best known as a legal term and a deadly insult, an accusation of passive homosexuality in Gmc., is found in ON in metathesized and umlauted forms, *ragr* and *ergi*. It is attested in all the major Gmc. dialects (OE *earh, earg*; OHG *arag, arg*; OS *arug*, Langobardic *arga*) also with umlauted forms, as in the MHG plural above (*ergen*).

In OF, the word *argot* is attested in the twelfth century in the plural, with the meaning 'spur.' OF *argaise* definitely means 'worthless growth,' as in a directive from Valenciennes (1445) ordering that one should deduct from the price paid for grain for the following: *rouisses* (rotten parts), *espines* (thorns), and *argaises*. From the nature of the other things mentioned, *argaises* could well be ergot. F *ergot* itself means 'small portion of a dead branch on a fruit tree' as well as 'spur on an animal's foot' and 'ergot.' An unumlauted form, *argoter*, means 'to cut off the dead branches of a fruit tree,' thus corresponding

[38] Jöran Sahlgren, "Förbjudna namn," *Namn och Bygd* 6 (1918), 11–12, quotes this saying (without giving a source). Cf. also the insulting "*argan* . . . goðvarg" of the *Kristnisaga*.

in meaning to G _wölfen_. The Walloon adjective _årgoté_ has the meaning 'rusé, malin' (deceitful, wicked). Morphologically, the adjective _årgoté_ is the unumlauted form of F _ergoté_ as used in _seigle ergoté_ 'diseased rye.' I posit an original adjective _argoté/ergoté_ with a later specialization of forms: the umlauted form being limited to plant disease, and the nonumlauted form conveying an abstract sense of moral depravity and being the linguistic and semantic equivalent of G _arg_. Thus, _ergot_ would be an umlauted form based on Gmc. _arg_, an ancient term of abuse, an accusation of shape and sex change, an accusation made most often in ON mythology against the two werwolf shapechangers (and sex changers), Odin and Loki. Like _warg_ and the word _wolf_ itself, it has very early disease associations, the most important being 'disease of rye.' Whereas it has generally been assumed that the disease meaning of _ergot_ was secondary, coming from analogy to the cock's spur (the meaning of _argot_ in its first attested OF form), hence E "spurred rye" and "cokyll," the evidence indicates that the development was precisely the reverse. Semantically, _ergot_ parallels _Wolf_; _arg_ is a term for depravity used for the ON wolf deities and used at least three times in explicit connection with _warg_.

The linguistic connection may be even closer. The Walloon adjective _årgoté_ has been linked with OF words for 'rye,' cf. Walloon _rgõ_; OWall, _ragon, rugon, regon, rogon_; Provençal _raon_, which reflect a Frankish _*roggo_.[39] If _årgoté_ is a form based on _arg_ and is related to _rgõ_, then Gmc. _arg_ is related to G _Roggen_ 'rye.' Further, it has been argued that the Indo-Iranian name for 'rice' is related to the European word for 'rye.'[40] The general term for 'rice' in Sk. is _vrīhí_, which presupposes _*wriĝhi_. The related Gk. ὄρυζα 'rice' seems to be a borrowing from the Persian. Now, the Thracian word for rye, according to Galen, is βρίζα, which would indicate an older _*wrugya_. The western European words for 'rye' fall into two groups (according to Kluge):

G _Roggen_
OHG _rocho_
MHG _rocke_ } < Gmc. _*ruggn_ < _*rug-n_
OS _roggo_
OFr. _rogga_

39 Cf. Otto Jänicke, _Die Bezeichnungen des Roggens in den romanischen Sprachen_ (Tübingen, 1967), pp. 165–168: _*roggo_. See also standard OF dictionaries for _argaise, regon_.

40 Jarl Charpentier, "Der Name des Roggens," _Arkiv för nordisk filologi_ 46 (1930), 63–73.

E *rye*
OE *ryge* } < Gmc. **rug-iz*
ON *rugr*

The Balto-Slavic forms (cf. Lith. *rugỹs,* ORuss *rŭžĭ*) would derive from a Pre-Gmc. **ruĝhi,* according to Kluge. If the Gmc. forms are borrowings from Balto-Slavic, where *wr-* becomes *r* at a very early period, Kluge's Pre-Gmc. **ruĝhi* could be revised to **wruĝhi.* (Except for the absence of initial *w,* Lith. *rugỹs* is very close to Thracian *βρίζα* < **wrugya*). With restoration of initial **w,* the I-E root for G *Roggen* would then be **wreĝh-,* that is, the *Schwebeablaut* variant of **werĝh-.* It is possible, then, that the Gmc. words for *rye* are linguistically related to Gmc. *warg.*

Heinrich von Veldeke's rhyme, "Cerberus der *arge* / end alle sine *warge,*" is, at any rate, no coincidence. *Arg* is not merely a convenient rhyme for *warg*; it is specifically chosen because both words denote physical and spiritual corruption, a hideous diseased growth on an organism. Cerberus, the pestilential hound of hell, is a magnificent fusion of classical, Gmc., and Christian traditions. (And it is perhaps not insignificant that Veldeke undoubtedly lived near the modern Liège, where the heaviest frequency of Gmc. 'rye' words in OF is found.) As for rye itself, it is a kind of outlaw among cereal grains. The first reference to it in classical antiquity is in Galen, who states that certain people in Thrace make a foul-smelling black bread from a grain called *βρίζα.* Always a staple among Gmc. and Slavic peoples from earliest times, rye was the staple crop of European peasantry because it was much more easily cultivated than the fragile wheat. It yielded dark, inferior flour and was much more susceptible to ergot infection. Thus, literally disease-ridden, dark, "hairier" than wheat, it was associated with spiritual foulness, in contrast with other grains, for example, in these late MHG and early NHG texts:

> all stend hand sich usz dem fluch zogen
> drumb wachzt also der fulkeit rogen.
>
> (because all classes are tainted by original sin,
> the rye of corruption flourishes.)

Luther states:

> nu ist on allen zweifel niemand, der da wolt, das jm rocken auf korn, bose wahr auf gute wahr gelichen wurde.
>
> (surely none would wish to receive rye in return for wheat, bad for good)

The association with evil and corruption is inherent in the Gmc. word 'rye' (*Roggen*) itself, almost independently of the actual grain, for Walloon *rgõ* is used not only for 'rye' but for inferior types of rye, where the F *seigle* 'rye' is used (<L *secale*).

Arg and *warg*, *Roggen* and *ergot*, whatever the exact linguistic relationships may be, are all intimately related to the idea of the raging werwolf as concrete embodiment and as human or demonic cause of disease. The disease and outlaw meanings of *warg* unite in the concept of the monstrous wolf as the agent of destruction, whether he appears as Cerberus, Grendel, Fenrir, or *Roggenwolf*.

CONCLUSION

The continuity of the outlaw as werwolf from Hittite law to medieval Gmc. law and literature, as manifested by the use of Gmc. *warg*, reflects the attitude of the primitive I-E community toward the criminal: the outlaw was originally no popular hero, but one whose deed polluted the community so much that he was considered a monstrous evildoer who had shown himself to be "not human" as defined by his kin group. He who violated the blood tie, through oath breaking, killing of a kinsman, or violation of a sexual taboo, was transformed legally into a wild beast. The archetypal beast for the Indo-European, as for many peoples, was the wolf, the crafty howler, death-dealing foe of domestic existence, feeder on the putrefying flesh of corpses. Paradoxically, the wolf was also the animal embodiment of those qualities most desirable in the I-E warrior: virility, superhuman strength, and frenzy in battle. Many scholars, most notably Wikander, Przyluski, and, of course, Dumézil, have traced the cult of the wolf-god among the warrior brotherhoods of I-E societies and have emphasized the erotic-macabre nature of their initiation rites.[41] In particular, Iranian sources offer striking parallels to Gmc. tradition: the *mairya*, members of a cultic *Männerbund*, are called "two-footed wolves, worse than the four-footed kind"; they are accused of eating carrion, and certain troops of *mairya* are said to be composed of warlocks and witches. An ambivalent attitude toward the *Männerbund* is clearly expressed. The main cultic duty of the young males was to ensure the virility of the community, to defend society against supernatural foes, such as demons of disease, just as their actual duty was military defense against human foes. And yet, because of its essential characteristic of frenzy, the *Männerbund* was a constant threat to society.

Germanists have frequently noted the similarity between *berserk*/warrior and *warg*/outlaw in Gmc. tradition, and yet the exact nature

[41] Stig Wikander, *Der arische Männerbund* (Lund, 1938); Jean Przyluski, "Les confréries de loups-garous dans les sociétés indo-européennes," *Revue de l'histoire des religions* 121 (1940), 128–145; Dumézil (most recently) in *The Destiny of the Warrior* (Chicago, 1970).

of their relationship has never been carefully analyzed. The ON *berserk* stands clearly in an ancient tradition of warriors who were shapechangers, capable of transforming themselves into raging werwolves in battle. It is this common characteristic of magical shapeshifting which links the Gmc. warrior with the *warg* and connects the two with the sorcerer. The sorcerer changed shape to blight crops and render men and animals barren; the warrior underwent a change into animal shape as part of his initiation rite, and the fiercest, most fanatical warriors retained this ability to change shape. This magical change into loathsome raging werwolf, voluntary and temporary for the initiate warrior, was an involuntary and permanent condition for the Gmc. outlaw, the *warg*, doomed by magico-legal pronouncement to wander as a frenzied werwolf in the wilderness beyond the boundaries of the community, in the realm of witchcraft and disease. Etymological and semantic as well as mythological evidence leads to the conclusion that the relationship between the *warg* and disease is not merely one of analogy or association, but that he is the visible embodiment of the forces of plague and destruction, a hideous outcast, a diseased wolf who gratuitously wreaks evil. The Gmc. *warg* is ultimately the human representative of the *Roggenwolf*, the dread and mysterious disease wolf, the supernatural demonic wolf who is the negative aspect of the wolf-god who protects the fertility of the community, allows the grain to grow, and punishes criminals.

Runes, Mandrakes, and Gallows

JEANNINE E. TALLEY, *University of California, Los Angeles*

In his *Deutsche Mythologie* Jacob Grimm sought to identify the Germanic goddess Aurinia, mentioned by Tacitus, with *alrûna* (mandrake).[1] He noted that Aliruna is one who has skill in magic and writing and speaks secret words. The Gothic historian, Jordanes, writing in the mid-sixth century, used a similar word in a passage describing the origin of the Huns.[2] He remarked that women called *aliorunas* were noted as magical women who cohabited with forest fauns. The ferocious offspring of these unions were the Huns. Grimm further associated these women with legendary traditions about the mandrake which preserved some beliefs dating back to the earliest Greek and Roman writers. He concluded that *alrûna* originally referred to wise women who prophesied, and that the term later became the name for the mandrake which perhaps played some part in their ritual.

The relationship between the *alraun* and the mandrake has periodically attracted scholars preceding and following Grimm.[3] In 1912 Alfred Schlosser concluded that the *alraun* was a sacred plant that bestowed fertility, and he suggested that the mandrake, which was reputed to grow from the semen of a gallows victim, was connected

1 *Teutonic Mythology* (New York, 1966), I, 404–405; III, 1202 (hereafter cited as Grimm).

2 Grimm, I, 404, quotes the passage from Jordanes (chap. 24).

3 The earliest attempt to collect scattered information about the mandrake was Schmidel's *Dissertatio de Mandragora* (Leipzig, 1655), and shortly thereafter another dissertation by J. Thomasius (*De Mandragora* [Leipzig, 1669]). The only comprehensive English study of the folklore and medicinal aspects of the plant is Charles Brewster Randolph's "The Mandragora of the Ancients in Folk-Lore and Medicine," *Proceedings of the American Academy of Arts and Science* 40, no. 12 (1905), 487–537, which contains many pertinent citations of classical authors.

to the Old Norse god Odin.[4] Adolf Taylor Starck in *Der Alraun* brought together copious information about the folklore of the mandrake, its literary treatments, and its development in classical botany.[5] After weighing his findings Starck took Schlosser to task for assigning the same meaning to myth and superstition.[6] Starck maintained that one single archaic trait had more meaning than dozens of examples from contemporary folklore, which he considered to be a kind of potpourri of popular beliefs, legends, and mythology which could never be disentangled.[7] His conclusions were that beliefs and legends about this plant began in the Orient, were transmitted to Egypt and North Africa, and came via the Greeks and Romans to Europe where they were assimilated and combined with indigenous materials.[8]

Five decades after Starck's investigation the amount of direct information about Germanic antiquity and myth has not increased, but comparative Indo-European mythology has begun to bridge the gap between fragments of Germanic myth recounted by early historians such as Tacitus and Jordanes and later historical documents and Scandinavian literature of the Middle Ages. By comparing other Indo-European myths with these fragmented accounts it has been possible to begin a reconstruction of Germanic myth. Because of these limitations we can hardly afford to dismiss any potential source. No matter how remote folklore may be considered to be from mythology, no cause is served by rejecting it (as Starck did) as undecipherable because it is the product of a *Lust zum Fabulieren* (delight with inventing fables).[9]

Partly at issue here are methodology and the arbitrary distinctions commonly made among myth, folktale, and legend, which all too frequently lead to the exclusion of valuable material. The tendency has been to think of myth as representative of an older period, as being a vivid and fairly accurate reflection of antiquity, and to consider folklore as a thing of the recent past. For the student of Germanic mythology and folklore, an area where reliable sources for myth are meager and folklore abounds, these arbitrary distinctions are a serious hindrance to investigation. It would be absurd to deny that the vicissitudes of oral tradition do result in accretions, deletions, and crisscross-

[4] *Die Sage vom Galgenmännlein* (Münster, 1912).

[5] *Der Alraun* (Baltimore, 1917) (hereafter cited as Starck). Another extensive treatment of the mandrake is Hugo Rahner's "Die Seelenheilenden Blumen: Moly und Mandragore in antiker und christlicher Symbolik,"*Eranos-Jahrbuch* 12 (1945), 117–239. Rahner's focus, which is in the domain of the psychological symbolism of the mandrake, falls almost entirely outside the scope of this study.

[6] Starck, p. 72.

[7] *Ibid.*

[8] *Ibid.*, p. 79.

[9] *Ibid.*

ing of material, but it is equally injudicious to ignore the stability that is frequently maintained by this type of fluid transmission.

While Starck's study is a concise statement of the complexities of this subject, as well as an attempt to chart the origin and diffusion of the folklore regarding this magical plant, it does not clarify the similarities between the legendary mandrake and Odin's self-immolation on the Yggdrasill as it is related in the Old Norse *Hávamál*. In addition, Starck makes only superficial reference to an etymological relationship between the words *alrúna* and *rune* and offers no explanation as to why the mandrake was known as *alrúna*. Both of these facets are pertinent to Odin's voluntary sacrifice on the gallows.

The derivation of ON *rún* (rune) remains problematical.[10] In addition to Old Norse the word also occurs in Gothic, Old Saxon, and Old High German as *rūna* and Old English *rūn*, all meaning 'secret' or 'advice' and 'letter of the alphabet.' In Celtic languages Old Irish *rūn* and Welsh *rhin* have the meaning 'secret' or 'charm.'[11] The word turns up in numerous ON compounds: *aldr-rúnar* (life-runes), *gaman-rúnar* (pleasure-bringing runes), *biarg-rúnar* (birth runes), *sig-rúnar* (victory runes) and *ǫl-rúnar* (beer runes).[12] These compounds give some idea as to the variety of uses of runic magic. We know from Old Norse literary passages that runes were carved on wood and that, apparently, verbal incantations or charms were said over pieces of wood to engender magical potency in them. A frequently quoted passage from Tacitus, written in A.D. 98, tells that the Germanic peoples practiced augury and divination by lot by lopping off a branch from a fruit tree and making marks on the wood.[13] Whether these peoples were notching the wood with characters of the *futhark*, the runic alphabet, cannot be determined from the description given by Tacitus.

Divination and incantation were practiced in remote antiquity, but it is not known if runic magic—that is, inscribing on wood, stone, and bone with accompanying incantations and charms—is an inherited Indo-European tradition or a Germanic innovation. The literature dealing with magical and religious practices in antiquity remains silent on this point, with one exception: the mention of Buddhists

[10] J. de Vries, *Altnordisches etymologisches Wörterbuch* (Leiden, 1962), pp. 453–454, provides a summary of current views including G. Dumézil's suggestion that *rune* is derived from **wrūnā- (Les dieux des Germains* [Paris, 1959], p. 64).

[11] D. E. Martin Clarke, *The Hávamál* (Cambridge, 1923), p. 37.

[12] Hans Kuhn, *Edda: Die Lieder des Codex Regius nebst verwandten Denkmälern*, II (Heidelberg, 1968), 169.

[13] Alfred John Church and William Jackson Brodribb, trans., *The Complete Works of Tacitus* (New York, 1942), p. 713.

using *phurbu,* a nail, against demons.[14] The nail was usually made of wood and was inscribed with mystic syllables or words. Yet the word itself is Tibetan, not Indo-European.

The oldest Scandinavian inscriptions are thought to date from the third century A.D.[15] Their distribution extends from Iceland down through the British Isles, across Scandinavia, and to the south where one inscription has survived on a marble lion from Athens. Sweden is the richest in runic carvings, but in the four Scandinavian countries runes were used for charms and memorial inscriptions well into the sixteenth century.[16]

When comparing the terms used in various Indo-European languages for the mandrake root, one notices that they fall into two groups. ON *alrúna,* OFr. *alrûne,* and OHG *alrûna, alarûn, alerûna,* as well as modern Danish *alrune,* Swedish *alruna,* Norwegian *alruna,* and Dutch *alruin,* form the *alrūna* group.[17] The second group, in which both Old and modern English, French, Italian, and Latin are present, is derived from Greek *μανδραγόρας* (mandrake).[18] The Greek word has the look of a compound. The first element sounds like the word *μάνδρα* 'stall' or an 'enclosed area,' and the second part of the compound recalls the verb *ἀγείρω* 'gather.'[19] In the fourteenth century the French *mandagoire* became *main-de-gloire* 'hand of glory.'[20] Sometime in the tenth or eleventh century the Latin word occurs in the Anglo-Saxon leechdoms: *Ðeos wyrt þe man mandragoram nemneþ* (the herb that one calls mandrake).[21]

The historical development of the *alrūna* words is unclear. Several OHG glosses use *alrûna* and *alrun* for mandrake.[22] One such gloss is for the Vulgate version of Genesis, 30, the account of Ruben gathering mandrakes for his mother Leah.[23] The occurence of *alrûna* in OHG glosses reveals that at least the concept of a root that conferred fertil-

---

[14] James Hastings, *Encyclopaedia of Religion and Ethics* (New York, 1959), III, 412.

[15] Anders Baeksted, *Målruner og Troldruner, Runemagische Studier* (Copenhagen, 1957), p. 194; also E. O. G. Turville-Petre, *Myth and Religion of the North* (New York, Chicago, and San Francisco, 1964), p. 2.

[16] E. V. Gordon, *An Introduction to Old Norse* (Oxford, 1927), p. 162.

[17] Doornkaat Koolman, *Wörterbuch der ostfriesischen Sprache* (Wiesbaden, 1879; repr. 1965), I, 27; also Jan de Vries, *Altnordisches etymologisches Wörterbuch s.v.*

[18] E. Hoffmann-Krayer und Hanns Bächtold-Stäubli, *Handwörterbuch des deutschen Aberglaubens* (Berlin, 1938–1941), I, 313 (hereafter cited as *HDA*).

[19] Is. Teirlinck, *Flora Magica* (Antwerp, 1830), p. 78.

[20] *HDA*, I, 314.

[21] *The Oxford English Dictionary* (Oxford, 1961).

[22] As Starck points out (p. 30), glosses of the eleventh and twelfth centuries give names such as *friedelwurz* (husband or lover root), *twalm* (narcotic drink), and *minnewurz* (love root), all reflecting the use of *alraun* as a love potion or soporific.

[23] Grimm, III, 1203.

ity was current among the southern Germans in the eighth or ninth century. Certainly the mandrake plant, indigenous to the Mediterranean and the Near East, was not to be found growing in Germanic territory prior to the Middle Ages. Other roots were commonly substituted for the mandrake during the medieval period. The most common of these was briony.[24] Old High German did not borrow the Greek or Latin *mandragora* or the Hebrew *dudaim* when glossing the biblical passage, indicating that the term was present in the language prior to the glossing.

In many respects the most tentative, yet most promising, evidence comes from Scandinavia. When trying to establish a chronology for *alrûna* in Scandinavia, one is confronted with a baffling situation. Several words totally unrelated in meaning could have contributed the initial word of the compound. Rather than outline all the possibilities, it will be more economical to confine the discussion to the most productive and cogent line of reasoning.

ON *ala* (Go. *alan*) means 'to beget, to bear.'[25] The evidence suggests that runic inscription on roots and limbs antedates the Gothic migration. From the preservation of numerous words compounded with *rún* it can be inferred that runic magic became highly specialized. Since birth is a matter of deep concern to any society, it is not unlikely that a rune for conceiving or begetting must be of considerable antiquity. The term *ala-rúnar* (birth rune) very plausibly could have been contracted to *alrúna*, but this development is impossible to pinpoint. Conceivably the term could have arisen at any time between the premigration period and fifth or sixth century A.D.

If the word is as old as I have suggested, which implies it was common to all Germanic languages, then the question arises: Why is English the only Germanic language, aside from Gothic, which has no attested forms of *alrūna*? The Goths are more easily dismissed because of the limited number of Gothic texts than the Germanic tribes who migrated to the British Isles. For the British Isles there are only two possibilities: either they had the word in their vocabulary and replaced it, or it was not part of their vocabulary. At first glance the alternative that *mandragora* replaced *alrūna* does not seem highly probable, since in general a culture does not borrow a word if it already possesses a word for a certain item. In this instance, however, there is a circumstance that could have upset this general rule.

As early as the eighth century the learned medical practices of Greece and Rome were beginning to penetrate the British Isles.[26] By

---

24 *HDA*, I, 316.

25 Kuhn, *Edda*, II, 14.

26 Probably the richest and most comprehensive historical view of the transmis-

the eleventh century the *Herbarium* of Apuleius Platonicus had been translated into Anglo-Saxon. In this work *mandragora* is given for mandrake.[27] What is essential to note is that classical medical practices were in distinct contrast with earlier medical practices which for the most part were magical. Platonicus emphasized the medicinal uses of the mandrake, not its magical properties.[28] Under these circumstances it is possible that *mandragora* usurped the place of *alrūna*, at least in the learned medical tradition. Whether this is true or not does not lessen the probability that special runes carved on roots and known as *alrūna* were used by continental Germans and the Scandinavians at least five to six centuries prior to the Old High German glosses. Consequently *alrūna*, a rune employed to facilitate conception, was easily associated with the mandrake and its name applied to the root, as the Vulgate text of Genesis testifies.

Contextual determinancy as evidenced in the selection of terms in Old English and Old High German is a frequent phenomenon, particularly in regard to plant names. Botany was a considerably less systematic science in classical antiquity than it is today, and the confusion of one plant with another was frequent, especially when knowledge of a particular plant moved from one geographic area or one linguistic group to another. The mandrake was no exception.

From the earliest known reference in Genesis to the present day the mandrake has been reputed to facilitate conception and noted as a drug and an aphrodisiac. It is probably these attributed characteristics that were conducive to the amalgamation of its legendary aspects with Germanic cultic practices and myths. In turn, as mandrake legends from the Middle Ages to the present day attest, the legend shared certain features found in sacrificial rites and myths of pre-Christian Germanic peoples. The primary accretion to the legend is that the mandrake comes from the urine or semen of a thief hanged on the gallows. Both modern German *galgenmännlein* 'little gallow's man' and modern Icelandic *thjofarót* 'thieves' root' are terms for mandrake derived from the legend. Before discussing this feature in greater detail it is necessary to reconstruct the sacrificial rite that is echoed in Odin's self-sacrifice on the gallows.

During recent decades Indo-Europeanists, following the comparative approach established by Georges Dumézil, have contributed overwhelming documentation affirming the antiquity underlying social

---

sion of classical medical learning to the British Isles and the transmission of medical practices is presented by Wilfrid Bonser, *The Medical Background of Anglo-Saxon England* (London, 1963).

27 C. J. S. Thompson, *The Mystic Mandrake* (London, 1934), p. 57.

28 See *ibid.*, pp. 107–113, for excerpts from Platonicus.

patterns reflected in various Indo-European myths. Several investigations have dealt with human and horse sacrifice among the Indo-Europeans and have alluded to the importance of these ceremonies as fertility rites.[29] Although parallels between the *puruṣamedha* (human sacrifice) of Vedic religion and Scandinavian accounts of sacrificial rites have been demonstrated, there has been little direct discussion or interpretation of Scandinavian rites as having any kind of connection with fertility. The result is not surprising since literary documents have all but obscured anything of sexual or erotic nature. The famous description Adam of Bremen gave of the sacrifices at Uppsala hints obliquely at the sexual nature of the ceremony. At the conclusion of this passage he wrote: "A Christian seventy-two years old told me he had seen their bodies [i.e., the bodies of sacrificial victims] suspended promiscuously. Furthermore, the incantations chanted in the ritual of a sacrifice of this kind are manifold and unseemly; therefore it is better to keep silence."[30]

A literary text that is commonly compared with Adam of Bremen's description is *Rúnatals þáttr* 'rune poem' of the *Hávamál*.[31] Here it is related that Odin hung on the gallows (*meiðr*) for nine nights without food or drink. Odin's self-immolation gave him possession of nine magic songs (*fimbulljóð*) which he gained from Bölthor, a giant. On the surface it is innocuous in respect to sexual matters. But a closer scrutiny of the text and a comparison with earlier Indo-European accounts of ritual sacrifice provide essential clues to parts of this passage which are both elliptical and enigmatic. Two questions that come to mind and must be dealt with: Why does Odin acquire knowledge beneath the gallows? Precisely what is the nature of this knowledge? Customarily Odin's knowledge has been characterized as consisting of spells or charms for curing illness, protecting men in combat, and settling disputes, and of countermagic against witches. What has remained deeply embedded and so obtuse as to be overlooked is the issue of fertility. For our ancestors life was perpetuated through life-giving forces. This concept is vividly disclosed when we observe the symbolic importance of semen in the sacrificial account of the Indic Prajāpati, lord of progeny. Prajāpati sacrifices himself to himself (as does Odin) in the form of a horse. The following description

---

29 These points are well established by Jaan Puhvel, James L. Sauvé, and Donald J. Ward in their articles in *Myth and Law among the Indo-Europeans*, ed. Jaan Puhvel (Berkeley, Los Angeles, and London, 1970).

30 For a translation of the complete passage by Adam of Bremen see F. J. Tschan, *Adam of Bremen: History of the Archbishops of Hamburg-Bremen* (New York, 1959), Bk. 4.

31 The entire text in Old Norse and its English translation are given by Clarke in *The Hávamál*.

of the sacrifice has been given: "... when Prajāpati became the sacrificial horse who was to prepare for his voluntary immolation, he contained his semen for a length of time equivalent to a year. Upon its release, the semen *became* the year . . . , which, we are told, had not yet existed."[32] The same constraint, that is, sexual abstinence, is required of the sacrificial victims in the *aśvamedha* and the *puruṣamedha*. For the early Indo-European peoples, perpetuation of life was not considered to be achieved through the victim's death, but rather through the life-giving forces he remitted during his ritual death, which was an untimely death when his procreative powers were prime. The symbolic cohabitation of the queen with the dead or dying animal in the *aśvamedha* ritual strongly underlines this point.[33] Medical evidence substantiating the reflex-conditional emission in hanged victims has been supplied by Willibald Kirfel.[34] This latter fact, along with the sacrificial victim's enforced chastity for a year prior to the ritual, suggests two very important things: namely, fecundity is not ensured through the death of a victim, but rather through his procreative powers, which—at least symbolically—have achieved maximal strength through sexual constraint. Here also is an explanation for the importance of hanging as the mode of ritual death. There are references throughout the literature that Odin lurked about the gallows and frequently visited such scenes in order to acquire runic knowledge. The concluding section of the *Hávamál* (st. 157) refers to such an instance:

þat kann ek iþ tólpta ef ek sé á tré	I know a twelth: if I see up on a tree
uppi váfa virgilná,	a swaying corpse on a gallows
svá ek ríst, ok í rúnom fák,	Thus I cut, and paint runes
at sá gengr gumi	so that the man walks
ok mælir viđ mik.	and speaks to me.

How are the runes cut and painted? *Grettir Saga* says that the runes were cut in wood and impregnated with blood while charms were recited. In stanza 142 of the *Hávamál* and stanza 13 of *Sigrdrífumál* the runes are cut by Hroptr (Odin). The latter source relates that Hroptr cut them by means of the liquid that had leaked from Heiđdraupnir's skull and from Hoddrofnir's horn. The liquid from the skull undoubtedly refers to blood, but what is the liquid from Hoddrofnir's horn? The name Hoddrofnir is a compound composed of

[32] James L. Sauvé, "The Divine Victim," in *Myth and Law among the Indo-Europeans*, p. 184.

[33] Jaan Puhvel, "Aspects of Equine Functionality," in *Myth and Law among the Indo-Europeans*, p. 161.

[34] *Ibid.*, pp. 161–162.

hod, a poetic word for 'hoard' or 'treasure,' and *drafnir* could be connected with the verb *drafna* meaning 'to break up.'[35] Ultimately the name Hoddrofnir appears to mean something like 'the one who breaks up treasure.' This may be a kenning for 'the one who violates virginity'? The liquid comes from his horn, an archaic term for the male reproductive organ.[36] ON *hornungr*, literally 'youth of the horn,' meaning 'bastard,' serves to confirm the antiquity of this association. I submit that the liquid from Hoddrofnir's horn is semen. Moreover, the first line of stanza 141 of the *Hávamál* is misleading in its usual translation of 'then I became fertile.' Such a translation for the sake of literary and poetic license is permissible, but unfortunately it has led to a broad interpretation which has obscured what may in fact be the central issue, Odin's renewal of his virility, as well as that of the whole community. Clearly, in the grammatical construction *þá nam ek fræváz, fræváz* is a noun, a cognate of Gothic *fraiw* meaning 'seed' or 'semen.'[37] A better translation would be the literal one, 'I took the semen.' There is a strong possibility that the bodily excrescences dropped by the victims (human and animal) during the fertility ritual were employed as blood was in runic inscriptions.[38]

A brief outline of earlier beliefs and legends about the mandrake and their transmission is in order. From biblical references in Genesis and Solomon until the time of Hippocrates there is no mention of the mandrake. Hippocrates (400 B.C.) remarked that a small amount of the mandrake would relieve anxiety but cautioned against the noxious effects of an overdose, which produced delirium.[39] Theophrastus, writing the first Greek history of plants about 320 B.C., included a rather detailed description of the ritual extraction of the mandrake. In collecting the plant one should stand in the direction of the wind and anoint oneself with oil in order to avoid swelling. The roots should be gathered only in the daytime, but before the sun has struck them. Theophrastus considered the mandrake efficacious in treating

35 Among other most constructive comments about this paper, Professor Edgar C. Polomé has suggested that the first element of the Old Norse compound might well correspond to German *Hode* 'testicle.' Although the word is attested only in Old High German and Old Frisian, the existence of an Old Norse word is not excluded. A number of cognates indicating sexual parts lend additional support to this idea.

36 Lester V. Berry and Melvin van den Bark, *The American Thesaurus of Slang* (New York, 1942), p. 457; see also John S. Farmer and W. E. Henley, *Slang and Its Analogues Past and Present* (repr.; New York, 1965), III, 351.

37 Kuhn, *Edda*, II, 63.

38 In his *Die germanischen Runennamen* (Meisenheim am Glan, 1956), Karl Schneider gives a general interpretation of runes and their connection with fertility (see esp. pp. 226–237).

39 Thompson, *Mystic Mandrake*, p. 51.

wounds, erysipelas, gout, and insomnia and noted its use as an aphrodisiac.[40] The Greeks frequently associated the plant with various magical women, just as Grimm suggested had happened among the Germanic tribes. The practice of drawing a magic circle around the plant before its extraction was also known by the Greeks. By the second century A.D. beliefs concerning the mandrake's powers had increased notably. Three contemporaries, Dioscorides, Pliny, and Flavius Josephus, are the main informants for this period. It is probably during this time that the mandrake achieved greater importance, owing primarily to a large corpus of beliefs dealing with the plant's extraction. Flavius Josephus, who wrote a history of the Jews about A.D. 93, appears to be the main source for medieval beliefs and legends. His additions were: (1) one must throw urine or menstrual blood on the plant to extract it from the ground; (2) a dog should be tied to the plant; after pulling up the plant the dog dies immediately, but it is safe for the person to pick it up; (3) the root expels demons.[41]

A legend collected from oral tradition in Schwarzwald and published in 1891 shows how faithfully the classical beliefs have been preserved, as well as the additions that appear to be derived from mythical reflections of human sacrifice.

> If a hereditary thief that has preserved his chastity gets hung, and drops water or seed from him, there grows up under the gallows the broad-leaved yellow-flowered mandrake. If dug up, she groans and shrieks so dismally, that the digger would die thereof. He must therefore stop his ears with cotton or wax, and go before sunrise on a Friday, and take with him a black dog that has not a white hair on him; make three crosses over the mandrake, and dig round her till the root holds by thin fibers only; these he must tie with a string to the dog's tail, hold up a piece of bread before him, and run away. The dog rushes after the bread, wrenches up the root, and falls dead, pierced by her agonizing wail. The root is now taken up, washed with red wine, wrapt in silk red and white, laid in a casket, bathed every Friday, and clothed in a new little white smock every new-moon. Then questioned, she reveals future and secret things touching welfare and increase, makes rich, removes all enemies, brings blessings upon wedlock, and every piece of coin put to her overnight is found doubled in the morning, but she goes to the youngest son, provided he puts a piece of bread and a coin in his father's coffin. If he dies before his father, the mandrake passes to the eldest son, who must in like manner with bread and money bury his brother.[42]

From this legend it is not difficult to see the obvious parallels with Odin's sacrifice. The mandrake grows from the semen of the gallows

[40] *Ibid.*, p. 54.

[41] For an account see Ph. Kohout, *Flavius Josephus Jüdischer Krieg* (Linz, 1901), pp. 778 ff.

[42] Grimm, III, 1202–1203. For the German text see Leander Petzoldt, *Deutsche Volkssagen* (Munich, 1970), pp. 267–269.

victim and in a sense replaces the rune, which, as we have seen, if not indeed coming from the semen very probably was inscribed with it as well as blood. It is noteworthy that the victim is one who has preserved his chastity, a feature shared with the Vedic and Indic sacrificial victims. The legend also tells of the divining powers of the mandrake, certainly reminiscent of the use of runes for the same purpose. Significantly, the folklore and superstitious beliefs of the mandrake tradition rest on archaic modes of thought. The notion of sacrifice is prominent in the method by which one is instructed to gather the plant. According to Flavius, one must first anoint the plant with urine or menstrual blood, both of which are closely associated with fertility.[43] This latter functions as an etiology of the plant's power to confer fertility and embodies the notion of sympathetic magic. The second point made by Flavius (the dog dies after extracting the mandrake) carries with it the idea of sacrifice in order to receive the benefits of the plant. An inversion of the ritual sacrifice has taken place in the folklore. It is no longer a sacrificial victim on the gallows (in classical sources) whose life essence coerces the powers that be to reassure an endless life cycle; rather, one gathers these essences from an anonymous source and the unsuspecting dog forfeits his life for another's gain.

Several conclusions may be postulated on the basis of the evidence at hand. During the prehistoric period the *alraun* was connected with fertility magic. The exact nature of the *alraun* is unknown and is perhaps unknowable. One could conjecture that it might have been an amulet worn by those desiring offspring. As an amulet it might well have been carved into a human figure, not at all unlikely when we recall the importance of sympathetic magic. It could have been a root or a piece of wood on which magic symbols were inscribed, and, possibly, wise women acted as the custodians of fertility magic which included the *alraun*.

The undeniable similarities between human and horse ritual sacrifices and Odin's hanging point to an Indo-European fertility rite that persisted into the Christian period in Scandinavia.

During the prehistoric period the *alraun* and the sacrifice were independent of each other. The former, if indeed it was a type of

---

[43] In *HDA* (III, 1472) there is an article on urine as the seat of life forces (*Lebenskraft*). Throughout folklore, and in folk medicine in particular, there is constant reference to blood, spittle, urine, and semen as the life essences. There is, moreover, frequent confusion between urine and semen. One could no doubt find a medical basis (i.e., certain infections affect the urine) for some confusion between the two fluids. J. Bourke, *Scatalogic Rites of All Nations* (New York, 1891), points out numerous instances in which urine is drunk to promote fertility. For these reasons it is no surprise to find urine and semen associated with the mandrake.

fertility magic, was a custom participated in individually; the latter was a ritual in which the society took part as a group.

Starck's thesis that the dissemination of mandrake beliefs and legends was from east to west and then northward is reasonable and conforms with the general geographical pattern of cultural movement. His conclusion that the motif of a magical plant with human form which grew from the semen of a sleeping or dead man had its origin in Mesopotamia or Persia raises an interesting question. Is this motif the folkloric expression of a sacrificial ritual? In view of what we know about the Vedic and Indic rituals this possibility is very interesting. If the mandrake motif is a secondary manifestation of the ritual sacrifice, then a curious thing happened. As we have seen, the mandrake became *alrūna* among the Germanic peoples because both the plant and the *alraun* imparted fertility (and one or both had an anthropomorphic shape). Simultaneously the motif of the plant's origin from the seed of a sleeping or dead man was easily associated with the Indo-European ritual sacrifice as practiced in Scandinavia. Somewhere the motif was significantly qualified by the notion that the mandrake grew from the seed of a gallows victim.[44] This trait is likely the legacy of the Indo-European sacrificial ritual from the Germanic area which merged with mandrake legends and beliefs from classical sources.

---

44 Schlosser (*op. cit.*) maintained that this origin of the mandrake was first given by Avicenna in the tenth century. Starck quoted Schlosser but said that he was unable to find the instance cited by Avicenna. What Schlosser in fact said was: "Vor allem kennt er [Avicenna] eine gar wunderbare Abstammung der Pflanze [mandrake]." Immediately following this statement Schlosser said: "Brunfels berichtet in seinem Kräuterbuch [*Herbarum vivae eicones* (Strassburg, 1530), App., p. 184], das dem 15. Jahrhundert angehört nach ihm also: 'Die Alraunwurzeln werden gegraben unter dem galgen, kumen von der Natur (sperma) eines harnenden Diebs' " (p. 29). (Before others he [Avicenna] knew an entirely fantastic origin of the plant [mandrake]. Brunfels reported in his *Pharmacopoeia*, which belonged to the fifteenth century, according to him there: 'The *Alraun* is dug under the gallows, comes from the sperm of a urinating thief'). A search through *Flores Avicenne* revealed no information of this nature. The most likely place for this attributed motif to show up is in Avicenna's *Al-Qanun* (*Canon*) where, according to Henry Corbin (p. 211), Avicenna devoted an article to the mandrake. The Venice 1507 translation of *Liber Canonis* contains a treatment of the mandrake but has no mention of its origin (Liber II, cap. ccclxviij). It is of course possible that in one of the twenty-eight medieval Latin translations of *Al-Qanun* (Meyer, III, 199) this particular origin might be found, but this possibility is highly unlikely. Ultimately one would have to check Avicenna's original manuscripts.

Georges Dumézil and the Rebirth of the Genetic Model: An Anthropological Appreciation

C. SCOTT LITTLETON, *Occidental College*

A few years ago, in the subtitle of a book (1966) about Georges Dumézil's achievement, I used the phrase "An Anthropological Assessment." In the interim, thanks in some small measure to that book and to the fact that English translations of his works are now beginning to appear, Dumézil's ideas have become better known among my colleagues, and it now seems fitting for me as an anthropologist to express my professional appreciation to Professor Dumézil for having opened up some important new avenues in anthropological theory and method, avenues that I hope my colleagues will not be slow to explore. Hence the subtitle of the present paper.[1]

The particular avenue I should like to explore here leads to what in my opinion is one of the most significant and far-reaching implications of Dumézil's work[2] for my field: the extent to which the genetic

[1] I should like to thank Professor Kees Bolle, who gave the formal response to the first draft of my paper after it was read at the symposium, for his most helpful comments and suggestions, many of which have been taken into account in what follows. A similar debt is owed to the other participants who were kind enough to comment on the initial presentation.

[2] Professor Dumézil's long list of published works is well known and need not be reviewed here. Perhaps the best overview of his central ideas is still *L'idéologie tripartie des Indo-Européens*, Collection Latomus, vol. 31 (Brussels, 1958), although more recent works, such as *Mythe et épopée* I, II, and III (Paris, 1968, 1971, and 1973) and *La religion romaine archaïque* (Paris, 1966), have added new and important dimensions to these ideas. Recent English translations include *Archaic Roman Religion* (Chicago, 1970), *The Destiny of the Warrior* (Chicago, 1970), and *From Myth to Fiction* (Chicago, 1973). For a general introduction and appraisal of

model[3] can fruitfully be applied beyond the narrow confines of historical linguistics. But before discussing this matter, it is necessary to comment briefly upon the several models traditionally utilized, at least in this century, by anthropologists in approaching the explanation of extralinguistic, cross-cultural parallels.[4]

For the most part, when confronted with a set of such parallels, anthropologists have brought to bear one of two basic models. For my purposes these may be labeled the *independent-invention model* and the *diffusion model.* The independent-invention model is fundamentally predicated upon the assumption that common conditions, especially ecological conditions, will produce generally similar cultural features. As developed in modern times by Steward, Wittfogel, Service, and others, this model has yielded impressive results and has permitted us to make important generalizations not only about the relationships among specific cultural sequences, but also about the nature of cultural evolution per se.[5]

The diffusion model, which had its modern origins in the German geographical school of the nineteenth century (that is, in the works of

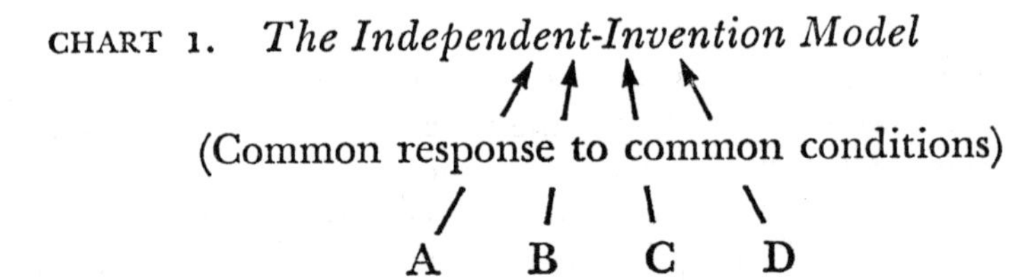

his achievement see my *The New Comparative Mythology: An Anthropological Assessment of the Theories of Georges Dumézil* (Berkeley and Los Angeles, 1966; 2d ed., 1973).

[3] I should emphasize that the term "genetic model" as used in this paper has no reference whatsoever to any biological processes or relationships. Rather, it is used in the more general sense commonly employed by linguists and others to refer to the relationships among linguistic and other cultural traits that derive from a common prototype; cf. *Webster's New Collegiate Dictionary* (p. 345) which defines "genetic" as "Pertaining to the genesis of *anything,* or its mode of development" (italics mine). Cf. also E. Vogt's use of the term "genetic model" in his analysis of the relationships among Middle American cultures, in "The Genetic Model and Maya Cultural Development" in *Desarrollo cultural de los Mayas,* ed. Evon Z. Vogt and Alberto Ruiz (Mexico City, 1964).

[4] It should be pointed out that the several models discussed in this paper, including the genetic model, do not in themselves provide *causal* explanations—in the Aristotelian sense—of the features whose similarity has been noted. Rather, their application to a given body of cross-cultural data is a necessary first step toward such an explanation. They form, as it were, the analytic frameworks within which these data may be ordered so as to understand the character of their temporal and/or spatial relationships to one another.

[5] Julian H. Steward, *Theory of Culture Change* (Urbana, 1955); Karl Wittfogel, *Oriental Despotism* (New Haven, 1957); and Elman R. Service, *Primitive Social Organization* (New York, 1962).

Ratzel, Hahn, the Finnish folklorists, et al.) and was developed in the twentieth century by Boas and his students in the United States and by Schmidt and others in Europe, has also yielded impressive results (I discount, of course, the long since discredited single-diffusionist theories of G. Elliot Smith and Lord Raglan), and it continues to be a major focus of comparative studies. Although a common basic assumption—that items or traits invented or discovered in a given culture tend to be borrowed by other cultures—is operative in all cases, it is necessary to subdivide this model into three fairly distinct subtypes. The first may be termed *the straight-line diffusion model,* wherein a feature invented in culture A is borrowed by culture B and in turn is passed along to cultures C, D, E, and so on, in a linear pattern of movement. The second subtype of the diffusion model may be labeled *the wave diffusion model*: a feature or trait invented in culture A diffuses simultaneously to cultures B, C, D, and so on, the pattern of movement being analogous to that of the ripples caused by a stone dropped into a pond. The third subtype is the *composite diffusion model*: an item invented in culture A, for example, may move in a straight line to culture B and then move simultaneously to cultures C, D, and E. In all instances, of course, it is generally assumed that the item or trait will undergo at least some modification as it moves from culture to culture, no matter who or what the specific agent (or agents) of diffusion may be.

CHART 2. *The Straight-Line Diffusion Model*

A → B → C → D — n

CHART 3. *The Wave Diffusion Model*

B
↑
E ← A → C
↓
D

CHART 4. *The Composite Diffusion Model*

C
↑
A → B → D
↓
E

In brief, then, these are the several models and submodels that have been brought to bear by most anthropologists in their attempts to explain parallels in form and/or function manifested in cultures wholly distinct from one another in time and/or space (see charts 1 through 4). To be sure, the models in question have frequently been combined in a single study, and a few phenomena, such as the parent-child incest taboo, have generally been held to be universal.[6] But with a very few exceptions these two fundamental models and the subvariations thereof form the whole of the methodological arsenal drawn upon by the majority of my colleagues when it comes to the explanation of cross-cultural parallels.

As I indicated at the outset, however, this arsenal need not be limited to independent invention and diffusion. For there is yet another fundamental model that can be brought to bear. It is the *genetic model,* a model fundamentally predicated upon the assumption of a common heritage, that is to say, on the assumption that each member of a given set of cross-cultural parallels bears independent witness to a common prototype that existed in what may be termed a parent culture. At first glance it might appear that the genetic model, predicated as it is upon the assumption of a common prototype, is almost identical with the wave variant of the diffusion model. But the differences are indeed profound. The wave model assumes that the several cultures concerned (A, B, C, etc.) are and always have been distinct from one another, whereas the genetic model assumes that the cultures in question all stem ultimately from a single parent culture and that the features being compared have all developed *independently* through time to the points of their respective attestations. Perhaps two simple examples—the distribution of Christian religious beliefs and practices and the distribution of legal systems based on the common law—may help to clarify this distinction. The spread of Christianity from Palestine to much of the world in the course of the past two millennia involved (and continues to involve) at any given point in time the simultaneous penetration of a number of autonomous cultures, from western Europe to the Pacific; thus the most applicable model is the wave-diffusion model. On the other hand, the distribu-

CHART 5. *The Genetic Model*

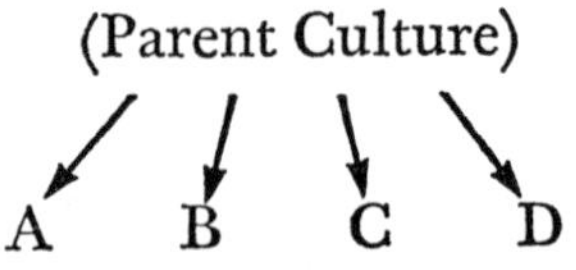

(Parent Culture)

↙ ↓ ↓ ↘

A B C D

[6] E.g., George Peter Murdock, *Social Structure* (New York, 1949), p. 12.

tion of the common law, from Australia to South Africa, involves everywhere cultures that trace their legal systems, at least, back immediately to a single legal system, that of England in the late eighteenth century; thus the relationship here is best characterized as genetic rather than as the result of wave diffusion. The British legal system is the common prototype of the several systems concerned.

The genetic model is by no means new. Indeed, under a variety of labels, it has been the fundamental model for the historical relationships among languages since the inception of historical linguistics at the beginning of the nineteenth century. And in the latter half of that century the *Stammbaum* model, as Schleicher called it, was liberally applied to extralinguistic phenomena, especially in the explanation of mythological and religious parallels, and it became the principal prop of classical nineteenth-century comparative mythology, the mythology practiced by Max Müller, Adalbert Kuhn, and others. I need not remind my readers of the cul-de-sac in which this "old comparative mythology" found itself at the beginning of the twentieth century, a cul-de-sac that has, unfortunately, discredited the extralinguistic application of the genetic model ever since among most anthropologists, folklorists, and historians of religion.

Now, thanks primarily to the efforts of Professor Dumézil, this long-neglected model—neglected, that is, by anthropological folklorists and mythologists—has received new luster; it has been reborn, as it were, in the "new comparative mythology," freed from the naturistic assumptions and dependence upon etymology which sullied it toward the end of the Victorian era. In Dumézil's hands the model in question has yielded a fundamentally new picture of the Indo-European tradition. It has provided the means by which to delineate the common underlying structure of this tradition, to say nothing of the extent to which it has facilitated the interpretation and the understanding of various figures within it, from the delineation of the trifunctional distribution of gods and heroes to the specific interpretation of such diverse characters as Neptune and Heimdallr.[7]

I do not mean to imply that the other two models are irrelevant to the new comparative mythology. Far from it. There are indeed a great many parallels among the ancient Indo-European-speaking communities which cannot be efficiently explained in terms of the genetic model. Perhaps the most obvious example is the close simi-

7 Dumézil's interpretation of the Indo-European character of Neptune, to whom he compares the Iranian figure Apąm Napāt̰ and the Irish hero Nechtan, was made in the course of a seminar given by him on Roman religion at the University of California, Los Angeles, January–March 1971. It is published in *Mythe et épopée* III (Paris, 1973), 19–89. For Heimdallr, see G. Dumézil, "Remarques comparatives sur le dieu scandinave Heimdallr, *Études celtiques* 8 (1959), 263–283.

larity between Greek and Roman religion in the years immediately preceding the Christian era; we have, of course, long known that the likeness was the result of diffusion from Greece to Rome, both directly and, in earlier times, via the Etruscans. Another example wherein the genetic model cannot be applied efficiently is the parallel between the cosmogonic use to which Puruṣa's remains are put in *Rig Veda* 10.90 and the essentially similar use made of Ymir's corpse in the Norse tradition. While it is possible that these two traditions are the result of diffusion from the Near East—the Babylonians, it will be recalled, had a similar tradition about the fate of Tiamat, whose corpse provided the raw materials from which the world was formed (*Enuma Elish* 4.130–140)—it is equally possible that these two traditions reflect a common response to a common circumstance (the presence of a giant's corpse) and that the parallelism between them can best be explained in terms of independent invention.[8] The important point here is that the genetic model is not the most efficient explanatory model in either of these contexts.

There are, thus, a number of factors that must be weighed in deciding which of the several models should be applied in the interpretation of a given body of cross-cultural materials. When the parallels are of a general nature and involve cultures otherwise remote in time and/or space, the independent-invention model is more often than not the most probable of the three. A good case in point is the presence of a primal earth mother–sky father pair who are forcibly separated, a theme found both in the Near East and in Polynesia. The specific differences and distance involved would almost certainly indicate that the Near Easterners and the Polynesians were both reacting to a common environmental feature: the physical relationship between earth and sky, wherein the former occupies a "female" relationship to the latter. The same kind of thing can be said for the general similarity between flood myths in Australia and the Near East; flash floods in arid or semiarid regions are awesome and dangerous, and they are likely, it seems to me, to give rise to similar kinds of myths. Again, it is a matter of a common response to a common condition.

If the parallels are more specific and detailed as to form and/or function, the choice is usually narrowed to either one or another of the variants of the diffusion model or the genetic model. The latter would seem to be least efficient in explaining technological parallels, for it is abundantly clear that technology is the most easily diffused aspect of culture; the evidence for this fact is massive indeed and

---

[8] C. Scott Littleton, "Some Possible Indo-European Themes in the *Iliad*," in *Myth and Law among the Indo-Europeans*, ed. Jaan Puhvel (Berkeley, Los Angeles and London, 1970), p. 391.

need not be recapitulated here. And when diffusion is effectively ruled out by vast distances and the presence of major barriers to movements (e.g., oceans, deserts, high mountains), the independent-invention model is usually preferable to the genetic model, even when the similarities are fairly specific. Indeed, similar ecologies usually produce closer similarities in technology than in any other aspect of culture (see above); the presence of remarkably similar irrigation systems in pre-Columbian Peru and most of the arid river valleys of the Old World (Thor Heyerdahl to the contrary notwithstanding) is an excellent example.

But when the parallels one has noted are specific as to form and/or function, when they are drawn from widely separated cultures (but not so widely separated as to preclude migration from a common intermediate region over a reasonable period of time), and when they concern social and ideological features, then the genetic model becomes much more probable, especially in the context of an established linguistic relationship like the one that obtains among those languages, ancient and modern, which we refer to as Indo-European. In such contexts, to insist that similarities in the character of divinities or heroes, to say nothing of rituals and other magico-religious phenomena, can be the result only of diffusion or of independent invention, as some anthropologists are still wont to do, or to assert that the genetic model does not apply outside purely linguistic contexts,[9] is unlikely and unscientific in the extreme. For, as Dumézil and his colleagues have amply demonstrated, the ancient Indo-European-speaking communities, distributed as they were from Ireland to the Bay of Bengal, abound in circumstances wherein sheer distance and the presence of intervening non-Indo-European peoples clearly preclude borrowing, and where the environments are so dissimilar (e.g., Ulster and the Punjab) that a "common response to common ecological conditions" is effectively ruled out. All the foregoing is reinforced when the parallels in question fall naturally into a *common structure*, as is true of most of the parallels Dumézil has isolated.

In short, in some contexts the most scientifically relevant model is the genetic one, and these contexts are not, of course, limited to the ancient Indo-European-speaking community. On the contrary, such contexts can be found within any widespread speech community. The Bantu family in sub-Saharan Africa should offer excellent opportuni-

[9] This observation is not based primarily upon anything specific that has been published—indeed, the genetic model has largely been ignored in discussions of the relative merits of diffusion and independent invention (cf., for example, M. Harris, *The Rise of Anthropological Theory* [New York, 1968], pp. 377–378)—but rather upon discussions with several of my colleagues in the course of the past decade.

ties for those scholars who would apply the genetic model à la Dumézil, for the orders of distance and the differences in environments (e.g., from the Congolese forests to the grasslands of South Africa) are comparable to those obtaining in the ancient Indo-European-speaking domain. The same thing may be said for the Uto-Aztecans in the New World, who inhabit regions as varied and as distant from one another as the Valley of Mexico and the San Joaquin Valley of California; in fact a common Uto-Aztecan ideological structure has begun to emerge, one predicated upon quadripartition rather than upon tripartition.[10]

In addition to the fundamental assumption, noted earlier, that a set of cognate cultural features derives from a common prototype, the genetic model is also predicated upon several other basic assumptions. One of them is that the speakers of a common, mutually intelligible language will necessarily share a common culture, at least when it comes to such basic features as religion and world view. I think few of my colleagues would deny this today, thanks to the efforts of Whorf and others and the emergence in recent years of ethnosemantics and other linguistically oriented methodologies. It is also necessary to assume that elements of the common culture, though modified by altered circumstances, will persist among the several speech communities that split off from the parent culture and that each of these communities will exhibit a patterned uniqueness. Indeed, given more intensive research, it should be possible to isolate systematic distributional patterns analogous to the isoglosses characteristic of a set of genetically related dialects and languages.[11] Such a project would seem to be especially relevant for genetically related ideologies, and I suggest that serious attention be given to the matter by my fellow anthropological folklorists.

It follows, then, that *no* set of genetically related ideologies, social systems, or whatever, will ever present a mirror image, so to speak, of their prototypes in the parent culture.[12] As I have noted elsewhere,

---

10 This observation is based upon the preliminary results of an investigation of Nahuatl and other Uto-Aztecan materials now in progress.

11 I am indebted to Dorothy D. Haas, of the Program in Indo-European Studies, University of California, Los Angeles, for this most interesting suggestion.

12 There is, perhaps, a subtype of the genetic model which might be labeled, for lack of a better term, the *drift variant*. It would be applicable to situations where no clear prototype can be reconstructed, but where a circumstance—social, environmental, or the like—which affected the parent culture can be said to have set in motion a common drift, as it were, among the daughter cultures. Dumézil's theme of a "war between the functions," in which representatives of the priestly and warrior strata (first and second functions) defeat representatives of the agricultural stratum (third function) (e.g., the Sabine War, the war between the Aesir

several basic processes would seem to be at work here: one concerns acculturation, a fusion of cultures which necessarily occurs when any two (or more) autonomous communities come into sustained face-to-face contact.[13] Thus, when the first Indo-European-speaking bands migrated into eastern and central Europe, they necessarily entered into an acculturative relationship with the indigenous "Old European" population—the archaelogical record provides good evidence of this fusion of cultures during the third and second millennia B.C.[14] —and the end result was a set of traditions (Celtic, Germanic, Italic, etc.) differing widely from those that emerged out of the acculturative situations that developed in north India and Iran. In some situations the effects of this acculturative process will serve to blot out much of the common heritage; the absence of a clear-cut Indo-European ideology among the Greeks and Anatolians is most likely the result of this kind of situation. A second process involves what linguists often refer to as "intrafamilial borrowing," that is, interchange among two or more already distinct albeit genetically related cultures. Perhaps the best single example among the ancient Indo-Europeans would be the previously noted Greek impact upon Rome and the subsequent Roman (or more broadly, perhaps, Greco-Roman) impact upon the Celts. A third process involves what may be called, for lack of a more precise term, the emergent genius of the tradition, considered independently of all outside influences, whether intra- or extrafamilial. I refer here to the internal dynamics that will necessarily affect the social and ideological evolution of any unique culture, regardless of its genetic affiliations or the impact of its neighbors upon it. A good example is the uniquely Roman tendency to historicize the common mythology, which cannot be explained by reference to any common Indo-European tendency, for the process is not commonly encountered elsewhere among the attested Indo-European traditions.[15]

Another assumption underlying the application of the genetic model is that the farther removed in space the parallels, the more likely they are to reflect the character of the prototype. This assump-

---

and the Vanir in Norse myth, and, as I have recently suggested, the Trojan War), may possibly reflect this type of genetic relationship rather than the more usual one involving a prototype. For a discussion of these matters see Littleton, *The New Comparative Mythology*, pp. 12–13; and Littleton, "Some Possible Indo-European Themes in the *Iliad*," pp. 232–233.

[13] Littleton, *The New Comparative Mythology*, pp. 209–212; 2d ed., 233–237; and Littleton, "Toward a Genetic Model for the Analysis of Ideology: The Indo-European Case," *Western Folklore* 24 (1967), 37–47.

[14] Marija Gimbutas, *Bronze Age Cultures in Central and Eastern Europe* (The Hague, 1965), p. 23.

[15] G. Dumézil, *La religion romaine archaïque*, pp. 28–32.

tion has guided linguistic reconstruction for generations, and it is equally—if not more—relevant to extralingustic applications of the model.

Yet another assumption involved in the application of the genetic model is that it may very well be operative in the broader context of the independent-invention or even the diffusion model. For example, one of the most distinctive and best attested Indo-European mythological themes is the theme of the divine twins. It has long been abundantly clear that the Greek Dioscuri, the Vedic Aśvins, the Norse Freyr and Njördr, and so on, all stem from a common prototype and are thus genetically related. Yet as Ward has pointed out, all human communities are characterized from time to time by multiple births, and almost all mythologies reflect in one way or another this universal biological phenomenon.[16] It is therefore necessary to consider this genetically related set of twin figures in the larger context of what Ward terms "universal dioscurism,"[17] to consider the extent to which the Indo-European version thereof manifests elements that have been independently invented elsewhere. It is also sometimes possible to demonstrate that the prototype of a set of genetically related features entered the parent culture via diffusion. For example, the world-tree concept, which occurs in several ancient Indo-European traditions (e.g., the Norse Yggdrasill, the Indian concept of the Tree of Life), may be ultimately derived from a very ancient central Asian concept which diffused to the Proto-Indo-European community before it broke up. (In this connection it should be noted, perhaps, that from the standpoint of the cultures into which the Indo-Europeans intruded—"Old European," Dravidian, etc., in ancient times and, more recently, the American Indian, African, and other cultures affected by modern European imperialism—the genetic model is necessarily correlated with the diffusion model, for the process of "Indo-Europeanization" included everywhere the diffusion and assimilation of Indo-European beliefs, customs, social structure, etc. From this perspective, then, the Indo-Europeans, like the Bantu and other linguistically related peoples who have spread over large areas, have served as the agents of wave diffusion.)

Finally, it must be assumed that any given set of genetically related phenomena, whether linguistic, ideological, social, or even technological, will necessarily reflect a common system or structure, one that lies beneath a fairly wide range of surface variations. As the new comparative mythology has shown, this last assumption is certainly borne

---

[16] Donald Ward, *The Divine Twins, An Indo-European Myth in Germanic Tradition*, Folklore Studies, 19 (Berkeley and Los Angeles, 1968), 3–8.

[17] *Ibid.*, p. 3.

out among the ancient Indo-European-speaking traditions, and I think it would also be borne out were other linguistically related traditions to be subjected to the same kind of analysis (cf. the quadripartite Uto-Aztecan ideology referred to earlier).

An important distinction must be made between the specific parallels to which one applies the genetic (or any other) model and the tales or bounded narrative structures in which they manifest themselves. For the latter often serve as frames for a wide variety of themes and motifs that lie outside the range of the model in question. Moreover, the linear structures of a set of narratives that otherwise contain variants of a common ideology may be very different and may stem from wholly unique historical and environmental circumstances. A good case in point is suggested by a comparison of the *Iliad* and the *Mahābhārata*. As epics, the two narratives are wholly distinct in linear structure and context; the events of the *Iliad* unfold against the background of a warfare between two more or less distinct ethnic communities, Achaeans and Trojans, while the *Mahābhārata* concerns a dynastic dispute between two closely related branches of a royal house, and no ethnic antagonisms as such are present. The circumstances and contexts are thus very different, and the epics themselves are not, it seems to me, genetically related. As I have attempted to demonstrate in a recent essay,[18] however, each in its own way seems to manifest the common Indo-European ideology in the interrelationships among several (but by no means all) of its major characters. Achilles and Arjuna may well be genetically related in that both may reflect the second or warrior function, just as Hector and Paris may be cognates of Nakula and Sahadeva and reflect the third function, despite the fact that the respective frames in which these figures act out their parts are wholly unique and outside the purview of the genetic model. This distinction is an obvious one, but it is all too frequently overlooked by those who would push the new comparative mythology beyond its effective limits.

These, then, are some of the factors that must be taken into consideration when applying the genetic model. In his own application thereof Dumézil has indeed taken these matters to heart, and in doing so he has provided a sound base for anthropologists to build upon, no matter how remote their special competencies may be from the ancient Indo-European-speaking world.

[18] Littleton, "Some Possible Indo-European Themes in the *Iliad*."

On the Relations of Dumézilian Comparative Indo-European Mythology to History of Religions in General

MATTHIAS VERENO, *University of Salzburg, Austria*

The following observations presume no more than to mention a few directions in which further investigations might be conducted. None of the latter are explored here, since to do so might impair the homogeneity of the present volume, dedicated to the particular field of studies in which Georges Dumézil, whose presence was the motivating occasion of the symposium, is so competent a specialist.

The title of this contribution, however, does not speak accidentally of "history of religions *in general.*" This phrase means that I am not dealing with the relation between two disciplines, which would be reciprocally external. Their relation is rather seen as one having its place within the other. Indo-European linguistics (philology), on the one hand, and history of religions, on the other, meet and interpenetrate precisely in comparative Indo-European mythology. Whatever the findings in this particular field are, they will have to be reflected upon within the wider range of comparative linguistics in general (ultimately beyond even the limits of Indo-European studies) and also within all the various aspects of the study of religion and the history of culture in its widest sense.

Such a drawing out of the lines traced by comparative mythology, such a "second reflection"—if I may use this somewhat philosophical term—will not only make available the concrete findings of this more specialized research to the wider field of related studies but will also shed new light on the findings themselves, introduce stimulating questions into the actual discussions, and influence the direction of further research.

Besides and beyond this basic and necessary correlation between comparative mythology and various other approaches in religious and cultural studies, there can hardly be any doubt that it is precisely the life work of Georges Dumézil, more than that of any other, which lends itself to the actual establishing of such correspondences and interactions, since he himself has insisted upon the correlation of various levels of investigation, that is, the correlation of mythology (or mythic "theology"), of epic tradition and literature, and of social structure and organization. Thus he himself considers a given historical culture as a whole, and that it has to be studied as such. And herewith quite naturally he invites cooperation and response from various fields, such as analysis of religious ideas, history of literature, and sociology.

In the following sections I present examples of possible further inquiries which take their inspiration from the questions raised by Dumézil, aiming at a wider view of man as a religious and historical being and at a deeper understanding of diverse, yet interrelated, cultural traditions.

I

Dumézil's "tripartite ideology" provides an ideal pattern for understanding functional interactions within given societies. Yet it should not be considered a static frame within which societies can neatly be divided into those that do and those that do not fit. Rather, in Dumézil's own tripartite structure there is an element of variability, capable of turning the structure into an instrument of perceiving, judging, and interpreting changes far beyond the patterns of "archaic" society. This element is the notion of sovereignty.

Sovereignty as such is not identified with any of the three basic functions, although Dumézil himself obviously associates it closely with the first, the sacred function; he even sometimes uses it as this function's very designation, speaking of it as the "function of sovereignty." This association is justified by the actual historic situation he is dealing with, where and when sovereignty and sacred function coincide. Yet, what happens when they separate?

This event occurred in early India in the crystallizing of the two leading castes—Brahmins and Kṣatriyas—the former retaining in every respect precedence over the latter, even though clearly renouncing the exercise of sovereignty. Varuṇa/Mitra, the embodiment of sacred sovereignty, steps back, and Agni comes to the fore, divine ideal of the priest, while Indra, the warrior, acquires the attributes of royalty. The more complete the transfer of sovereignty from the first to the second function in any given culture and at any given time, the sharper the distinction between sacred and secular. The modern doctrine (or "ideology") of secularism, pluralism, and separation of church and state constitutes the extreme opposite to the archaic notion of sacred sovereignty.

Dumézil's second category is ideally the warlike function. But exactly in proportion to the separation of the notion of sovereignty from the first, the sacred function, the offices of wise government and administering of justice merge with the second. The second function, then, becomes the "political" function in its totality. The unity of the political function was maintained in Rome beyond the time of the kings. In the republic, the career of public office included assignments in various fields (military as well as financial, administrative as well as judiciary), and the consuls bore the highest responsibility in the affairs of both war and peace. This situation contradicts, once again, the modern Western assumption that in public leadership and responsibility military and civilian functions should be strictly separate, with the former being subordinate to and controlled by the latter.

Modern understanding presupposes a further shift of sovereignty which leaves the warring function, like the sacred function, to specialists who retain a somewhat marginal, if exceptional and respected, position in society as a whole. This next shift confers sovereignty on the third function, that is, the people at large. Regarding the third function, Dumézil admits a certain oscillation: on the one hand, it represents a very characteristic quality and activity; on the other hand, it is just "the people," everyman. This ambivalence remains so long as we limit our inquiry to a given ethnic or cultural group, excluding foreigners from serious consideration. For instance, the Vaiśyas are the Āryan common people, but simultaneously free people, and as Āryans are "twice-born." The *dasyu*, on the other hand, are simply others, or outsiders, and when they are incorporated into the Āryan system they become Śūdras. In Athens, the freemen who had the leisure to concern themselves with public affairs retained certain traits of the contemplative; in the Germanic world, the freemen, though producers, were identified as those who would bear arms.

Once more we find a contradiction in principle between ancient and modern views of the body politic, of democracy. In ancient times freedom was considered as an excellence; now it is understood as the natural property of man as such, of man as biological being. And in this freedom, in the second sense, are placed the root and the justification of sovereignty. The modern vision of society may be seen as related to the tripartite structure and may be understood against its background, yet actually it breaks its frame or transcends it. Nevertheless, many modern phenomena and developments may be seen as residues or survivals of one or the other element of that age-old structure, or as attempts at their reassertion (for example: the Communist ideologists as the educators of the people, their claim to ultimate control of administrative as well as military functions).

II

Dumézil bases his arguments mainly on material collected among the Indo-Iranians, on the one hand, and among Romans and Scandinavians on the other. It would be rewarding to study both Eastern and Western wings in the context of later historical developments which cease to be dominated by the tripartite mythology. In such a study one discovers a strangely inverse problematic in East and West.

1) The sacred Indo-Iranian tradition—I use this double term to indicate a yet undivided Proto-Vedic stage—experienced, in historical times, two major religious upheavals or reforms: that of Zarathustra and that of the Buddha, respectively in the Western and the Eastern parts of the common dominion. The spiritual and social structures originating from these two reforms entered, in later centuries, into intimate contact with non-Indo-European traditions: Zarathustrian Persia was conquered by Muslim Arabs; Indian Buddhism conquered the Far East. These historical developments suggest three sets of questions.

a) What was the fate of the tripartite structures under the influence of these two reforms? How did the effect of these new impulses differ on the three levels of mythology, epic tradition, and social organization? We may assume, as a hypothesis, that the most strongly affected level would be the mythological one, the epic tradition suffering lesser inroads and the social functions being most likely to maintain an essential continuity. In what did the two reforms differ? Dumézil himself has dealt with the transformation of the system in Iran and its reassertion under new names and within a new overall framework. It appears that Buddhism did not so much attempt to replace the Devas by "archangels," who would inherit basic qualities of the former, but rather to downgrade them; nevertheless, one might ask whether Mahāyāna mythology did not bring a partial reassertion of old structures under new names? And what about the other two levels, epic and social, here and there?

b) What structures that might be considered as corresponding to the manifestations of the tripartite ideology on the three levels can we delineate in those societies that were the partners in the two great encounters, that is, the non-Indo-European peoples in the Near East and the Far East? In this connection, we would have to take into account the demythologizing effects of Islam (and, of course, of Judaism and Christianity) on the one hand and of Confucianism and Taoism on the other.

c) What were the dominant structures, on the three levels, which emerged from the religiocultural syntheses in Western and in Eastern Asia? What, if any, continuity with the ancient Indo-Iranian conceptions can we observe?

2) In Europe, the Latin and the Germanic branches of the Indo-Europeans were the ones that had the largest share in the creation of the specific Western culture and civilization. Here, analogous questions could be raised, *mutatis mutandis,* as with regard to the Indo-Iranian tradition.

The Celtic contribution must have been considerable, but it is difficult to ascertain, since so little pre-Christian material is available and so little of the once great Celtic-Christian tradition and of the Celtic languages has survived in later European history. The Hellenic branch did not provide Dumézil with much material from ancient strata, and, as a result, the tremendous impact of the Greek heritage enters only somewhat marginally into the framework of our particular question. It has, nevertheless, to be considered mainly under a double aspect: (1) that of its contribution to the Christian synthesis, joining the biblical, originally Hebrew, tradition; (2) that of its influence in the later secularization process, in consequence of the demythologization brought about by the philosophers, here again joining the biblical heritage with its emphatic distinction between creator and creation and the accentuation of history over nature.

Compared with the fate of the Indo-Iranian heritage, we observe an opposite, inverse movement in western Europe. There we have the differentiation of two distinct traditions out of what was originally one common brand; here we have two clearly separate branches, Latin and Germanic, which meet and merge (to a certain degree) in historical times in order to create a new synthesis, or rather a bifocal, elliptic dynamic whole that continues to produce ever new syntheses and polarizations.

III

Western European history shows one most interesting trait, a closer consideration of which might lead to interesting conclusions. I mean the split of the whole social body according to ethnolinguistic divisions.

In virtually all Western countries, as a result of the great migrations, there was established a Germanic warrior class, while the first, the sacred function, remained almost as exclusively in the hands of the Latins. Even when later on more and more Germanic-speaking people were admitted to the ranks of the clergy and the religious orders, they were completely assimilated into the structures of church life, which were thoroughly Roman and Latin, not only in language. The church was heir to and continuator of classical (which meant concretely Roman) civilization. On the other hand, Germanic tradition remained practically equivalent to the tradition of nobility as such, even in the later stages of more advanced cultural amalgamation. While the warriors from the North readily admitted the superiority of Roman civilization and tried to assimilate it, especially its language, they retained consciousness of their particular biological heritage and pride in their noble blood, which was the criterion of their tradition and the standard of assimilation of originally non-Germanic elements (by intermarriage or in a merely fictitious way, e.g., by transference of titles).

Starting from this point of departure, many lines of investigation could be pursued. To name a few:

1) In a general situation where the warrior function would have absorbed to a large degree the administrative and judiciary functions, the symbiosis with the more sophisticated classical heritage caused an abandonment of the major part of these activities to the representatives of the first function, leaving the notion of sovereignty as such with the second function, but in an always precarious position, thus giving rise to complaints about clerical intrusions into foreign domains and to anticlerical sentiment.

2) The taking back of already partly desacralized functions by the clergy (secular and monastic) led to a certain desacralization and intellectualization of the latter, thus instigating a dialectic of laical intellectual protest and emancipation, clericalism and anticlericalism inciting each other to ever new intellectual desacralization and secularization.

3) Both leading functions appear rather indissolubly intertwined: the sacred function by necessity caught up in politics, the warrior function tied to a still somewhat sacred, universal notion of sovereignty. The bitter conflicts arising from this abnormal situation may to some degree account for an even sharper and more radical division of the two spheres in modern times.

4) One might consider, in this context, the medieval concept of the three offices of Christendom: *sacerdotium*, *imperium*, and *magisterium*, with their centers of gravity in Italy, Germany, and France respectively.

5) It might be rewarding to compare, in the light of these factors, the developments in the West with the developments in non-Western Christianity (particularly the Byzantine world).

IV

Another line of investigation would be to pursue the relation between the three functions and the three cosmic qualities, that is, the *guṇas,* "threads," of the Sāṃkhya system, a notion not confined to this system, but quite generally Indian, and not lacking striking parallels in other cultures. This, of course, implies the relation seen by Hindu authorities themselves between the *guṇas* and the castes. Thus, the *Manusmṛti* describes the Brahmins as predominantly *sattva,* the Kṣatriyas as a mixture of *sattva* and *rajas,* the Vaiśyas as a mixture of *rajas* and *tamas,* and the Śūdras as predominantly *tamas,* an interesting way of correlating a triadic and a quaternary structure. There are added symbolic colors: white for the Brahmin, red for the Kṣatriya, yellow for the Vaiśya, and black for the Śūdra. I submit that the designation of the basic castes as *varṇa,* "color," may not only indicate the consciousness of a color bar between Āryan invaders and the *dasyu,* but may also refer to such symbolic color associations.

In Tibet and Mongolia another triad of cosmic principles has been evolved, the Mongol designations being *khi, shara, bagdan.* To what extent does this concept depend on Buddhist influences? and, as Buddhist, on Indian influences? and, as Indian, on Āryan influences? And can it be traced historically to the three *guṇas*?

The main difference from the *guṇa* triad would appear with respect to the third principle. *Khi,* as the mainly intellectual principle, and *shara,* as the mainly voluntary principle, could, without too much difficulty, be homologized to *sattva* and *rajas* (although, certainly, they could not simply be equated). But *bagdan* is all else but dark or obscure. It is, rather, the principle of goodness: goodness as being, or quality; and goodness of attitude and action, or love, grace, gentleness, and care. It might also be described as the substantial principle, underlying the more articulate principles of cognition and volition, bearing or carrying them, as it were, and thus easily to be overlooked. It might be considered as a female principle, even as a material principle. But then it would indicate the luminous substance, principle of harmonious vibration, immediate correspondence, and receptive response, rather than matter as the principle of inertia or even resistance against the spiritual impulse.

It may be that we have here two dimensions of a cosmological and ontological structure: the *guṇas* representing our vertical vision, one quality superimposed over the other, of increasing value and excellence; the Lamaistic principles representing a horizontal vision, all three at the summit of equal perfection, interpenetrating one another completely and allowing for indefinite degrees of reduced participation in the fullness of consciousness, power, and goodness.

V

Another interesting comparison, involving an element of classical Indian systematics, would be the one that relates the fourfold caste structure to the four ends of life of the Hindu traditions: *kāma, artha, dharma,* and *mokṣa.* Here one might apply another method of relating triadic and quaternary structures, different from the one observed with respect to the correlation of castes and *guṇas.* The *Manusmṛti* is not explicit on this point, but we might try to pursue the following line of thought.

Excluding the Śūdras as not fully participating in the structure, we might correlate *kāma,* sensual satisfaction in the widest sense, with the Vaiśya; *artha,* success and wealth, with the Kṣatriya; and *dharma,* duty, that is, pursuit of righteousness, with the Brahmin. Certainly such correlations could not be mutually exclusive. The less so, since the fourth aim, transcending all three, would be equally accessible to all three castes, and thus the mystic attraction of *mokṣa,* ultimate liberation, would provide also a point of integration for the three preparatory aims. Their common striving for liberation would unite men and women of all three castes (at least of the twice-born which are considered here) and let them participate in all three preparatory life aims. The ultimate ideal of liberation would also establish a hierarchy among those other aims, depending on their respective closeness and instrumentality to that highest and ultimate aim.

Here a comparison seems to be in tune with Plato's hierarchical structure of the body politic as described in the *Politeia* and with his use of the four virtues as they had already been articulated in earlier Greek thinking. Through Plato they became the cardinal virtues of the Latin-Christian tradition: *σοφία/prudentia, δικαιοσύνη/iustitia, ἀνδρεία/fortitudo,* and *σωφροσύνη/temperantia.* Of these four, three are related to the main social strata: *σωφροσύνη* to the common people, *ἀνδρεία* to the warriors, *σοφία* to the philosopher-kings. The virtue related to the lowest class, the people at large, is distinct from the other two in that it is described not so much as exercise of a psychic quality (*ἀνδρεία, σοφία*), but rather as overcoming or controlling a psychic quality, namely, *ἐπιθυμία,* "desire." This virtue, then, corresponds exactly to *kāma* in the Hindu scheme. And the somewhat negative character of the third virtue is stressed even more in its Latin designation *temperantia* (*moderatio*).

The main difference between the Greek and the Hindu model, however, is expressed in the fourth virtue, δικαιοσύνη (the second in the classical sequence of cardinal virtues, but clearly set aside, over against the other three, in the *Politeia*). This belongs to the whole polis, but it is actually possessed and administered by the first class; from the virtue exclusively proper to them, σοφία, "wisdom," derives justice as their wisdom applied appropriately and proportionately to the two other groups, the principle of *suum cuique*. There, then, we have the striking difference to the fourth life aim. *Mokṣa* surely serves somehow as a spiritual force of integration, but only in a secondary and indirect way. Primarily and explicitly it tends to call all men to rise beyond the three other aims and dedicate themselves to the fourth. The Brahmins, the teachers of *dharma*, are necessarily—if they teach *dharma* in the fullest sense of universal order—also teachers of *mokṣa*. Thus they, as representatives of the first, the sacred, function, cannot be kings themselves: Are they not teaching the relativity of all worldly pursuits, including those of royalty? Yet if the fourth principle, integrating the others, is not *mokṣa* but δικαιοσύνη then the wise men are, and necessarily must be, the rulers of the whole social body, which by this very fact becomes the body politic in the real and full sense. Here the highest pursuit is the one that turns back to the others.

VI

We have considered principles, qualities, and virtues, not only because they characterize in one way or another the various social classes, but also, and above all, because such concepts to some extent replace the older mythological imagery. The ancient divinities as well as the metaphysical and cosmological symbols constitute the transcendent correspondence to the organically and hierarchically structured society; I say "correspond" because I do not wish in any way to pass judgment on a supposed dependence of the one level on the other. The intermediate level, that of heroic epic tradition, obviously finds hardly an adequate continuation once the gods of mythology are replaced by metaphysical and cosmological principles.

It remains to suggest one more direction of inquiry: to consider the merging of such principles with the notion of God, the union, as it were, of metaphysics and theology.

In Christianity, and in biblical tradition in general, God is described as all-knowing, all-powerful, and all-merciful (the last attribution is somewhat narrowed down; in German there is the perfect parallelism: *allwissend, allmächtig, allgütig*). To these three essential attributions correspond three activities or effects: God enlightens, he strengthens, and he cares for (the most impressive and immediate image of his caring is that he feeds his creatures). Between the third and the two preceding activities, we observe a marked difference. The enlightening and the strengthening aspects grant participation in the divine nature, pure and simple; that is, they constitute the analogy between creator and creatures: he is light, and in the act of enlightening he grants of this light to the creature; he is strength, and in the act of strengthening he grants of his strength. But the third action stresses not the similarity, but the dissimilarity; not the analogy but the encounter. Certainly, being fed by God may result in being strengthened and enlightened. But the act of feeding is not the assimilation of the creature to the creator, but rather the revelation of their radical difference: essential want here, overflowing plenty there; God being active, man passive, or rather receptive. Mainly two images for this third relationship have been elaborated: that of the mother suckling the child, and that of intimate union between man and woman.

The above, of course, is only one way in which one can relate the triadic structure to certain traditions of Western theology. In another perspective, God the Almighty could be seen as the sovereign judge, separating the goats from the sheep; God the merciful would certainly be no less sovereign, but he would manifest his sovereignty in letting his sun shine on the just and unjust alike; in his enlightening action God allows man again and again to transcend as well as to synthesize this rational contradiction.

As these brief reflections have hopefully indicated, Dumézil's studies in comparative Indo-European mythology have raised intriguing questions and fascinating comparative problems for the history of religions in general.

Bibliographical Note

Several extensive bibliographies dealing with modern-day Indo-European comparative mythology have recently been published. For a nearly complete listing of Dumézil's publications to 1960, see *Hommages à Georges Dumézil*, Collection Latomus, vol. 45 (Brussels, 1960), pp. xi–xxiii. For publications of Dumézil to 1966 together with a listing of scholarly works on Indo-European comparative mythology, both in support of and in opposition to Dumézil, see C. Scott Littleton's bibliography in his *The New Comparative Mythology: An Anthropological Assessment of the Theories of Georges Dumézil* (Berkeley and Los Angeles: University of California Press, 1960), pp. 215–233. For a comprehensive bibliographical summary of work in Indo-European comparative mythology to 1970, see Jaan Puhvel, ed., *Myth and Law among the Indo-Europeans* (Berkeley, Los Angeles, and London: University of California Press, 1970), pp. 247–268. For the most recent summary of material (to 1973), see the revised bibliography in the second edition of C. Scott Littleton's *The New Comparative Mythology: An Anthropological Assessment of the Theories of Georges Dumézil* (Berkeley, Los Angeles, and London: University of California Press, 1973).

The best general summary of Professor Dumézil's overall perspective continues to be his own *L'idéologie tripartie des Indo-Européens*, Collection Latomus, vol. 31 (Brussels, 1958). The most spirited criticisms of Professor Dumézil's work are Paul Thieme, *Mitra and Aryaman*, in *Transactions of the Connecticut Academy of Arts and Sciences* (New Haven, 1957), pp. 1–96; Jan Gonda, "Some Observations on Dumézil's views of Indo-European Mythology," *Mnemosyne* 4 (1960) no. 13:1–15; and John Brough, "The Tripartite Ideology of the Indo-Europeans: An Experiment in Method," *Bulletin of the School of Oriental and African Studies* 22 (1959), 69–86. For Dumézil's equally spirited and convincing rejoinder to Thieme, see his "Aryaman et Paul Thieme," appendix to *L'idéologie tripartie des Indo-Européens*, pp. 108–118; and for his excellent rejoinder to Brough, see his "L'idéologie tripartie des Indo-Européens et la Bible," *Kratylos* 4 (1959), 97–118.

For an assessment of the place of Dumézil's work and Indo-European comparative mythology in the general history of religions, see Jan de Vries, *The Study of Religion*, trans. Kees W. Bolle (New York: Harcourt, Brace and World, 1967), pp. 181–186; and Mircea Eliade, "The History of Religions in Retrospect: 1912 and After," in *The Quest* (Chicago: University of Chicago Press, 1969), pp. 12–36, and esp. pp. 32–34.

For an evaluation of Dumézil's work from the perspective of the field of anthropology, see C. Scott Littleton's *The New Comparative Mythology: An Anthropological Assessment of the Theories of Georges Dumézil.* For an interesting comparison of Dumézil's work with that of C. Lévi-Strauss, see P. Smith and D. Sperber, "Mythologiques de Georges Dumézil," *Annales économies, sociétés,* civilisations, 26 (May–August, 1971), 559–586.

Finally, some general works in the area of myth which range beyond specifically Indo-European comparative mythology but which relate in significant ways to some of the issues raised in this volume are the following (in alphabetical order): J. Campbell, *The Hero with a Thousand Faces* (New York: Pantheon Books, 1949); E. Cassirer, *Language and Myth* (New York and London: Harper and Brothers, 1946); M. Eliade, "Remarks on Religious Symbolism," in *The History of Religions: Essays in Methodology,* ed. by M. Eliade and J. Kitagawa (Chicago: University of Chicago Press, 1959); R. A. Georges, ed., *Studies on Mythology* (Homewood, Ill.: Dorsey Press, 1968); S. H. Hooke, ed., *Myth and Ritual* (London: Oxford University Press, 1933); C. G. Jung and C. Kerényi, *Essays on a Science of Mythology* (New York: Pantheon Books, 1949); S. Langer, *Philosophy in a New Key* (Cambridge; Harvard University Press, 1942); B. Malinowski, *Myth in Primitive Psychology* (New York: W. W. Norton, 1926); H. A. Murray, ed., *Myth and Mythmaking* (Boston: Beacon Press, 1960); R. M. Ohmann, ed., *The Making of Myth* (New York: G. P. Putnam's Sons, 1962); R. Pettazzoni, "Myths of Beginning and Creation Myths" and "The Truth of Myth" in *Essays on the History of Religions* (Leiden: E. J. Brill, 1954); T. A. Sebeok, ed., *Myth: A Symposium* (Bloomington and London: Indiana University Press, 1958).

Index